Presidential Management of Science and Technology

An Administrative History of the
Johnson Presidency Series

Presidential
Management of
Science and Technology
The Johnson Presidency

By W. Henry Lambright

University of Texas Press, Austin

First Edition, 1985

Requests for permission to reproduce material from
this work should be sent to Permissions, University
of Texas Press, Box 7819, Austin, Texas 78713.

Library of Congress Cataloging in Publication Data

Lambright, W. Henry, 1939–
    Presidential management of science and technology.

    (An Administrative history of the Johnson presidency series)
    Bibliography: p.
    Includes index.
    1. Science and state—United States—History. 2. Technology
and state—United States—History. 3. United States—Politics
and government—1963–1969. 4. Johnson, Lyndon B. (Lyndon
Baines), 1908–1973. I. Title. II. Series: Administrative history
of the Johnson presidency.
Q127.U6L29 1985   338.97306   84-28420
ISBN 0-292-76494-4

To Nancy, my closest and strongest support

Contents

Foreword

This is the third of a group of publications designed to form the series An Administrative History of the Johnson Presidency. The first study, by Emmette S. Redford and Marlan Blissett, *Organizing the Executive Branch: The Johnson Presidency*, was published in 1981. The second study, by Richard L. Schott and Dagmar S. Hamilton, *People, Positions and Power: The Political Appointments of Lyndon Johnson*, was published in 1983. Ten to twelve special studies, including the first three and an overall volume, are planned.

Our objective is to provide a comprehensive view of how a president and those who assisted him managed the White House and the executive branch to achieve the objectives of law and presidential policy. Administration will be studied as part of the responsibility of a president—in this case, President Lyndon B. Johnson.

The view taken of administration is comprehensive. It includes the interrelations among policy, administration, and program development. It encompasses administration in its various aspects: development of the infrastructure, including structuring and staffing the executive branch and budgeting for its operations; implementation of policy; and presidential management of the executive branch.

We aim for an authentic and adequate historical record based primarily on the documentary materials in the Lyndon B. Johnson Library and on interviews with many people who assisted President Johnson. We hope the historical record as presented from a social science perspective will amplify knowledge of administrative processes and of the tasks and problems of the presidency.

The study is being financed primarily by a grant from the National Endowment for the Humanities, with additional aid from the Lyndon Baines Johnson Foundation, the Hoblizelle Foundation, and the Lyndon B. Johnson School of Public Affairs of the University of Texas at Austin.

The findings and conclusions in publications resulting from this study do not necessarily represent the view of any donor.

Emmette S. Redford
Project Director

James E. Anderson
Deputy Project Director

Preface

In 1978, Emmette Redford of the University of Texas invited me to Austin to begin discussing a study of the relationship of the Johnson presidency to science and technology. This was to be part of a series for which he was responsible on the Administrative History of the Johnson Presidency. Having written a book on the relationship of the federal agencies and departments to science and technology, I saw this opportunity to focus on the presidency as a natural next step in my own work.

Thus, periodically, over the next few years, I spent considerable time in the Lyndon B. Johnson Library in Austin and the National Archives in Washington. There I went through a variety of documents of the Johnson presidency concerned with this field. These documents were both multitudinous and revealing. They provide insights into the decision-making processes of the White House that are possible in no other way. They are a particularly rich resource for showing the contributions of the various individuals and organizations around the president that seek to influence his decisions. These documents were the most important resource in researching and writing this book. Combined with secondary sources and interviews, they have made it possible to investigate the inner dynamics of the presidential institution in a way that is seldom done.

This study is intended to fill a gap in both the presidential and science and technology policy literatures. The relationship of the presidency to science and technology is important and continuing. It is deserving of more attention than it has received. Through intense study of the Johnson presidency, it is hoped that major issues are highlighted that will encourage others to give further time and attention to this area.

In writing this book, I have had the help of many. The National Endowment for the Humanities provided necessary financial support. Those who read the entire manuscript include Donald Hornig, former science adviser to President Johnson, now with the Harvard School of Public Health; William Carey, an official of the Bureau of the Budget under Johnson, who is presently executive officer of the American Association for the Advancement of Science; James Anderson of the University of Houston; Michael Reagan of the University of California, Riverside; various anonymous reviewers; and Emmette Redford. All provided insights and helpful criticism. The staff of the Lyndon B. Johnson Library and the National Archives gave assistance that was both efficient and essential. Richard McCulley, who served the Johnson Administrative History project in a professional research capacity, was extremely enterprising in the work he performed on this particular volume. Two Syracuse University research assistants, Elma Boyko and Mary Roy, helped greatly at different points along the way. Various drafts of the manuscript were typed by Alfreda Lakins and Joyce Falk. Ms. Lakins' work, as always, was excellent. Ms. Falk, in particular, found the "LBJ project" an activity with which she was associated closely (sometimes arduously) from the time she came to work with me. Her efforts in going beyond typing to thoughtful advice aimed at perfecting the manuscript are deeply appreciated.

Finally, to my wife, Nancy, and sons, Dan and Nat, I give the thanks of one who knows that his preoccupations have been a burden to others. My family provided support that was needed over the long time it took to move from conception to completion of this project. To all who helped, in so many different ways, I am grateful. The book is better for what they have done. Any faults are mine alone.

W. Henry Lambright
Syracuse, New York

Presidential Management of Science and Technology

1. Introduction

This is a study of the presidential management of science and technology policy. It is an examination of the president as chief executive, and of the presidency as the institutional embodiment of this role. The presidency constitutes "top management" of the federal executive branch. It provides leadership and initiative in public policy. There is no area of national purpose that is not touched by presidential decision. It matters immensely how the presidency decides and who exercises influence within the institution. This is true in every realm touched by governmental action, including that of science and technology.

Science and technology (technoscience) policy decisions embrace the continuum of activity from basic and applied scientific research through technological development to the application of the latest technologies to the problems of war and peace. Science and technology can be a great force—an instrument of national policy. For better or worse, government has a dominant role in guiding the scientific and technological process. The federal government itself is a major investor in science and technology, spending many billions on missions cutting across virtually every agency of government, from the Department of Defense (DOD) to the Department of Housing and Urban Development (HUD). The implementation of these research and development (R&D) programs utilizes federal laboratories, industry, universities, and nonprofit "think tanks." Through regulation, patents, and tax incentives, government indirectly influences R&D investments and technological applications in the private sector. Because government is so deeply involved, the presidency is inextricably drawn into attempting to manage this federal technoscience enterprise.

Every presidency must face an unending series of choices involving science and technology: the development and deployment (or arrestment) of new weapons, the acceleration of key energy technologies, the role of the United States in outer space, the preeminence of American science and technology vis-à-vis other nations.

Such issues come to a presidency in various forms. How a particular president structures his presidency to cope with them differs. But issues of programs, priorities, resources, and direction in science and technology are inescapable. They have been major concerns at least since World War II, when Franklin Roosevelt made his most critical technological choice: to develop the atomic bomb. They are central today—in civilian as well as military areas. They will be present in the future. No matter who is president, science and technology will be part of the presidency's agenda. It is an important aspect of many of the most significant executive decisions with which any presidency must cope. The modern presidency must deal with science and technology. How well it does so is critical.

The Problem

There is a need for better understanding of presidential management of science and technology. How do issues that are science and technology–intensive become important to a particular presidency? Which issues gain priority? How? Why? What is the role of the presidency in the adoption of national policies affecting science and technology? What is the presidency's role in implementation of science and technology programs? Under what conditions does the presidency try to curtail or even to eliminate certain programs or to rescue programs Congress might seek to terminate? How does presidential implementation of a program adopted by an incumbent president vary from implementation of an inherited program? Such questions as these go to the heart of science and technology policy. They entail critical presidential decisions.

To a remarkable degree, the relevant literatures do not deal with such matters. There is a literature on the presidency, and there is one on science and technology. Seldom do they converge. Heclo, referring to the presidential literature, has noted, "To a great extent, presidential studies have coasted on the reputations of a few rightfully respected classics on the Presidency and on secondary literature and anecdotes produced by former participants. We still have remarkably little substantiated information on how the modern office of the President actually works."[1]

Recent studies of presidential personality by Barber have made it clear how the styles of presidents shape the decision modes of a presidency,[2] but they have not gotten at the variations or commonalities in the large institution of which the president is a part. An emphasis on presidents, rather than the presidency, "promotes the illusion that it is only what they do that matters." Such a perspective should be broadened, Heclo argues, "to communicate the reality of complex interactions involving many people." There is a "need to look at what has been going on around and beyond presidents, often without their knowledge, comprehension, or interest."[3] Some writers, such as Cronin, have sought to do so, indicating differences and similarities in presidential decision making across major policy spheres. He suggests that the work of the modern presidency can be divided into three major areas: 1. foreign affairs and national security; 2. aggregate economics; and 3. domestic policy, or "quality of life" issues.[4] Some work by presidential scholars has delved into the "complex interactions" in these spheres. A recent book edited by Heclo and Salamon includes a major section on "policy management." The policies receiving attention are the same ones noted by Cronin.[5] While research on these areas is needed, such a concentration obscures other important presidential policy areas. One that has received very little attention from presidential scholars is science and technology.

Writers on science and technology policy, for their part, have only begun to investigate the role of the presidency.[6] To some extent, this is because they have been primarily interested in the place of scientists in top-level decision making. In the 1960s, this emphasis was seen in Snow's *Science and Government*,[7] Gilpin's *American Scientists and Nuclear Weapons Policy*,[8] and Price's *The Scientific Estate*.[9] The theme of "scientific advice" was continued and given new richness in the 1970s when two former special assistants to the president for science and technology produced books on their experience: Kistiakowsky, *A Scientist in the White House*,[10] and Killian, *Sputnik, Scientists, and Eisenhower*.[11] In the decade of the 1980s, there have been two additional volumes of this genre: Burger, *Science at the White House: A Political Liability*,[12] and a book-length issue of the journal *Technology in Society*, devoted to "Science Advice to the President."[13]

Significant as scientists (and scientific advice) may be, they are only components of presidential decision making. Who and what else are relevant? In the mid-1970s, in *Governing Science and Technology*, I pointed up the importance of the role of the large science and technology–oriented agencies.[14] Later in the decade, in *Presidential Politics and Science Policy*, Katz delved directly into presidential decision making.[15] In a broad survey of presidents from Eisenhower to Carter, Katz showed that there was more to presidential decision making than scientific advising—for example, the Office of Management and Budget (OMB). The Katz volume was rare in taking the kind of perspective it did. It represented an important beginning. There were limits, however, arising from the very breadth of the book. It was not possible to provide the depth of analysis that would reveal intricate relationships among such entities as OMB, the science adviser, and agency administrators, and between these and the president himself.

It is in these basic relationships within the presidency, and between the presidency and its political environment, that the most fundamental gaps in knowledge remain. This is where both presidential and science and technology literatures are weakest. Filling this gap is essential to understanding the presidential management of science and technology, which will illuminate broader issues in presidential governance.

Central Issues

The management of science and technology raises a number of issues about the relationship of the presidency to the agencies and departments, and about its very capacity to provide policy guidance to the executive branch. These issues are raised in other fields, but they are perhaps highlighted particularly in this area. There are four that stand out, which are addressed in various ways in this book.

The first issue is the *dispersion* of the science and technology enterprise. Some functions of government are largely embraced by one or two agencies. Thus, in national security, a relatively concentrated function, the presidential management problem relates primarily to the State and Defense departments. In agricultural policy, the Department of Agriculture looms large. But in science and technology, there are many agencies that have a role.

For example, the National Science Foundation (NSF) and National Institutes of Health (NIH) are principal forces in basic science policy. The Defense Department, National Aeronautics and Space Administration (NASA), and Department of Energy (DOE) have major missions in technological development. Virtually all the agencies, however, spend funds for research and development to some extent, and all are interested in the application of new technology to the problems under their purview.

There are some countries where science and technology is centralized under a Ministry of Science and Technology, or its equivalent. The United States has chosen an extreme pluralistic approach. This provides a model of organization of general relevance. However, it also raises the issue of how the presidency manages such a dispersed function.

The second major issue that is raised in this policy area is the *sequential* nature of presidential decision making. In many areas, the president can make a decision to adopt a program and can largely ignore the issues of implementation. This is because they become highly diffused and/or show up only after a decade or more. Within the science and technology policy area, however, there are a class of programs that by their very nature press visibly for sequential presidential attention over a shorter period of time.

These are the programs that embody large-scale technological development projects. At what point should research give way to the launching of a development program (project)? Once under way, should such a program be accelerated, slowed down, reoriented, killed? At what point does development move to demonstration or operational deployment? Who is to say? Often, for very large-scale technologies, it is the president.

Because a new technology is being built in the developmental phase, there is a tangible object upon which decision making can focus. Large-scale technological programs can cost billions—Apollo cost $24 billion—and decisions to move a technology from one stage to the next in the developmental cycle are significant national decisions. They are often controversial. Moving from one stage to the next is debated—as in the shift from development to demonstration of the breeder reactor, or to deployment of the MX missile. What is technically feasible may not be politically possible, and vice versa.

The president may be pulled into decision making as the technology advances. Because such technological programs frequently extend beyond one president's tenure, different presidents may be in office at various stages of a technology's advance or end. Kennedy launched Apollo; Johnson implemented it; and Nixon presided over its completion (demonstration and termination). The stages do not necessarily go smoothly. Hardware projects have technical (and political) problems along the way, and because so much money is involved, the president is drawn in, usually when a project is in trouble. Hence, it can be said that presidential management must deal with the sequential nature of many science and technology programs, certainly with the large-scale developmental projects that are expensive and visible.

A third major issue is the capacity to *integrate* scientific, political, administrative, and budgetary aspects of presidential technoscience advice and decision. A particular burden falls upon those "under" the president who aid him in synthesizing knowledge. For that reason, this study highlights the role of the subpresidency in the overall presidential management system. The subpresidency includes those official advisers and administrative aides (and, possibly, certain unofficial advisers) who help the president exercise his role as chief executive.

Subpresidencies vary with the policy area. Thus, there is one for national security and aggregate economics, as there is one for science and technology. In each subpresidency, there are those who represent the specialized professional knowledge associated with the policy area. But this specialized knowledge (e.g., science advice) is usually not enough. It must be integrated with other kinds of knowledge, including that concerning political acceptability. The president, of course, is the ultimate synthesizer, but the subpresidency can facilitate or inhibit the integrating process. This is a particularly difficult process in the policy area at issue, since few scientists have political backgrounds, and few presidents are knowledgeable in matters of science and technology. The problem is that the nature of modern public problems forces scientists and presidents together and adds enormous complexity to decision making. The capacity to integrate knowledge is thus a central issue for the presidential management of science and technology.

Finally, there is a fourth issue in presidential policy management: whether there is a coherence to the policy (or policies) to be managed. Is the policy *strategic?* Or is it de facto, ad hoc, an aggregate of the actions of agencies, subpresidential actors, and president? In ad hoc, reactive policy, presidential management is short-term in outlook and piecemeal in approach.

A strategic approach would deal with the other issues mentioned: dispersion, sequence, and integration. It would link science and technology, as a means, to broader national ends. The presidency would be master of the technoscience tool, even as it developed, and use that tool for public purposes.

Was there a strategic science and technology policy in the era of Lyndon Johnson? If not, what were the characteristics of the policy that the Johnson presidency formulated and carried out? The coherent nature of the policy (or policies)—its strategic or nonstrategic flavor—is thus the fourth issue of presidential management this study seeks to bring out.

These issues overlap at many points. All converge in presidential decision making. They are issues of relevance beyond science and technology. But science and technology policy is one of their most significant and difficult meeting grounds.

The Johnson Presidency

To study these major issues, we focus on the Johnson presidency. The administration of Lyndon Johnson extended from late 1963 to early

1969. A spotlight on any one presidency has its drawbacks, owing to uniqueness. However, given how little is known about this institution vis-à-vis science and technology, a study of one presidential management system has utility in permitting in-depth exploration of major questions concerning presidential action. It allows identification of key roles, relationships, processes, and outcomes that can later be used to compare decision making across presidencies. All presidential administrations must now deal with science and technology. They do so in ways that are alike and that also differ. The Johnson presidency thus provides one example, with which others can eventually be contrasted.

The Johnson presidency is important in the history of government/science and technology relations. Lyndon Johnson presided at a time of transition from rapid growth in federal R&D spending to funding that was stable with inflation, or even declined in buying power. This was a time when the subpresidency concerned with science advice reached a new stage in its evolution, even as the personal relationships between presidency and science adviser went from close to distant. It was a time when presidential ambition led to activism in many science and technology areas. It was also a time when that very activism in some fields led to disillusionment and criticism of science and technology from other quarters of society. It began as a time of hope. It ended as a time of frustration.

When Johnson became president, science and technology was still riding a special wave of interest that had begun in 1957 when the Soviet Union launched Sputnik, an event that raised the priority of science and technology as a presidential issue in a way that was as unprecedented as it was dramatic. Congress, the media, and the public in general demanded "action" from the presidency, and the Eisenhower administration responded. Science and technology became a goal in and of itself. The enlarged space program—replete with a new agency, NASA, as its host—was but a symbol of what was taking place. Throughout the government, old science and technology programs vied for new monies, and new programs sought to be born. The environment, to say the least, was conducive to growth in the federal science and technology establishment.

The technoscience surge was continued and given further impetus by President Kennedy. His 1961 decision to launch the Apollo program gave an awesome new goal to America's space effort, as well as a symbol for America's science and technology emphasis: to recapture "preeminence."

Aside from space, the major areas of growth were defense, atomic energy, and health. But basic science, the universities, and education in general also gained from the mood. In the period following Sputnik, federal research and development expenditures soared, approximating an annual growth rate of fifteen percent per year at the time Lyndon Johnson became president. These were "golden years" for science and technology that extended, for a while, into the Johnson era.

The organizational capacity of the presidency to manage science and technology was enhanced during the Eisenhower and Kennedy years. At the time of Sputnik, there was an existing Science Advisory Committee (SAC) in the Executive Office of the President. However, SAC reported to a subordinate official under the president. After Sputnik, this body was elevated to a President's Science Advisory Committee (PSAC). A group of fifteen to eighteen eminent scientists and engineers, PSAC met as a whole for two days each month.

New to the subpresidency was another Eisenhower creation, a full-time special assistant for science and technology (known as the science adviser). A bureaucratic equal to other top White House aides, the science adviser was also chairman of PSAC. In addition, he presided over a subcabinet-level body, the Federal Council for Science and Technology (FCST). This was composed of top science and technology officials of the various agencies and departments. All that was needed to complete this core of specialists within the president's technoscience management structure was a permanent, full-time staff. This was supplied by Kennedy in 1962, when he established an Office of Science and Technology (OST) within the Executive Office. Like PSAC and FCST, the OST was headed by the science adviser.

Thus, by the time Johnson came to power, there had been a considerable wave of innovation in government relations with science and technology. This had meant more money and more programs at the agency level. It had also meant more institutional innovation within the presidency.

The wave of change probably crested under Kennedy, but it was still a considerable force in the early Johnson years. Growth continued, but at a slower pace. When the full financial impact of Vietnam hit home near the end of Johnson's administration, funds for research and development actually declined. Even before, as a consequence of tighter funding, there was more emphasis on management concerns during the Johnson years than earlier. There were no Apollo-scale decisions, but there were many others of major science and technology significance.

Johnson's orientation toward domestic social goals (the Great Society) inevitably had its effect on science and technology policy. Efforts were made to apply science and technology to a broader range of ends. Indeed, applications in general received great attention in the Johnson period. Science and technology remained a presidential priority, less because it was seen as a primary presidential concern in and of itself than because it was instrumental in achieving other policy goals.

This shift from a direct to a more indirect or derivative kind of priority was subtle and slow. It meant that the science adviser's role also changed. Because science and technology per se was not accepted without question as a priority, there was a greater need for advocacy. Yet advocacy made the science adviser suspect in the eyes of other subpresidential aides. Perhaps the changes were inevitable, for the surge that began with Sputnik and Apollo could not have been maintained indefinitely. Midway through the Johnson years, it could be seen clearly that the momentum behind science and technology was ebbing.

From the vantage point of the present, the Johnson years appear more typical than atypical of presidency/science and technology relations. That is, science and technology has been one among many interests clamoring for presidential attention. For President Nixon, there was too much clamoring, or perhaps not enough that was supportive of his pet projects, such as the supersonic transport and antiballistic missile. He dismantled the science and technology element of his subpresidency. Gerald Ford, however, resurrected the science adviser and much of the institutional apparatus surrounding him. Succeeding presidents, such as Carter and Reagan, have found this subpresidential unit of use.

As might be expected, certain policy issues have made science and technology a matter of concern for particular presidents. For Ford and Carter, it was energy. For Reagan, it was national security and economic recovery. But all presidents—including Nixon—have had to grapple with science and technology policy matters. They have had to make decisions affecting basic research, large-scale development, and application of new technologies to pressing problems. This is not because, as some allege, science and technology has a mind of its own. Rather, this is because it has become a major force in modern government and society. It is one that creates problems and opportunities for the president, often at the same time. This is a reality with which modern presidents must deal, one they try to manage through policy decisions. How the Johnson presidency did so is the subject of this book.

The Approach

The approach I use is that of presidential decision making. "Presidential" refers to the institution called the presidency. By "decision making," I mean the process by which choices are made to consider, create, carry out, or diminish science and technology–intensive programs. In using this approach, we can link presidential and science and technology scholarship with relevant work on decision making (e.g., Allison, *Essence of Decision*)[16] and the policy process (e.g., Lasswell, *A Pre-View of the Policy Sciences;*[17] Brewer, "The Policy Sciences Emerge: To Nurture and Structure a Discipline";[18] and Jones, *An Introduction to the Study of Public Policy*).[19]

We can also build on the rich tradition that analyzes the dynamics of policy systems and subsystems. As long ago as 1939, Griffith, in *The Impasse of Democracy*,[20] pointed to the utility of studying the "whirlpools" of policy interaction. He found such relationships among interests within and outside government to be more significant than those among congresspeople generally or among administrators generally. Cater later investigated *Power in Washington* in terms of whirlpools he called "sub-governments."[21] Likewise, Freeman in *The Political Process: Executive Bureau–Legislative Committee Relations* wrote of "subsystems."[22] They saw policy making as devolving largely to special-interest alliances of bureaucrats, legislators, and lobbyists. There are many critics of such "iron triangles," and many observers who see the president as a needed point of integration in an otherwise bottom-heavy and fragmented system of government.[23]

However, as various writers have shown, that integration is not easily accomplished. The presidency itself is a conundrum of relationships. In a given presidency, there is a sense of transiency as well as permanence, competition as well as cooperation. Viewed horizontally, the policy system is one of agency, congressional committee, and interest group. It is a system of long-term associates sharing a common orientation. Viewed vertically, from the standpoint of the presidency as it relates to bureaucracy, executive politics in Washington can constitute what Heclo calls *A Government of Strangers*.[24]

What we are examining in this study is another kind of policy system.[25] It is not the bureaucracy-centered system of agency, congressional committee, interest group described by Griffith, Cater, and Freeman. Nor is it the system of relationships between political appointees, in general, and high level bureaucrats, in general, that is the focus of the Heclo study of executive politics. Rather, it is the policy system of the science and technology presidency, the top management of the executive branch as it relates to this specific policy area. We are concerned with the internal dynamics of this policy system, and also with its external relations with other forces.

What is the nature of the presidency as a decision-making institution? Who influences what it does or does not do in managing federal science and technology? The presidency is an institution, but it is informal in the sense that it does not have fixed administrative boundaries. The structure of the presidency, as a working body, is determined not by a static organization chart, but by a particular president. Who is "in" the presidency is similarly uncertain. This depends upon the president, the particular decision at issue, and the motivations of those wishing to participate. Having a place in the Executive Office of the President or cabinet can help, but it does not assure a role in presidential decisions.

Presidents inherit certain structures and institutions. But, as Destler notes, "they also create their own through how they operate, whom they work with, and what they demand. Their day-to-day signals condition, over time, their senior officials' responses, the relative power of these officials and their agencies, how these officials deal with their subordinates, and so on." A president's operating style and personal relationships, as much or more than formal institutions, structure a presidency, and how it deals with policy.[26]

Who is in the presidency and has power therein varies with the particular set of issues or "policy sphere."[27] There are differences in who is present and active among the various functional presidencies: national security, aggregate economics, domestic quality of life, science and technology, and others. What they have in common is a basic structure growing out of the requirements of presidential management. That structure includes the president and the subpresidency.

The President

The president is not just another actor. He is special, qualitatively different in power from all others in the presidency. This was certainly true in the case of Lyndon Johnson. Born in 1908 in Stonewall, Texas, Johnson was fifty-five when he succeeded John Kennedy as president. Virtually his whole adult life had been spent in government and politics, commencing in 1931 when he became secretary to Congressman Richard M. Kleberg of Texas. He was elected to Congress as a representative in 1939 and became a senator in 1949. As majority leader in the 1950s, he was widely described as the second most powerful man in government. He was an active vice-president under Kennedy.

Johnson had a bachelor's degree from Southwest Texas State Teacher's College. While highly intelligent, he was manipulative, not contemplative in manner, and not given to reading for the sake of intellectual pleasure. His educational background and personal style made for some distance from the scientific community, including those who served him as science adviser. But these attributes did not detract from his interest in what science and technology could do. As a legislator, he had dealt with a range of science and technology issues over the years—biomedical science, atomic energy, and, especially, space. He had led the drive to respond to the Soviet Sputnik with a strong U.S. space program.

His orientation, as reflected in his space policy, was competitive and nationalistic. This was true in military and civilian technology, and also in basic science. He believed in American preeminence in science and technology. At the same time, he was highly pragmatic and concerned with visible "payoffs" in the short term. He had a populistic bent and was anxious to see science and technology, as a resource, benefit parts of the country that lagged economically. He knew little about the technical details of science and technology, but he had faith in its potential for the nation and world. His policies therefore were those of a believer and activist in science and technology policy. He was also pragmatic about science and technology's place vis-à-vis other priorities. When it was necessary to cut back in federal programs, he did not spare technoscience.

Johnson was a consummate politician, one who constantly gauged decisions in terms of his power stakes. He was particularly concerned with Congress, and the next election. However, the fact of his being chief executive meant that considerations other than pure politics had to enter into his decision making: the government had to be run. How factors other than the purely political entered the White House depended greatly upon the role and capacity of the subpresidency.

The Subpresidency

There are five basic elements represented in the official subpresidency.[28] They vary in the degree to which they are oriented to the president as a person (the personal presidency); to the president as an office (the institutional presidency); or to some outside referent. Closest to the personal presidency are the *principals*. This is a role that is independent of formal title. It can be filled by various individuals in the subpresidency. Some aides are principals some of the time on some of the issues; others are principals much of the time on many issues; still others are never in the mainstream of presidential policy management. The principals are those upon whom the president most relies in making particular policy decisions. Those who are principals most often include policy generalists on the White

House staff who are capable of blending sensitivity to the president's political needs with policy advice. Ideally, they can span the personal and institutional presidencies. Examples of such inner-circle aides during the Johnson years were William (Bill) Moyers and Joseph Califano. These individuals cut a wide swath across domestic policy matters and involved themselves in science and technology on occasion. When they did, it mattered.

A second group includes the *budgeteers*. The budgeteers are based in what is today the Office of Management and Budget (OMB) and during the Johnson era was called Bureau of the Budget (BOB). The director of OMB may well be a presidential principal, but his organization has a perspective that relates more to the institutional than to the personal presidency. The organization is composed primarily of highly skilled civil servants, who continue from one presidency to the next. They adapt to different presidential perspectives, but develop their own points of view and give continuity to presidential management. The chief budgeteer, the director of OMB (BOB), is potentially extremely powerful. Three different BOB directors served Johnson: first, Kermit Gordon; then, Charles Schultze; and, finally, Charles Zwick. They were an extension of presidential power by virtue of their centrality to the president's use of the budget as a primary management tool. Since science and technology programs invariably cost money, the budgetary aides became major participants in technoscience decision making.

The third group in the subpresidency consists of the *professionals*. These individuals and organizations may seek to reflect what a particular president wants, or what they think the presidency needs. But they have another outside referent—their professional calling. They may be in the subpresidency not because they are close to the president, but because they bring a specialized knowledge he needs to make certain kinds of decisions. As commander-in-chief, for example, the president may require the advice of military professionals—the Joint Chiefs of Staff. In making economic policy decisions, he may rely on information provided him by the Council of Economic Advisers (CEA). And, as one who must make decisions with a high content of science and technology, he has what Price has called the "scientific estate."

Price makes a distinction between scientists and professionals. Scientists, he says, are a group concerned solely with truth for its own sake, "for a basic approach of modern science has been to purge itself of a concern for purposes and values in order to deal more reliably with the study of material phenomena and their causes and effects."[29]

Professionals, he says, make use of the sciences, but they go beyond truth for its own sake to add a purpose. The scientific estate, in its subpresidential role, must relate to the president's problems, and this requires a professional stance. It is more accurate to conceive of the scientific estate as another set of professional aides than as a unique group with a special claim to truth. Scientific certainty may be possible in the laboratory, but it is seldom found in the White House.

As a professional contingent of the subpresidency, the scientific estate is one among a number of groups vying for presidential access. Its relative influence is especially significant for our purposes, since it is the one element of the subpresidency with a potentially comprehensive perspective on science and technology. Other groups may deal with technoscience, but they usually do so piecemeal, off and on, or from a very particularized point of view (e.g., budgetary). Hence, the place of the scientific estate, as a bellwether of the technoscience presidency, is critical.

When Johnson became president, the science adviser was Jerome Wiesner, an engineer from Massachusetts Institute of Technology (MIT). Wiesner had made a decision to return to MIT, and his successor, Donald Hornig, a forty-three-year-old Princeton chemist, had already been formally selected by President Kennedy on November 7, 1963. Stressing continuity and with no candidate of his own—in itself a significant fact—Johnson accepted Hornig, a virtual stranger. Hornig was sworn into office on January 24, 1964. As a White House aide, he was a principal in form. However, he seldom had that status in fact. Hornig later called his relationship with Johnson "friendly but arm's length." He wrote, ". . . I had little feeling for the strong dominant personality who saw everything in political terms, and President Johnson had little feeling for academicians and scientists, although he always held them in great respect."[30] Nevertheless, the two men found ways to work together, especially in the first two years. If Johnson was not close to Hornig personally, he found Hornig and the scientific estate useful as professional aides. At least, when Hornig sought to leave, Johnson urged him to stay. Always the master in finding the right incentive to get another person to do what he wanted, Johnson warned that if Hornig left, he would make OST part of the Bureau of the Budget. Hornig recollects that he did not know whether Johnson would follow through, but he took the admonition "very seriously."[31]

Hornig was one of the very few top presidential assistants who stayed throughout Johnson's tenure. In doing so, he walked a thin line between his loyalties to Johnson and the expectations set by his outside professional peers. Every science adviser has had the same problem, and it is typical for all the president's professional aides.

In the fourth group are the *administrators*. These include the heads of the independent agencies and departments. No group has a greater problem in identification than the administrators. They are appointed by the president and expected to represent presidential perspectives to their agencies, as well as to advise him on policy. Administrators are supposed not only to support the president, but also to administer their agencies. The latter task frequently results in a conflict of interest. What is good for the agency may not be good for the president.

What is true in general is not always the situation in specific cases. In the Johnson presidency, there was great variation in the ability of administrators to play subpresidential (in contrast to agency-oriented) roles. Robert McNamara, secretary of defense, was usually in the subpresidency—not only on White House weapons decisions, but also in matters relevant to another presidential concern, the supersonic transport (SST). In the latter case, Johnson gave him a special role. This permitted him to do what other administrators generally could not do, namely, advise the president in areas beyond their own agency's purview.

A more typical case was that of James Webb, administrator of NASA. Webb's influence was essentially limited to the space agency's jurisdiction. Within that jurisdiction, his influence was great. When Johnson thought about space policy, he looked first to advice from Webb. However, Webb felt the conflicts of simultaneously being both an aide to the president and a spokesman on behalf of his agency. Johnson, for his part, recognized the problem, and dealt with Webb accordingly.

So it was with other key administrators under Johnson. These included such individuals as Glenn Seaborg, an eminent chemist, who was chairman of the Atomic Energy Commission (AEC) throughout the Johnson years, as well as Najeeb Halaby and W. F. "Bozo" McKee. Halaby was administrator of the Federal Aviation Administration (FAA) until March 1965, when he was succeeded by McKee. These individuals had responsibilities for SST. Like Seaborg in atomic energy, Halaby and McKee in SST matters were expected to represent Johnson's views, but they also had a program to champion. The president solved the problem, in part, by giving McNamara a subpresidential SST assignment.

There were many other administrators with science and technology interests, such as Stuart Udall, secretary of interior, and John Gardner, who headed the Department of Health, Education, and Welfare (HEW) for a period during the Johnson years. Sometimes such individuals could be seen as members of the subpresidency; at other times they were not. Their role depended on how the president saw them at a given time. There were certain administrators who were almost never involved in presidential decision making, even though they were in charge of significant technoscience enterprises. Among these was Leland Haworth, director of the National Science Foundation. The head of NSF was not perceived as a subpresidential actor. His views had to be represented by one who was—namely, the science adviser.

The fifth element in the subpresidency is the *vice-president*. The ambiguity of the vice-president's role is well known. He (or she) is the only other elected official (besides the president) in the executive branch. But he has little constitutional power. He is a principal to the extent that the president lets him be. Various presidents have treated their vice-presidents in different ways. Johnson let his vice-president, Hubert Humphrey, play a limited subpresidential role, but it had some important science and technology elements. Like Johnson under Kennedy, Humphrey headed the National Aeronautics and Space Council (NASC), formed at the same time as NASA to coordinate civil and military space policy. The vice-president also chaired the National Council on Marine Resources and Engineering Development (Marine Council), an interagency committee to provide advice and coordinate policy in the field of oceanography. In this capacity, Humphrey was a forceful subpresidential presence.

These, then, are the key subpresidential actors—principals, budgeteers, professionals, administrators, and the vice-president. They are the officials who are part of presidential decision making on most issues, most of the time. On occasion, there may be unofficial advisers so close to a president that they are de facto members of his subpresidency. In science and technology policy, however, these occasions seem very few and far between, and the official subpresidency is the one that operates. Together, subpresidency and president make up a presidential management system. They merge the executive branch's top management around a policy area, in this case science and technology. They constitute a collective decision-making apparatus, the technoscience presidency. Decisions by the technoscience presidency reflect the dynamics within; they also reflect the pressures from outside actors.

The Political Setting

The presidency decides in a political setting. There are many outside actors that affect behavior inside the presidency. The scientific com-

munity is an important constituent of the science adviser. The bureaucrats are key constituents of the administrators. Professional
interest groups and bureaucracies are but two of the forces that impinge on any presidential decision-making process. Others are the
media, foreign nations, and the general public.[32] The most pervasive
outside interest directly active and influential in presidential science
and technology policy, however, is Congress.

Like the presidency, Congress has evolved a structure for addressing science and technology issues. Congress regards itself as
having a claim equal to the president's in science and technology
policy making. It has various committees, subcommittees, and individual legislators who have specialized in technoscience areas. Most
of these relate directly to line agencies that spend the dollars that
fuel science and technology programs. They pull particularly at administrators and constitute a centrifugal force countering the cen-
tripetal pressures of the president.

For example, there are specific House and Senate committees/
subcommittees concerned with military, space, and energy technologies. In the Johnson era, there was an exceptionally powerful Joint
Committee on Atomic Energy (JCAE). The existence of such a structure gave those legislators with strategic positions in one or more
of those committees special influence in science and technology
affairs. Thus, Senator Clinton Anderson (D, New Mexico), who was
chairman of the Committee on Aeronautical and Space Sciences and
a member of the JCAE, had leverage in two key technoscience fields.
When Anderson wished access to the president, he readily got it, as
did other legislators with similar key roles in technoscience.

Influence came not only from the authorization committees,
but also from appropriations committees. A single legislator, such
as the chairman of an appropriations subcommittee controlling the
budget of a technoscience agency, could threaten the best-laid plans
of a president and subpresidency. With Johnson, a former legislator,
in the White House, the presidency was especially sensitive to congressional points of view.

Thus, outside interests make a difference. Our concern is not
with these interests in their own right, but with their impact on the
decision-making institution we are studying: the presidency.

Policy Decisions

The various interests—internal and external to the presidency—
cooperate and compete in a myriad of ways to influence the course of
presidential decision making. Who has influence, under what conditions? Who is in the subpresidency? Who is out? Who is a principal

aide? Who is not? To get at these questions we focus on presidential decisions affecting the course of major science and technology programs under Lyndon Johnson. The great bulk of public management decisions impacting on technoscience programs are made by the bureaucracy.³³ The presidency interacts with the science and technology programs, however, at the key milestones of their evolution. Presidential policy decisions tend to be critical decisions.

The critical decisions studied are those concerned with 1. agenda setting; 2. adoption; 3. implementation; and 4. curtailment. These are not single decisions. Rather, they are decision processes, often lasting years. They are processes in which the president, as an individual, may be involved only intermittently. Those direct presidential interventions are all important, however, since they set the tone for what the subpresidency does before and after. The many decisions leading up to and from a personal presidential choice are usually made by subpresidential actors. Both president and subpresidency are influenced in their decisions by congressional and other outside interests.

Also, as noted earlier, the science and technology process itself—the factors emanating from the shifts along the continuum from research to development to demonstration to operational use—is a force impacting on presidential decision making. At particular stages, the president is frequently drawn in: to adopt a new development program; to implement one already under way; to curtail one that is not going well or that is costing more than intended. There is a rough parallel between the processes of presidential policy and those of science and technology. One influences the course of the other.

Agenda setting is conceived as a process by which general problems or opportunities in the society are brought, and sometimes kept, before the presidency for a decision. Agenda setting does not necessarily require decisions by the president per se. It does require awareness at the subpresidential level of a problem or opportunity related to science and technology. Awareness, however, is not action.

A problem is more or less defined in presidential terms, but policy resolution in the form of concrete programs can be a distant goal. It usually takes some trigger internal or external to the presidency that catalyzes decision making by getting the president's personal attention and thus raising the priority of the problem for the institution as a whole. The president authorizes a search on the part of certain components of the subpresidency to identify alternative ways to solve the problem (or to respond to the opportunity). The search is undertaken and available options are given attention, including those which would launch a government technoscience program.

Gradually, this latter option gains favor, and the search shifts from what to do to planning how to adopt. The particular option moves ever higher on the subpresidency's agenda, a process mirroring and influencing its place among the president's personal priorities.

Adoption occurs when a policy is made to establish a techno-science program. Adoption entails the authoritative allocation of resources. The sense of legitimacy that is conveyed is critical to adoption. The president must be personally involved. A presidential adoption may be enough to get some forms of administrative action, but legitimacy is partial. For full legitimacy, legislation is usually essential. Indeed, the presidential decision to adopt may be in response to the pressure of a previous congressional adoption. Complete adoption carries both presidential and congressional authority.

Implementation takes place when a program that has been adopted is set in motion. Programs are the administrative embodiment of policy. A new organization may be formed or an old one revamped to carry out the policy. The program is executed and given direction. There is delegation to line agencies, which increases as the program evolves. Funds are provided. There may be an evaluation as to how the program is progressing. If all goes well, implementation continues and leads to a successfully completed program as the policy goals are met. If the evaluation reveals problems, but the presidency wants to keep the program, changes are made. How a presidency implements a program may depend to a considerable degree on whether it sees the program as its own. A distinction may be usefully drawn between implementation of programs begun under an incumbent president and implementation of programs begun under a predecessor.

Agenda setting, adoption, and implementation may be regarded as stages in a process that take place in sequence over time. The stages are by no means precise in the sense of having clear-cut beginnings and ends. One overlaps with the next. Implementation can give rise to adoption through the feedback of impacts to adopters. Yet there are differences in central tendency, and, over time, stages can be detected. Indeed, actors who are present at one stage may not be at another.

There is another class of critical presidential decisions that can take place at any point, at any stage. These are decisions involving *curtailment* of science and technology efforts. Curtailment can take place in agenda setting. Many possible scientific and technological issues do not ever reach the agenda of the president; they are screened-out or held back by subpresidential aides. Not all proposals that do reach the agenda are adopted. Many are rejected. Finally, many programs are terminated during implementation; they are canceled outright.

As programs can be curtailed at any point along their life cycle, so they can also be curtailed in varying degrees. Curtailment can be partial or complete. A partial curtailment takes place when a program is cut back rather than cut out. There are many more instances of partial than of complete curtailment once implementation is under way. This is attributable, in part, to sunken presidential costs— particularly where programs have their genesis under an incumbent president.

Agenda setting, adoption, implementation, curtailment—critical decisions of this kind are basic to presidential management of science and technology. They are made during every presidency. Our focus is on how the Johnson presidency made its critical choices, and who influenced their making. Decisions do not just happen. They occur because an insider or outsider becomes an advocate or policy entrepreneur behind a particular choice, then builds a coalition of support around that choice. Getting the president in that coalition— whether he comes with enthusiasm or reluctance—is a major goal in the politics behind presidential policy management.

The Cases

To investigate the role of various actors in presidential technoscience, I have based the analysis on twenty-four case histories of specific decision processes occurring in the era of Lyndon Johnson. These involved programs such as Apollo, supersonic transport, nuclear accelerators, the antiballistic missile, Mohole, the Manned Orbital Laboratory, nuclear desalting, chemical defoliation, the electronic barrier in Vietnam, and others. The cases are used to illuminate aspects of the presidential policy process. They are not meant to be in-depth case histories covering all points of view in a given experience. They represent a presidential management perspective on these various science and technology programs, clarifying central issues of dispersion, sequence, integration, and strategy in decision making.

The use of case histories for purposes of gathering data on the policy process is well established in the political science and public administration fields. Cases are a primary method for testing existing hypotheses about decision making as well as exploring new conceptions about who does what, how, and when. Given our objective— better understanding of the processes of presidential management in a relatively uncharted area—cases are an appropriate tool for analysis.

The cases chosen represent different science and technology programs in various stages of development.[34] They include both civilian and military examples and cut across the various government agencies. They were selected to cover a range of both critical decisions and decision arenas. The arenas are those of scientific research, technological development, and technological application. While many actual and potential programs have elements that could place them in more than one arena of decision, most can be classified in one of these three in terms of emphasis. Arenas matter, since issues and actors differ.

Key questions in *scientific research* relate to the division between basic and applied research. Basic research is ordinarily favored by the scientific community and universities. They want the maximum funds with the minimal governmental controls. Applied research targets science more toward societal missions, and it places government more in charge of research priorities and direction.

Presidential decisions affect basic and applied research in the aggregate through the budget process. While most federal agencies sponsor basic research, the agencies most closely associated with this type of program are the National Science Foundation and the National Institutes of Health. Presidential decisions concerning these agencies are particularly salient to academic scientists.

Some scientific decisions are especially presidential in scale: those that entail massive expenditures for very large, unique facilities. Such facilities are viewed by scientists and political officials as regional prizes. In these "big science" decisions, presidential choices go beyond questions of "whether" and "how much" to those of "where."

The second arena of choice involves *technological development*. Decisions here resemble scientific decisions insofar as they entail budget preferences and locational politics. Big science is big because it requires large-scale technology (e.g., high energy physics' use of nuclear accelerators). However, while the goals of science are diffuse and its organization is typically flat and decentralized, the nature of technological development raises different issues. Decisions on technology entail presidential choices to build specific new products or to develop particular novel capabilities. The cost of such developmental efforts are often in the billions, whereas science typically requires millions, at most. Decisions on technology usually involve industry rather than universities. They also raise ideological issues (e.g., the government's role in developing technologies that may ultimately inure to commercial benefit). They involve different agencies from those concerned primarily with basic research, including those of defense, energy, and space. Because the decisions involve a bigger dollar impact and visible, tangible hardware, they are also usually more politicized than are those concerned with science per se.

Finally, there is the arena of *technological applications*, decisions to use advanced technology for practical purposes. This is in the gray area between R&D and operations. It is where a policy *for* science and technology gives way to science and technology *in* policy. It is also where scientists and engineers may yield to operating officials in terms of expertise. Applications may or may not be classified under the R&D category. A project demonstration may be the end of R&D or the beginning of application. The application decision is placed in the realm of science and technology by the novelty of the technology employed. Innovation is entailed: new technology being used for the first time, generally, or for the first time in a new way.

Application decisions are often not as obvious in presidential choices in science and technology except where particular applications become controversial. Thus, the application of new military technology in war or the deployment of very expensive weapons systems can gain visibility and notoriety. Less visible, but also in the arena of applications, are decisions to apply new technologies to the problems of cities (e.g., housing, urban mass transit, pollution control, etc.) or to transfer technology to developing countries. Here questions abound as to how much is enough, not just in money but in the overall government "push" as contrasted with reliance upon the market "pull" to accomplish a transfer. These nonmilitary application decisions can involve the president and those around him with such civilian agencies as Housing and Urban Development (HUD), Department of Transportation (DOT), and the Environmental Protection Agency (EPA). They also bring him and his associates into decisions concerning the Agency for International Development (AID) when foreign technology transfer is at issue.

The cases selected involve all three arenas of science and technology policy: research, development, and applications. They are analyzed in succeeding chapters in terms of the decision-making framework discussed—agenda setting, adoption, implementation, and curtailment. Who is influential in the presidential management of science and technology depends both on the nature of the critical decision involved and on the arena of policy choice. It also depends on the relative power resources that those who wish to be influential can mobilize in a particular decision context.

This approach permits a broad understanding of presidential

management issues, both specific to the field and of a more general kind. The science and technology policy process is complex. It is characterized by decision making that is dispersed, sequential, and requiring an unusual blend of scientific and political considerations. It is a process deeply influenced by presidential decision making. How the presidency attempts to manage that process is examined in the pages that follow.

2. Agenda Setting

New science and technology policies begin as problems or opportunities. They get on the agenda of the presidency and are transformed into issues for White House decision. The manner in which the process works can be convoluted and complex. How agenda setting worked in the era of Lyndon Johnson highlights the issues of policy management raised earlier: the dispersion of the science and technology function, the sequential nature of many technoscience decisions, the need for integrating scientific and political considerations in decision making, and the strategy (or lack thereof) behind the decision making in question.

Every presidency must establish an agenda (or agendas). What it puts on its agenda may or may not be new to the government. Indeed, there are initiating and continuing presidential agendas. Issues on the initiating agenda are those with which the presidency concerns itself as a potential adopter. These are policies that are new to a particular presidency. Issues on the continuing agenda are those with which a presidency is concerned as an implementer. These are issues that relate to the administration of policies established by previous adoptions. The adoptions may be a given presidency's own or they may be those of a predecessor, in which case the presidency is placed in a position of implementing policies adopted by a predecessor. Thus, a distinction may be made between the initiating and continuing White House agenda. This chapter is concerned primarily with the initiating agenda.

Presidential agenda setting begins with awareness by some actor within the presidency of a particular problem or opportunity. Awareness may last quite a while before there is any action. Customarily, this action is a process of searching and planning for a solution to a perceived problem. (Exactly what to do about the opportunity can also be seen as a problem.) Often, a key variable in the speed with which the president personally deals with the issue and gives it priority is some "trigger" for policy making. The trigger can be inside or outside the presidency. It can be an event or a decision by an individual or group or the president's personal interest in a matter. It gives an issue priority within the presidency, making it stand out from the multitude of items considered day to day. The trigger is an "action forcing" occurrence.

Triggers can spur action quickly or slowly. Perhaps the classic example of a "fast trigger" was the Soviet Sputnik of 1957. All of a sudden, space technology became a top-priority problem for the Eisenhower administration. On the initiating agenda of Eisenhower, space took its place on the continuing agendas of his successors, including Lyndon Johnson. Gradualism, however, is the norm. Problems have to be developed and sold within the presidency as worthy of the attempt to achieve adoption. Coalitions cutting across actors and involving outside alliances must be forged. This takes time. Some issues succeed in moving up the initiating agenda and remain high on the continuing agenda of a presidency. Others must await a better opportunity under a later incumbent. Still others fall from grace over time.

Many issues that a given presidency places on its agenda are those that were at a low priority among a predecessor's concerns. They are new to "a" presidency, but not necessarily new to "the" presidency except in terms of the ranking assigned them. The fact that certain participants within the subpresidency carry over from one president to the next provides some institutional memory that can ease the process of agenda setting. There is already awareness of a problem within the presidency. It is necessary to persuade the president of the importance of dealing with this issue as an item on his initiating agenda.

Many issues get presidential rhetoric but not serious attention. Among those that do become serious agenda items, some get further than others. A distinction can be made in terms of the nature of presidential consideration. Consideration varies in intensity and span of time. There is a *temporary* agenda of issues that receive passing presidential attention. That attention can be slight or intense, depending upon many factors. Then there is an *emergent* agenda. This includes issues rising in terms of presidential (and perhaps national) interest. The emergence process can take a long time. An issue can stay at a low priority or emerge spasmodically to some decision (adoption) level. However, with emergent issues, there is not a sense that the issue has yet arrived. It involves problems or opportunities entailing decisions in the making.

The third type of initiating agenda is the *priority* agenda, involving issues still new to the presidency and, usually, to the government and nation. However, decision making clearly proceeds from awareness to search and planning toward adoption and beyond. There is a sufficient ground swell of support for action within and outside the presidency to say that the issue has arrived and has become established for at least the incumbent president. It is still on the initiating agenda, but it is a priority item and stays at that status for some time. The prospect is that formulation will give way to policy implementation and the issue will be a continuing agenda item of the next presidency.

In illustrating the various processes of agenda setting, I will draw from a number of cases in the Johnson experience. For temporary agenda setting, there are issues involving earthquake prediction/prevention and power-blackout/electric utility reliability. For the emergent agenda, there are oceanography and energy. For the priority agenda, environmental pollution stands out.

The Temporary Agenda

The most important temporary issues with which any presidency must deal involve crises, emergencies, and disasters. Foreign policy crises are frequent. Crises relating to science and technology occur less often. However, there are natural and technological disasters that do recur sufficiently often to be seen as more than unique events. That they tend to be treated as such on the temporary agenda suggests that our presidential decision-making processes have not kept pace with our disaster management realities.

The Johnson presidency had earthquakes and power blackouts with which to contend. In the case of earthquakes, an actual major event took place, the Alaskan earthquake of 1964. There also was the threat of another event in Denver in 1967. The principal presidential response to the former was to press the relevant emergency-assistance entities within the executive office and the bureaucracy to get on with the task of providing immediate response to the death toll and property damage visited by the quake on Anchorage, Alaska. From the standpoint of some technoscience elements within the subpresidency, however, there was a need to learn from the experience and to use it as a trigger to augment federal efforts in earthquake prediction. At Science Adviser Hornig's urging, Johnson asked the National Academy of Sciences to study intensively the various technical aspects of the event.[1] This was a temporary response to a temporary event.

At the same time, a President's Science Advisory Committee panel investigated the prospects for a potential program in earthquake prediction research. A $137 million program was proposed to

PSAC in 1965.[2] PSAC differed with its panel over emphasis on prediction, as contrasted with engineering (e.g., construction techniques).
PSAC also was divided over which agency should manage the program. Two agencies—the Environmental Sciences Services Administration (ESSA) and the U.S. Geological Survey (USGS)—were interested, and each had proponents on PSAC. Hornig informed Johnson
of the issues and problems. At the president's decision,[3] the PSAC
panel report was released by the Office of Science and Technology,
not the White House, without endorsement. Both ESSA and USGS
set up research centers to work on earthquakes, and their funding for
the field went up slightly. But no national program was developed or
advocated by the presidency. With PSAC itself at odds over the juris-
dictional issue, OST and the science adviser concluded that the time
was not right to push for a major program in earthquake prediction
research. As a scientific research program, earthquake prediction remained potential.[4]

In 1967, there was concern that an earthquake hazard might be
growing in the Denver area. There was never an actual prediction or
official warning. There was scientific worry, however remote. What
made the Denver earthquake more ominous was that it was seem-
ingly a consequence of human action. There had been an injection of
fluid wastes deep into the ground by the Rocky Mountain Arsenal
near Denver. A series of small, local earthquakes had been detected.
Was a larger, more damaging earthquake possible?

The risk of a more serious earthquake in Denver could not be
totally dismissed. A panel of technical experts, under the cognizance
of the science adviser, assessed the threat. The president was kept
informed.[5] Over time, the perceived danger diminished, and mitigat-
ing measures were largely left to nonpresidential agencies. However,
as with the Alaskan quake, the threat of a Denver earthquake was
tested as a trigger by some elements of the scientific estate. Hornig
mentioned to the president the possibility of more research on earthquake prevention technology, but the matter of a major program was
not pursued.[6]

The power blackout issue was another temporary agenda item
that arose during the Johnson years. However, this one moved further in gaining the personal involvement of the president as well as
other actors within and outside the technoscience presidency. Indeed, the president was among the first to become aware of the major
power outage that occurred during his administration: the Northeast
blackout of 1965.

It was the evening of November 9, 1965. Johnson was in Texas
listening to his radio.[7] He learned that a large portion of the North-

east, including New York City, was in darkness; thirty million Americans were affected. Johnson's initial concern was that the blackout might have been caused by sabotage, a situation which would have had national security implications. Normally, agenda setting *ends* with presidential action. In this instance, it *began* with the president.

Upon hearing the radio report, Johnson's first move was to call Defense Secretary Robert McNamara. Washington had been unaffected by the blackout, and McNamara had not heard about it. The technical nature of a vast electrical blackout made the issue a matter for the technoscience presidency. McNamara called Hornig, who was at his office. Hornig contacted a member of the OST staff to have him investigate what was happening. He also called Joseph Swidler, chairman of the Federal Power Commission (FPC). Swidler was not immediately available, but Hornig determined that the FPC staff was keeping in touch with the situation.[8]

Johnson was kept informed, with Hornig spending much of the night on the telephone collecting information and relaying it to the Texas White House.[9] As the night wore on, Johnson was reassured that there was no major defense or civil crisis as a result of the incident and that power in some areas was already being restored. The exact cause of the blackout had not been discovered, but it seemed relatively clear that no sabotage or conspiracy was involved. The blackout had been a consequence of a technological malfunction or human error, or both. A breakdown in the large, complex, interconnected system had given rise to a chain reaction of vast proportions. The problem was thus defined as not being one of national disaster. As Hornig telegraphed the president the following morning, "The most plausible hypothesis seems to be a malfunction of the automatic frequency control equipment in some part of the system, leading to the alternating current getting out of step with other parts. This, coupled with the inadequate circuit-breakers to isolate the various interlinked companies, could have led to a breakdown."[10]

The recovery from this event went through two phases. The first was the initial, overnight assessment of what went wrong, a process in which the science adviser was key. The second was a more in-depth study of the problem and search/planning for a long-term solution. Here FPC loomed large. On December 6, FPC provided Johnson with a report on the Northeast blackout and recommendations for action to prevent further blackouts.[11] FPC interpreted the issue as "electric power reliability." Stronger interstate transmission and generating links in the Canadian–United States pool were needed. FPC's regulatory power to set standards had to be augmented to be certain of reliability.[12]

For the scientific estate, this was primarily an applications issue, since better use of existing technology by utilities could help to improve reliability. Getting the utilities to use that technology was a regulatory problem, however, in the view of FPC. The difficulty was that the solution advocated by FPC (more regulation) was hardly welcomed by the utility industry or its friends in Congress. The president was not anxious to do battle at this point. Consequently, time passed, the memory of the Northeast blackout faded, and the blackout issue receded from the technoscience presidency's agenda.

A year later, the issue was revived. It was placed on the agenda by a Johnson principal and chief domestic aide, Joseph Califano. On October 14, 1966,[13] he asked Hornig to assemble an interagency task force to consider various issues concerned with electric power reliability that might require resolution by legislative means. Hornig quickly saw why a solution to the Northeast blackout problem had been put aside previously. "Whoever voluntccrcd me fur the Electric Power Study must have seen it as a convenient way to get me out of government," he wrote Califano, "because it is quite clear that, no matter how we turn, I will be embroiled in controversy with someone."[14]

On December 2, 1966, Hornig reported to Califano setting forth two alternative proposals aimed at creating more of a system out of the electrical supply network. As Hornig summed up, "In essence, the report recommends that we move in [the] direction of regional planning and systems integration. It presents two similar packages, one largely voluntary and one giving mandatory powers to FPC. A majority of the task force favor the latter, but no consensus was reached."[15] He urged in a follow-up memorandum, ". . . in any future public reference or presentation to the Congress, it [should] be emphasized that any controls to be given to the Federal Power Commission are designed to be standby controls only, not to be exercised unless all clse fails."[16]

FPC had prepared a bill in 1965 in line with its report to the president. It now revised that draft bill to take account of the views of the task force. Another power cessation helped trigger Johnson's attention to the blackout problem. This outage occurred during midday in the Pennsylvania, New Jersey, Maryland, Delaware area. Key members of Congress urged "action."[17] On May 1, 1967, Hornig told BOB that the FPC bill was fully consistent with the findings of the interagency group that he had chaired. He recommended that Johnson endorse the bill.[18]

Over time, an alliance between the science adviser and the chairman of FPC had been forged around an assessment of the problem and the solution needed to avoid future blackouts. However,

still missing was the strong political backing of Johnson for a measure that clearly was not favored by industry. In a memorandum
dated June 7, 1967, Califano advised "caution" and noted that the
bill was "controversial." Passage might be delayed, and there could
be many amendments. He suggested letting Lee White, the chairman
of FPC, send the bill up. In this way, Califano suggested that Johnson
"could avoid much of the controversy and still take credit for any
progress. . . ." Once it was transmitted, no one could accuse Johnson
of "not taking every appropriate step to prevent power failures." [19]

The necessary presidential support for adoption was thus weakened. The bill for electric power reliability went to Congress the
next day. The chairman of FPC was asked by the press whether this
was an FPC bill or an administration bill.[20] It was significant that the
question had to be asked at all. Equally significant was White's reply,
referring the inquiring reporter to the bill's concluding "boiler plate"
paragraph. This stated that the Bureau of the Budget advised that
there was no objection to the proposed legislation from the standpoint of the administration's program. He suggested that the inquiring reporter draw his own conclusions.[21] The bill did not pass.

Thus, for different reasons, earthquake prediction/prevention
and electric power reliability proved to be temporary issues for the
Johnson agenda. Earthquakes came and went, or threatened to come
and did not materialize. Power blackouts were taken seriously, but
proved temporary presidential interests. The regulatory solution developed to induce utility change faced political uncertainties. As
technoscience programs of the presidency, earthquake prediction/
prevention and electric power reliability remained in the realm of
potential.

The Emergent Agenda

Emergent issues are those that are given more than temporary consideration by the presidency. They are on the presidential agenda and
stay there. They are on the way up and may well experience some
adopted policies. On the other hand, they are not top-priority items,
and their place on the presidency's agenda is precarious.

There were a number of such emergent issues clamoring for attention during the Johnson years. Some of the key factors, indicating
why some got attention and others did not, are seen in the cases of
oceanography and energy. One represented an opportunity; the other,
a problem.

When Johnson became president in late 1963, the predominant
proponents of oceanography as a field of research and development

were outside the technoscience presidency. They were to be found in Congress, the universities, and industry. Whatever their differences, they could unite around a common complaint: the government was not doing enough to advance and apply knowledge in this field.

There existed a subcommittee of the Federal Council for Science and Technology, called the Interagency Committee on Oceanography (ICO). This unit worked with OST and BOB staffs in developing and coordinating oceanographic budgets and plans. As chairman of FCST, Hornig was the most visible White House aide in the oceanographic area. His general stance was to seek balance among competing scientific research enterprises, unless there was some overriding policy reason for raising one above the other. To oceanographic interests this made Hornig seem to be insufficiently enthusiastic about their field. These advocates despaired that oceanography as a scientific research program was fragmented among innumerable agencies. A program of many, it was a prime interest of no one agency in particular. They felt that it was an administrative orphan. There was no strong-willed agency head to advise the president on behalf of oceanography.

On May 19, 1964, Hornig responded to a congressional inquiry regarding a proposal to establish a national oceanographic agency. He commented that oceanography was important, but there was no need to combine all elements in a single agency. This would cause problems. It could best be handled by coordination, and his office and FCST were already doing this.[22] Oceanography was on the agenda; however, some thought its place inadequate. Being on the agenda of the technoscience presidency was not enough if oceanography had a low priority.

In June 1964, FCST, with Chairman Hornig in agreement, authorized ICO to look at oceanographic plans and budgets coming from the agencies and to recommend a more substantial federal effort if a study deemed this wise. ICO did so. It took a cross-cutting perspective that revealed gaps in agency funding. It put forth what advocates of oceanography wanted, namely, a comprehensive national program. A review by OST that was completed in September concurred with some ICO recommendations while rejecting others. However, in October 1964, FCST turned down all of its subcommittee's recommendations. It chose not even to concur with those items supported by the OST review.[23]

There was bound to be an unfavorable reaction from oceanographic supporters in Congress, among whom was Warren Magnuson, a powerful senator from Washington and friend of Johnson. At the request of Bill Moyers, a key principal aide to the president, BOB and

OST again assessed the matter. On December 18, 1964, BOB's Philip Hughes provided Moyers with a memorandum on the National Oceanographic Program in which he stated that an increase in funds was not justifiable. He questioned "the quality of science already being done" and stated that there was a "need to resolve internal operating problems such as organization and data collections before making additional investment."[24] On December 22, Moyers wrote the budget director, stating, "After reading this, it is my feeling we ought not to increase oceanographic research by any substantial amount."[25]

ICO's reaction to this turn of events was indicated by a report it issued in 1965:

> The National Oceanographic Program is at an impasse. Under its initial impetus, capital investments were made, training programs encouraged, and research possibilities explored. The implication of all this was the aim toward a program which would utilize this potential at a high energy level. Such a program must be bolstered by funds, and sufficient funds have not materialized. In effect, then, the plan has been turned off almost at the point where results might have been born.[26]

During 1965, a number of bills were introduced to raise the national priority of oceanography. Congressional hearings were held. The key legislation, introduced by Magnuson, would displace the existing locus of presidential oceanography with a new one modeled on space. There was a National Aeronautics and Space Council in the Executive Office of the President. Why not have a similar body for oceanography?

As the idea gathered momentum, Hornig resisted; so did BOB.[27] The OST and BOB engaged in a "quiet lobby" against legislative action, pointing out the strong possibility of presidential veto.[28] In May 1965, in a further attempt to stave off congressional action, Hornig formed a PSAC panel on oceanography and charged it with drafting a statement on national goals for this field, along with a set of programmatic proposals for carrying out those goals. He contacted various legislators, including Representative Herbert Bonner, chairman of the House Committee on Merchant Marine and Fisheries, saying that he was in favor of the goal sought by oceanography's advocates but that he opposed a special organization reporting to the president on oceanography when FCST and his own science advisory apparatus were already in existence.[29] He testified in Congress against such a new structure.[30]

Hornig wrote Johnson on August 19, 1965, that there was "a strong and urgent sentiment in both Houses of Congress for the passage of some legislation on oceanography."[31] By April 1, 1966, the president's science adviser was writing him that "a real need" existed "for a thoughtful and imaginative federal program to develop marine science and technology" and that he expected to present such a program to Johnson after the PSAC panel report had been discussed and evaluated by his science advisory committee.[32]

On June 2, 1966, before PSAC could issue its report, Congress passed the legislation. It did not set forth a program; rather, it created new presidential entities with limited periods of existence to espouse the oceanographic cause and to design a lasting administrative framework for this area of science and technology policy. After letting the bill sit for a considerable time, the president signed the Marine Resources and Engineering Development Act of 1966 into law.

The act created an interim National Council on Marine Resources and Engineering Development (generally called the Marine Council) and a presidential Advisory Commission on Marine Science, Engineering, and Resources. The Marine Council, as indicated, was placed in the Executive Office of the President and modeled after the National Aeronautics and Space Council. In effect, the commission displaced PSAC, and the Marine Council displaced OST. While the Marine Council included the heads of various agencies with oceanographic interests, it also had a staff directed by Edward Wenk, an engineer-administrator who came from OST. Most important, the head of the Marine Council was Vice-President Hubert Humphrey. This meant that the science adviser was being replaced by Humphrey as the president's chief aide for oceanographic policy. Thus, the scientific estate had been deemed a failure by oceanographic interests in Congress, and a new structure, with a different orientation, was put in its place. In a speech delivered before a group with oceanographic concerns on June 28, 1966, Hornig noted that he had been charged with "oceanographic unconstructivism." He denied guilt and wished the new units well so that they could "get on with the job."[33] Thus, Hornig's scientific estate bowed out, and an alternative source of professional advice to the president came in.

The purpose of these new entities was not neutral analysis; it was advocacy. Such a task fitted well the personalities and style of Wenk and Humphrey. Humphrey was an ebullient individual whose energies were constrained by the limited role and resources of the vice-presidency. He had inherited Johnson's vice-presidential task as chairman of the National Aeronautics and Space Council. However, there was little room for a major policy role there, since space was Johnson's issue. In contrast, the Marine Council provided one of the few outlets that Humphrey had, one in which there was no competition from a strong agency head—or from the president himself.

The purpose of the Marine Council and the commission was to help trigger action on oceanography within the government by getting the support of the president. In a July 16, 1966, memorandum to Humphrey, Johnson asked for initial recommendations by January 1967 so that appropriate legislative proposals might be made early to the next Congress.[34] How serious was Johnson about this request? At this point in 1966, as Wenk later wrote, "The question was not how high [on Johnson's agenda] ocean affairs might be, but whether they were on his list at all." Hence, the first challenge for the Marine Council was to get Johnson's genuine attention. As Wenk explained:

> For marine affairs, the President was the locus of decision-making. But because of the competition with so many other issues, the challenge was something like a game played on amusement park merry-go-rounds, where passengers snatched at rings as they whizzed by a rack. The rings were of wood, except for one beautiful, shiny, and sought-after prize—the brass ring! In Washington, a similar game is played by government officials and special interests alike. In straining for visibility and funds for favorite programs, the brass ring is public support by the President.[35]

Knowing that Johnson was interested in applications, the argument of science for science's sake was deliberately suppressed in favor of more technologically oriented advocacy. On October 14, 1966, Humphrey sent Johnson a memorandum in which he stated that the Marine Council was "evaluating problem areas where redirection or increased emphasis in marine science affairs would immediately contribute to broad national interests and to the Great Society concept."[36] A month later, on November 19, Humphrey sent Johnson two memoranda: the first listed eight programs that the Marine Council believed should be emphasized; and the second concentrated upon the subject of food from the sea. The latter was singled out for special attention.[37]

The choice was strategic. Johnson had said, "Next to the pursuit of peace, the greatest challenge to the human family is the race between food supply and population increase. That race is now being lost."[38] The Marine Council saw "Food from the Sea" as a natural response to a declared presidential concern and developed a specific initiative to attack protein malnutrition.[39] In writing to the president, Humphrey called the initiative "a weapon in the war on hunger." It would involve:

> . . . a new policy for the U.S. to provide world leadership and begin a long-range program to exploit the oceans vigorously as an untapped source of protein concentrate. This five-year program will help less-developed nations to obtain high-quality but inexpensive protein.
>
> AID would be made project leader; Interior would develop the technology; other agencies would redirect on-going efforts, wherever appropriate, to support the program. Total cost of this five-year demonstration program to provide protein requirements for one million people in one country is $23 million, with a FY 67 and FY 68 start totalling $5 million.[40]

It was argued that it would be possible to convert whole fish into a nutritious fish protein concentrate that was not then available. The technology for doing so was at hand. In addition to helping the other nations, this program would help the U.S. domestic fish industry.

In this and various other ways, the vice-president, a politician, found the words to attract Johnson's eye. The organizational change creating the Marine Council provided a vehicle for getting oceanography on the president's personal agenda. For every Johnson interest, there was an oceanographic response. As Wenk later noted:

> In the area of urban decay, we argued in the first annual report that "urban development does not end at the water's edge." . . . We searched for marine solutions in coastal management and pollution abatement. Potential programs in tune with Johnson's interests were also examined in relation to unemployment and economic distress . . . long-range weather forecasting that could be improved to reduce the misery from unexpected and prolonged drought—a matter well understood in the heart of Texas. International cooperation in space had been one of Johnson's proudest achievements in his influence on drafting of the Space Act, and it had a marine analogue. One, of course, the Sea Grant program, was in harmony with Lyndon Johnson's deep-seated interest in education.[41]

Humphrey's enthusiasm for his oceanographic assignment was real. "Oceanography has more economic dividends than anything we're doing in the science area," he declared in February 1967.[42] He chaired every meeting of the Marine Council. With extensive prior briefings, he used the meetings to prod agency heads who were members of the council to move toward common objectives. Humphrey was not so much interested in the scientific problems as in science and technology policy questions.[43] Given his relatively easy access to Johnson, this made him an excellent intermediary between the Marine Council and the president.

Wenk and the Marine Council staff made maximum use not only of Humphrey but also of others with direct channels to the oval office, such as Joseph Califano in domestic affairs and Walt Rostow in the national security realm. The process of gathering ideas for the president's messages and legislative program provided yearly opportunities for the Marine Council to seek the brass ring. In 1967, Wenk recalls submitting twenty-two separate ideas in response to one Califano call. The twenty-two were ultimately trimmed down, with most being completely eliminated. However, one particular idea survived the screening process: the International Decade of Ocean Exploration (IDOE).[44] IDOE was a program to encourage all countries: 1. to develop their marine science opportunities through cooperative exploration; and 2. to develop new patterns of collaboration in the peaceful uses of the oceans that could be a factor in an eventual treaty.[45] It became what Wenk called "our greatest triumph by its identification in the 1968 State-of-the-Union Message."[46]

Not everyone was happy with the way the restructured presidential agenda setting process was working. Hornig, for example, was critical of the IDOE "triumph." As he wrote Califano on March 4, 1967, IDOE's announcement might raise expectations that would not be fulfilled: ". . . those promoting a 'Decade' as a new program (principally Marine Council staff) are concentrating on a presidential commitment that could be translated into substantially increased funds for Marine Science activities. The budgetary implications of a new program are unknown, but one Council committee staff estimate was $5.46 billion."[47]

There is no doubt that outside interests succeeded in stimulating the emergence of oceanography by changing the inside actors affecting presidential decision making. Not only were ideas generated that might not have surfaced otherwise, but also, more importantly, they were pushed by individuals with a definite set of views and skills. To be sure, congressional restructuring of executive office institutions does not necessarily always succeed. The president may be given a new adviser, but it is up to him to listen or not to listen. In this case, that adviser was the vice-president, who was supported by an astute technical professional. The president listened in spite of himself. As Wenk remarked, the elevated position of the Marine Council mattered. Its place in presidential technoscience gave it ". . . greater insight as to the presidential processes and timing and opportunity to follow an issue through this maze to the important finale of action. Even an issue that has become a candidate for presidential support has to be shepherded assiduously right up to mention in the State of the Union Address, for example, or in other important messages to Congress, where the President asserts his priorities."[48]

Oceanography became an emergent issue under Johnson. It did not become a top-priority issue; but, as the Johnson administration ended, it seemed to be moving in that direction. When the Nixon administration took over, it had the report of the Advisory Commission on Marine Science, Engineering, and Resources. This report was released on January 8, 1969, but it was judged to be a matter for action by the next administration rather than by Johnson.[49] Nixon did little with the commission's report, which suggested a variety of new national ventures in oceanography, and the commission soon vanished from the scene. The Marine Council lingered a while longer. With their demise, a new National Oceanic and Atmospheric Administration (NOAA) was established in 1970. This was not the large, independent, NASA-style agency that the oceanographic proponents had wanted. As a relatively small agency in the Department of Commerce, NOAA played the role of advocate for oceanography in the 1970s, but it was a weak and unappreciated base of activity.

In contrast to oceanography, where the science adviser was perceived by advocates as a barrier to placing an issue on the agenda, energy was a case in which the science adviser was the principal proponent behind the emergence of a presidential interest. It can be said of energy policy during the Johnson years that it was an extremely fragmented sector and that, to the extent that any official played an integrating role, it was the science adviser. The identification of energy as a science and technology policy issue came naturally, as the government's principal energy concern at this time was nuclear power. However, there was a growing awareness during these years that energy meant more than nuclear power and more than research and development. For the technoscience presidency, energy was a problem of great complexity and interagency strife.

At the subpresidential level, the science adviser attempted to give some shape and direction to this emergent issue but was limited by his power relative to other participants, as well as by his own tendency to see the future of energy largely in nuclear terms. This helped to keep the issue on the agenda, but it was in an emergent mode that was, if anything, less developed than that of oceanography. Studies became the principal means for policy action under the circumstances. Concrete proposals were few and far between.

When Hornig became science adviser, he inherited a major interagency study of energy that President Kennedy had set in motion under the guidance of his science adviser, Jerome Wiesner. The study was, in part, a response to a 1962 proposal by the Atomic Energy Commission for a massive, long-term commitment of federal funds to nuclear power, from improved design of conventional plants to development of new reactors. Questions were raised about public versus private roles in such plans. There were also issues of balance between nuclear and nonnuclear sources. AEC represented the nuclear bias, and the Department of Interior served as the governmental base for concerns about oil, gas, and coal.

Kennedy was persuaded to take an overarching view of energy priorities, especially from a research and development standpoint. With the science adviser in charge and the chairman of the Council of Economic Advisers as vice-chairman, an Interdepartmental Energy Steering Committee was formed. Ten agencies with energy interests were represented. The actual work was performed by a team of technical specialists headed by Professor Ali Bulant Cambel, head of the Department of Mechanical Engineering at Northwestern University.[50]

Draft after draft of the Cambel report, initially delivered in 1964, was prepared to meet objections from various agencies. The report was not officially completed until 1966. This was a sign of bureaucratic dispute, particularly between AEC and the Department of Interior, and the lack of urgency on the part of the subpresidential actors.

In 1963, an early draft indicated that the report's basic conclusion was that the United States had "adequate energy supplies for the foreseeable future, with no increase in . . . prices."[51] Such views concerned AEC, even though successive drafts were generally supportive of nuclear power. AEC believed that there was overoptimism with respect to existing fossil fuel resources and new discovery and production techniques.[52] On the other hand, BOB took the view that the report "should avoid, as far as possible, creating a feeling of urgency regarding an expanded research and development program for nuclear energy."[53] Thus, AEC was anxious to put a damper on the emphasis on fossil fuels (i.e., the Department of Interior), and BOB wanted to put a hold on the atom (i.e., AEC).

Under the circumstances, it took a long time to complete the report. When it was finally made public in 1966, there was no indication that energy was a problem requiring an immediate presidential decision. While it indicated possible long-term difficulties in energy resources and the need for increased R&D, the report found little danger of an imminent energy crisis. It stated, "Since no true emergency nor compelling opportunity is foreseen, the total energy R&D expenditure looks reasonable. Of course, if heavier reliance were to be placed on imported energy resources, the level of R&D expenditure should undoubtedly decrease."[54] The report saw "no grounds for serious concern that the nation was using up any of its stock of fossil fuels too rapidly; rather, there is a suspicion that we are using them up too slowly."[55] Given such views, conservation was "not an economic necessity."[56] Nor were crash efforts needed on such non-nuclear options as solar energy or geothermal energy: "Without significant technological breakthroughs, solar energy has little prospect of extensive civilian use except in special circumstances. . . . Presently, geothermal energy supplies only a minute portion of U.S. energy requirements. Because the need to develop geothermal resources is not urgent, a large R&D program is not essential."[57]

The Cambel report saw no emergency looming. It did not express particular dissatisfaction with the existing sense of R&D priorities. The nuclear option was supported, particularly the need to move ahead with the breeder reactor. On October 7, 1966, Hornig sent a final draft of the report to Johnson and listed the following as its major findings and recommendations:

—The Nation's total resources seem adequate to satisfy expected energy requirements through the end of the century at costs near present levels. There is no foreseeable shortage of either coal or nuclear fuels.
—The exhaustion of liquid petroleum and natural gas should be anticipated, but alternatives will certainly be available, such as those from shale oil and tar sands, and from the liquefaction of coal.
—Advanced technology can enormously expand the economically available resources of nearly all fuels, and can provide substitutes for many.
—In addition to domestic resources, the energy resources of other countries offer increased potential supplies for the U.S. in exchange for other products of the U.S. economy.
—Because of high risks, large capital expenditures, and long times involved, Federal Government is justified in continuing a reasonable level of effort to develop advanced nuclear power plants with improved fuel utilization. Approximately

50 times more energy is available from each pound of nuclear power than we are now getting.
—Although it has been argued that private enterprise will take
necessary action when the economic need is clear, some
government involvement in developing technology and sur-
veying resources is appropriate so that substitutes for oil and
natural gas can be available when needed.
—Environmental pollution associated with production and use
of energy resources, and especially with fossil fuel combus-
tion, is a serious national problem requiring government regulation and both government and private R&D.
—Government has a continuing role to play in developing a
number of energy-related technologies such as controlled nuclear fusion, more effective power grids, and underground
transmission of electricity.[58]

While somewhat diffused by the broader perspective of the Cambel report, atomic energy continued to get special attention. This
was epitomized and reenforced by a statement, jointly signed by
Hornig, Budget Director Charles Schultze, and Council of Economic
Advisers Chairman Gardner Ackley, released with the Cambel report
in late 1966:

The major energy issue is the size and direction of the atomic
power program, both in magnitude of government involvement
and in overall national significance. The most economical program should be pursued which will ensure flexibility and reap
the benefits of lower energy costs. . . . While private industry
will probably concentrate on improving existing commercial
reactors, the government should play a key role in developing
more advanced reactors with better fuel utilization . . . the
government should encourage development of more than one
breeder or near-breeder concept as a hedge against possible failure of any one approach.[59]

Thus, in 1966 as in 1963, when the Cambel study was launched,
the country had energy as an issue on its emergent agenda. However,
nuclear power was an issue on the presidency's continuing and priority agenda. This mattered when it came to going beyond words
to deeds. For example, in 1967, AEC selected the liquid metal fast
breeder reactor (LMFBR) as the lead design on the basis of breeding
efficiency, while continuing work on a limited number of backup
systems. The technoscience presidency generally accepted this ap-

proach. There was some contention among AEC, OST, and BOB over the number and nature of the backup systems.[60] However, on technical grounds, the LMFBR was selected as the most efficient system with which to proceed. The reasoning seemed to be: if the nation needed an energy source for the future, that source was going to be atomic energy. If atomic energy was to be the top priority, a breeder had to be developed. The type of breeder depended upon AEC. Given the costs and risks, the government would have to play the lead role in bringing advanced nuclear technology to fruition. This was the logic and the policy on nuclear energy. To a large extent, AEC's continuing agenda biased the presidency's capacity to initiate a broader energy program.

There were events in the presidential environment that might have sounded an alarm of a possible energy crisis at a much nearer term than anyone imagined. The 1965 blackout of the Northeast, including New York City, has already been discussed. As we have seen, the blackout was interpreted primarily as a problem in electric power reliability rather than a harbinger of resource scarcities in energy supplies. The blackout was viewed largely as an emergency and an aberration, something for the technoscience presidency's temporary agenda.

There was another event during the Johnson years that might have served as a trigger. This was the Six-Day War in the Middle East in 1967. For a brief period, the oil supply to the United States was interrupted. Again, there was concern but not a sufficient sense of urgency to stimulate a deep search or reconsideration of the energy problem. The war lasted but a short time, and there were reserves of oil on hand. Why worry? Why change?

A third event came in 1968, when the Department of State sent word to foreign governments that American oil production would soon reach the limits of its capacity.[61] Such governments needed to know that the extra capacity of the United States which could be called into production during an emergency was about to disappear. As Stobaugh and Yergin have written, "The end of an era was at hand."[62] The State Department memorandum did not become the necessary catalyst for change, however. Like the Cambel report, the blackout, and the Six-Day War, the State Department's concern did not cause the president to accelerate and adapt energy decision making.

The best that the subpresidency's scientific estate could do in this context was to try to keep the issue on the emerging agenda and to get a better understanding of the energy problem in all of its complexity. On December 20, 1966, in response to a memorandum from

Califano for draft material for the 1967 State of the Union message, Hornig suggestd that some language be included to indicate the president's concern about energy policies. He recommended that the president point out that:

> . . . although several federal agencies are responsible for different aspects of energy resources development and utilization, there is no provision for considering energy questions within a comprehensive framework of national objectives—rapid economic growth, efficient development and use of resources, satisfactory international monetary and resource relationships, and adequate resources for national security. . . . [and that the president] propose to establish within the Office of Science and Technology in the Executive Office of the President a small staff to analyze and coordinate the study of energy issues and to develop policy alternatives for decision-making, taking fully into account the interaction of the interests and objectives of the federal agencies involved.[63]

In his cover memorandum to Califano, Hornig pointed out that the statement "would also pave the way for Congressional support for an increased staff for this purpose in the Office of Science and Technology."[64]

On January 30, 1967, President Johnson issued a statement in an address entitled "Protecting Our National Heritage." He declared:

> The number and complexity of federal decisions on energy issues have been increasing as demand grows and competitive situations change. Often decisions in one agency and under one set of laws—whether they be regulatory standards, tax rules or other provisions—have implications for other agencies and other laws, and for the total energy industry. We must better understand our future energy needs and resources. We must make certain our policies are directed toward achieving these needs and developing these resources. I am directing the President's Science Adviser and his Office of Science and Technology to sponsor a thorough study of energy resources and to engage the necessary staff to coordinate energy policy on a government-wide basis.[65]

In November 1967, Hornig hired S. David Freeman, an experienced energy analyst with both an engineering and a legal background, to lead OST in its new energy role. OST got some preliminary work under way via a relatively small Resources for the Future study. At the same time, Hornig requested $500,000 for OST to initiate a more comprehensive study of all aspects of the energy problem. Although the president approved this request, Congress was not about to do so. This was the period of cutbacks in science and technology, and OST was deemed not to be immune to the need for austerity. Hornig wrote Califano on February 9, 1968, saying that questions had been raised at the House appropriations hearings as to whether the president considered this a priority item. He asked for help in reassuring Congress and in getting the necessary funds to carry out the president's January 30, 1967, directive. The help that Califano could give was not enough. He was supportive, but would not play the advocacy role. Hornig was left to struggle unsuccessfully for support.

Not only did Congress turn Hornig down, but Johnson did not include the $500,000 in the new budget he prepared in late 1968. On December 12, 1968, Hornig asked Califano to intercede with the president. Califano turned to Budget Director Zwick. "Can you do anything about this?"[66] Zwick responded, "I've done all I can. I am sure Don would appreciate any help you can give him."[67] Hornig wrote Johnson a final plea on January 3, 1969, but to no avail.[68] Energy might have reached the point where Hornig, Califano, and Zwick saw its importance, but it had not yet captured the priority concern of Johnson.

Thus, during the Johnson years, energy slowly emerged. It was always on the presidential agenda, but it was never quite ready for serious presidential action. The Cambel report did not alert the science adviser or Johnson to an impending crisis. There were budgetary and bureaucratic conflicts that tended to work against integrating and accelerating energy policy. There were signals along the way, but these were not perceived as forerunners of what was to come in the 1970s. Energy was important enough to win presidential rhetoric, but not important enough to get the needed money and staff to back up the words. Within the subpresidency, Hornig pushed much harder than most; but, as he later commented, "There was no time when . . . I went to the President and said, 'We have an energy crisis'—because it seemed clear to us that even the late 1980s allowed plenty of time to make some readjustments. What's more, at the time, the nuclear energy route looked like a very good one."[69]

Thus, throughout the Johnson administration, energy remained on the emergent agenda. It was too obvious a problem to ignore or abandon, but it was not immediate enough to get priority attention. That attention did not come until 1973–74, when the Arab oil boycott moved energy to the center of the nation's science and technology policy stage.

The Priority Agenda

This chapter is on the initiating agenda and those issues in science and technology policy that are new to a given presidency. Most agenda setting processes noted have dealt with issues struggling to gain and hold presidential attention. There are other issues that are new to a given presidency but gain top priority. They move to the forefront of the presidency's initiating agenda. Environmental pollution is an example of an issue that moved to a position of priority under Johnson. It also was one that mushroomed well beyond the technoscience presidency to become a concern of other functional jurisdictions. However, environmental pollution remained a subject with highly technical aspects. Therefore, it continued to have priority in the scientific estate and with others in the subpresidency concerned with scientific dimensions of the burgeoning environmental field.

Initially, environmental pollution was primarily a concern of the scientific estate within and outside the presidency. There was some political interest in Congress,[70] and administrative concern in the bureaucracy. However, at the level of the subpresidency, awareness began among the scientists, especially in PSAC. They were familiar with the work of Rachel Carson and others who were sounding the alarm of an environmental crisis. Carson's 1962 *New Yorker* articles, excerpted from her forthcoming book *Silent Spring*, were discussed at PSAC meetings. In May 1963, PSAC issued a report, *Use of Pesticides*, that dealt with many of her concerns.[71]

By the time Johnson became president, the technoscience presidency's scientific estate was convinced that something had to be done. As a chemist, Hornig was fully cognizant of many of the problems arising from the applications of his science. When Moyers, in 1964, called for ideas for the upcoming Johnson legislative agenda, Hornig had his own priorities well in hand. On May 29, 1964, he wrote:

> The variety of pollutants and their pervasiveness, coupled with the inherent toxicity of many of them, makes this one of the "big problems" of our times. Our ability to understand and control has not kept pace with our capacity to pollute. . . .
> We are just in the process of organizing a panel on "Environmental Contamination" with a distinguished membership to

look at the entire problem, including its management in the government.[72]

Moyers immediately saw the relevance of Hornig's idea to Johnson's Great Society interests. Moyers, a principal, could serve as broker between the scientific perspective of Hornig/PSAC and the political needs of Johnson.

There were a number of task forces to generate ideas that might produce specific presidential proposals for legislative action. The task force mechanism was a Johnsonian device for mobilizing the best thinking from within and outside government for his legislative program. His view was that, for genuine innovation in public policy, you had to get ideas from some place other than the bureaucracy. The task force notion was an outside-in approach that came to dominate much of the way that Johnson put his domestic program together. This time, rather than appointing a new task force, Moyers, at Hornig's suggestion, reconstituted the PSAC panel as a presidential task force on environment. This action lifted PSAC from its customary role of performing long-range studies to one of providing short-term advice for a possible specific Johnsonian initiative.

The PSAC task force met regularly from August through the fall and produced a nonpublic report that was delivered to Johnson on November 9, 1964. PSAC supplied broad ideas, in effect, a comprehensive view of the total problem. While PSAC was taking this approach, the staff organization, OST, was working with BOB on the formulation of specific efforts that might be placed in the FY 1966 budget. The president's deadline for submitting legislation helped to bring together the various subpresidential aides around a common goal. The scientific professionals of PSAC and OST emphasized technical information and analysis; the budgeteers of BOB focused on financial and organizational aspects; and Moyers and his staff screened what others did, in terms of their judgment of what made sense from the standpoint of Johnson's overall policies and personal stakes as president. In the process, many of the possible programs that the scientific estate suggested—programs involving major, expensive R&D initiatives—were dropped or reduced in order to make them more politically feasible for legislative enactment. A congressionally oriented president, Johnson saw legislation as the natural end point to presidential action, at least for domestic policy. He later expressed his philosophy to Califano, saying, "I wouldn't start something I couldn't pass."[73]

On February 8, 1965, Johnson tested the congressional waters through a Special Message on Natural Beauty. This message contained words on pollution that were largely drafted by OST: "I am directing the heads of all agencies to improve measures to abate pollution caused by direct agency operation, contracts, and cooperative agreements. Federal procurement practices must make sure that the government equipment uses the most effective techniques for controlling pollution."[74]

Shortly after the delivery of the message, Moyers held a meeting with representatives of various concerned departments:[75] the Department of Agriculture; the Department of Health, Education, and Welfare; the Department of Interior; BOB; the Council of Economic Advisers; and OST. The purpose of the meeting was to discuss details of a specific bill on water pollution that was to be placed at the forefront of Johnson's environmental program. This was going to be proposed as a follow-up to the presidential message of February 8.

The meeting was not without tension. HEW, which was to administer the proposed act, was somewhat resistant to certain aspects of its procedures. While the discussion was taking place, Moyers was called out of the meeting by Johnson.[76] Moyers took the occasion to note to the president that HEW was not altogether pleased. When Moyers returned to the meeting, he reported that Johnson wanted everyone to know that he had received a great deal of favorable comment on the special message and that he did not want anyone to think that the message was just rhetoric. Moyers made it clear that the president was serious and that environmental pollution was on Johnson's priority agenda. HEW's vocal opposition ceased.[77]

Success in gaining top priority for environmental pollution on the personal agenda of Johnson encouraged Hornig and PSAC to continue giving emphasis to environmental pollution. There was far more to do; they wanted this policy area to remain high on Johnson's set of domestic concerns and to result in a coherent group of programs aimed at coping with short- and long-term aspects of the problem.

The president's special message of February 8 had provided legitimacy for the scientific estate to stay in the policy picture. It had called for the review of the adequacy of the present organization of pollution control and research activities by the directors of BOB and OST. The message had also instructed Gordon and Hornig to recommend "the best way in which the federal government may direct efforts toward advancing our scientific understanding of natural plant and animal communities and their interaction with man and his activities."[78]

Thus, in contrast to other presidential task forces, the PSAC task force on environmental pollution (as it had become known) did not disappear. It continued as a standing PSAC panel and went still deeper and more intensively into the environmental pollution problem. In 1965, a PSAC report that came to be regarded as the definitive work in the field for the remainder of the decade was prepared and brought to Johnson's attention. It was entitled *Restoring the Quality of Our Environment.*[79] Johnson liked it. He added a presidential introduction and authorized its publication. In issuing the report, he declared, ". . . the technology that has permitted our affluence spews out vast quantities of water and spent products that pollute our air, poison our waters, and even impair our ability to feed ourselves. At the same time, we have crowded together into dense metropolitan areas where concentration of wastes intensifies the problem. Pollution is now one of the most pervasive problems of our society."[80]

Johnson called for more R&D effort to be devoted to the problem and requested responses from various agencies as to what they would do in view of the report's recommendations.[81] The president also had Hornig and the PSAC panel members hold a news conference when the report was issued in November 1965. Ideas contained in the report found their way into presidential messages in 1966 and into a considerable amount of subsequent environmental legislation, including the Air Quality Act of 1967.

In this way, a wide-ranging environmental program was launched by the Johnson technoscience presidency as an ongoing, national concern. While building on earlier efforts, the Johnson initiatives marked a major step forward in this area. Once on the presidency's agenda, environmental pollution stayed there and moved from its initiating agenda to its continuing agenda. Johnson remained an enthusiastic participant in keeping it a presidential priority.

Other actors, including a second working group on the environment under the leadership of the chairman of CEA, became involved.[82] The role of the scientific estate diminished, over time, as that of others became more prominent. The emphasis changed from science and technology to regulation and the use of economic incentives for pollution abatement. Administrative problems became more obvious. In 1966, under Reorganization Plan 2, water pollution was transferred from HEW to the Department of Interior, a move largely engineered by Califano, with the president's approval.

The technoscience presidency was called upon to adapt to these changes in emphasis. For example, the reorganization notwithstanding, there were many pollution programs outside the Department of Interior; for example, air pollution stayed with HEW. A Federal Council on Science and Technology Committee on Environmental Quality was established in June 1967 as an interagency coordinating mechanism. Hornig pressed Califano on December 15, 1967, for OST to become the president's staff coordinator for the science and technology aspects of environmental pollution.[83] In early 1969, Hornig was assigned this task, which included evaluating policies for setting technical criteria and standards for environmental control.[84]

By the time Johnson left office, environmental pollution had clearly arrived as an issue. It was on the nation's agenda, not just the agenda of the presidency. The National Environmental Quality Act was passed in 1969, and the Council on Environmental Quality became part of the Executive Office of the President. In 1970, the Environmental Protection Agency (EPA) was established in the bureaucracy. It was left for Nixon to consolidate what Johnson had innovated. Environmental pollution was now organized as a presidential function identifiable in its own right, independent of the technoscience presidency. Having developed under science and technology's auspices, it was on its own, with separate subpresidential professionals to provide advice to the president. The memorandum sent to Johnson by Hornig in 1964 had been prophetic. Hornig had predicted that environmental pollution would become one of the big concerns of our times. In this instance, the scientific estate helped to make that prediction come true.

Conclusion

How do policies that are new to the technoscience presidency get started? They begin first as issues: problems or opportunities, present or anticipated. Problems and opportunities abound. Cobb and Elder point out that while there are any number of issues "that are commonly perceived by members of the political community as meriting public attention and as involving matters within the legitimate jurisdiction of existing governmental authority," only a few make it to "that set of items explicitly up for the active and serious consideration of authoritative decision makers."[85] Fewer still, of course, become issues at the presidential level. Of these, only a fraction can become top-priority items for possible policy adoption. Most become mired in indecision or fall from the presidential agenda in time. Why?

Jones suggests that in agenda setting generally, government has three options. It can be passive, being open to those who wish to be heard, reacting to pressures as they come. This method favors those interests which are the best organized and most visible or have the most resources. A second method is one in which the decision-making unit takes a more activist role, encouraging pressures from certain groups. It helps create (or strengthen) the demands to which to respond in shaping an agenda. In the third option, government plays an even more active role, attempting comprehensively to define problems itself, weigh alternatives, and rationally set goals. The government anticipates and leads, rather than reacts, or encourages.[86]

The Johnson technoscience presidency seldom used the third option. At times, usually in the case of temporary issues, it reacted to the events of the moment. Usually, however, its style was a variation of the second option or model. This was because interests within the presidential policy system were advocates on behalf of certain agenda issues and, thus, certain outside interests. But they rarely were strong enough initially to achieve priority for their issue. There was active advocacy, but it was issue-specific and ad hoc, rather than comprehensive and "balanced." Moreover, it was successful only to the degree that initial advocates had help from allies inside, and outside, the presidential policy system.

This helps explain why the issues discussed in this chapter reached different points along the agenda setting continuum. As noted, earthquake prediction/prevention and electric power reliability were on the temporary agenda; oceanography and energy reached the emergent agenda; and environmental pollution achieved priority status during the Johnson years.

Issues on the temporary agenda of technoscience tend to be triggered by events such as natural or technological emergencies, real or potential. They may or may not have a constituency for action. Usually a constituency is concentrated narrowly in the affected area. There may be representation within the presidency, but this representation—and advocacy—tends to be temporary. The basic difficulty is that the problem itself is seen as short-lived. Space on the presidency's agenda for new issues is quite limited and contested. As Light has pointed out, presidents are sharply limited by their resources, including time in office, "in the amount of innovation they can produce."[87]

Ironically, in the case of some temporary issues, the president can begin as the main entrepreneur or advocate behind an issue. This was the case in the wake of the Northeast blackout that affected New York City. In this instance, the president was at the forefront of decision making. He was immediately aware of the blackout. He directed that a search diagnosing the problem and possible remedies be launched. Then he moved to other matters. The question was: whose issue was this? The science adviser was involved. But so was the Federal Power Commission. For a while it was not clear who was in charge. Gradually, the issue was taken over by FPC, and it became increasingly a regulatory rather than science and technology issue.

Since public interest in blackouts receded rapidly, there was no great political incentive for a rekindling or sustaining of presidential support. Thus, an issue initially on the presidential agenda, including that of the president himself, now essentially devolved to the agenda of a regulatory agency, FPC. The constituency advocating action had decreased, not increased, over time. As an agenda item of the presidency, electric power reliability largely went the way of earthquake prediction/prevention—away.

The emergent agenda is illustrated by the cases of oceanography and energy. Oceanography was seen by its advocates as an opportunity; energy was seen as a problem. Presidential organization was perceived in both instances as part of the necessary means to get the issues to a point where some action might be taken.

Friends of oceanography in Congress displaced the scientific estate with the Marine Council, and Hornig with Vice-President Humphrey. Oceanography soon had stronger inside support and key policy adoptions behind it. This congressionally inspired presidential organization did not last much beyond Johnson, however. The thrust to build an oceanography program on the model of space failed. There was never a Sputnik-like trigger to broaden the relatively narrow advocacy coalition. Also, there was continuing opposition to unwarranted special attention to oceanography within the techno-science presidency on the part of OST and the budgeteers.

Energy was a genuine problem and would become a crisis in 1973–74 with the advent of the Arab oil boycott. Unfortunately, the seriousness of the problem was not perceived during the Johnson years. The scientific estate saw energy as a long-term issue for which there would be an eventual solution, principally nuclear. There was enough of an inside coalition for energy to stay on the presidential agenda but not enough of a constituency to get policy action beyond studies. The Cambel report may have diminished the sense of urgency. Interagency competition, particularly between Interior and AEC, slowed down the Cambel study and added complications to getting issues resolved.

The science adviser became the primary subpresidential advocate for energy. He had some support from principal and budgetary aides; but he could not get Johnson to be part of a coalition for energy. This kept the issue low on the emergent agenda of the presidency, awaiting the necessary trigger from the outside that would raise it to a priority status.

As noted earlier, Johnson did not wish to start something that would not get legislative acceptance.[88] His reading of congressional indifference apparently influenced his own lack of activism on the energy issue. As a politician, he gauged "the art of the possible." What was possible in environment was not possible in energy. In environment, he saw the opportunity for significant legislation. Johnson joined a growing ground swell of support within and outside his technoscience presidency for making environmental pollution a high-priority national issue. This issue reached the priority agenda of the Johnson White House. It moved from an initiating to a continuing concern as a key component of Johnson's Great Society. There was a strong subpresidential coalition of scientists, budgeteers, and principals. In contrast to energy, Johnson joined this coalition. Thus, on environment, the major actors of presidential technoscience were united. Moreover, this coalition lasted. The result was a series of policy actions. Johnson innovated a range of pollution abatement programs; Nixon kept and consolidated many of these.

Constituency matters, both inside and outside the technoscience presidency; so does advocacy; and so does timing. They all constitute factors in getting issues on the presidential agenda and in getting them considered seriously, with some measure of priority. Gaining the personal attention of the president requires relating a proposed measure to his interests. An unprecedented power blackout that shut down the entire Northeast, including the nation's largest city, constitutes the kind of emergency issue that immediately captures the president's attention. It is also the kind of issue that may lose presidential attention once the emergency passes. Environmental pollution is an example of the kind of issue that takes longer to reach the White House, but, once it becomes a presidential priority, it can stay for years. The key was in becoming an aspect of the Great Society, and thus being linked with a continuing and personal concern of the president. Oceanography made headway to the extent that it was related to Johnson's interests in international cooperation concerning the world's food and population problems. Energy might have been the next step in Johnson's Great Society had he remained in office another term. It was at the very front of presidential awareness and attention. There had been some search and planning. There was subpresidential support. The absence of a trigger for action prevented its emergence as a priority item for Johnson. In the 1970s, the Arab oil boycott provided that trigger for Nixon.

In conclusion, decision making by the Johnson technoscience presidency reflects the second model suggested by Jones and discussed above. What got on the agenda reflected neither passive acceptance of all demands nor comprehensive planning. Nor was it rooted in the particular subject matter. Rather, it resulted primarily from the nature of an issue's constituency, particularly the ad hoc advocacy of specific interests inside the presidential policy system. Whether an issue was temporary, emergent, or received priority depended upon the capacity of the original issue advocates to build alliances among subpresidential aides and outside interests. The president was more likely to join an ongoing coalition within his policy system than to initiate one himself. This was especially the case when his own political sensitivities suggested that outside congressional support was available for what his subpresidential advocates wished to do.

3. Adoption

Adoption has been briefly mentioned in the previous chapter. It was discussed as part of a more general examination of how problems and opportunities get on the agenda of the presidency and are given priority, temporarily or over time. Here we discuss the process of adoption in greater depth. Many issues can get on the agenda, but relatively few reach the point of policy adoption—the authoritative allocation of resources. Adoption moves beyond the general discussion and searching of agenda setting to a major decision by the presidency. Adoption marks the point at which the president is more personally and critically involved in the decision-making process of the presidency. What is needed is the legitimacy to launch a new program, and this is supplied by a president's action.

The presidency matches a problem or an opportunity with a policy solution. The chief executive is involved, and either makes the decision himself or ratifies one made by a subordinate under his authority. Usually, the result is to allocate funds and assign organizational responsibility. The president is personally associated with the adoption decision, often in a formal way, such as in the signing of a new law. What he adopts may be quite specific (e.g., to build a new weapon) or more general (e.g., to give a different status to a particular R&D field). How he adopts can vary: he can do so with enthusiasm and high visibility or with reluctance and in relative seclusion; he can make one big decision or a series of minimal choices. Although adoptions differ, they have in common the president's personal involvement and authorization of a program of science and technology action.

Agenda setting can be limited to interactions between the president and subpresidency in the executive branch. Other than the president, the key actor in agenda setting may well be a presidential aide. Agenda setting is concerned with inputs to a possible adoption decision. White House staff and cabinet and agency heads may seek to influence the president's agenda. They may well set priorities for adoption in terms of what they perceive as presidential interests, but only the president can authoritatively adopt (i.e., confer legitimacy); and he can usually only do so partially in a constitutional system of separated powers. Because legitimacy and money are at the heart of adoption, Congress matters. Presidential adoption is presidential participation in the broader process by which bills become laws and new programs receive authorization and appropriations. Hence, the president must consider the congressional role in adoption: how much? to what purpose? how does it impinge on his own interests?

Adoption is the point at which the political estate dominates decision making by the technoscience presidency. The question is: which political estate is in charge? The president is the key political participant within the presidency. However, outside the presidency is Congress, very much a political body with its own role in adoption. Who governs? The answer, in adoption, is both, to some degree. Adoption, like the other stages, is a stage in policy making in which many can participate. The issue is: how, and with what influence?

There is a continuum of control in adoption. At one extreme, the president acquiesces to what Congress wants; at another, he adopts and gives the signal for implementation with hardly a nod in the direction of Congress. Between these extremes in behavior, the president can be a partner of Congress or a leader of Congress through arbitrating differences among legislative factions, which usually mirror bureaucratic rivalries in the executive branch. These different presidential adoption roles may be classified as *acquiescence, partnership, arbitration,* and *preemption.* Each role carries successively more presidential leverage over the adoption decision.

In the discussion that follows, acquiescence is seen in the case of oceanography, a field discussed in another context in the previous chapter. Partnership is illustrated in presidential-congressional decisions concerning the adoption of the 200 billion electron volt (200-BEV) nuclear accelerator. Presidential arbitration is revealed in the establishment of the man-in-space program of the Air Force, the Manned Orbital Laboratory (MOL). For presidential preemption, there is the adoption of two Vietnam War innovations: weather modification and the electronic barrier. Each of these cases highlights different aspects of presidential adoption, ranging from a situation in which the president follows to one in which he takes the lead; from cases in which legitimacy is clearly conferred by an act of Congress to ones in which it is at least partially sacrificed to other presidential values. A range of technoscience programs—scientific research, technological development, and technological applications—are included.

Acquiescence

The notion of presidential acquiescence seems wholly out of character with what is known about President Johnson. Johnson's career
was largely spent in Congress, and he was reputed to be a master of
that institution. Also, Congress is not known for taking collective
initiative; it speaks with many voices. It is a body more adept at reacting than at leading, particularly in more esoteric realms of public
policy such as those concerned with science and technology. Add
to these factors the climate of the 1960s, a time that would later
be called "the imperial presidency." Yet Congress did lead in the
adoption of certain scientific and technological policies in the era of
Lyndon Johnson. While the Johnson technoscience presidency may
have bargained and achieved some compromises, it nevertheless
found itself acquiescing.

Consider again the case of oceanography. By the time Johnson
took office, the elements in Congress that were pushing oceanography had already tried and failed to force adoption of a major new initiative in this field. Congress had passed a bill in 1963, only to have
it vetoed by Kennedy. Three years later, Congress tried again; this
time, there was presidential acceptance. Why did Johnson agree to it?
Key units of the subpresidency (the science adviser and BOB) were
opposed, and Johnson himself was hardly enthusiastic. One reason
was the nature of the policy embodied in the bill. Through bargaining between presidential aides and congressional staffs, the establishment of the Marine Council and Advisory Commission was
made temporary. The study commission was to set forth a program
of activities in oceanography eighteen months from the time it was
constituted. The Marine Council, the operating entity in the executive office, would cease to exist 120 days after the commission delivered its final report.[1] Thus, the bill to which the president acquiesced represented what was perceived as a transient threat to
presidential prerogatives.

A second reason for presidential acquiescence was the fact that
congressional backing for change was greater in 1966 than in 1963.
There was much more emphasis on marine resources and technology, on using rather than studying the ocean. Industry, not just
the universities, saw opportunities in oceanography. Also, one program in the field was of particular congressional interest: the concept of establishing a set of sea grant programs. Modeled after the
land grant idea, such sea grants would go to selected state universities and colleges to initiate and support efforts of education, training, and research in marine sciences activities. The sea grant notion

was a specific concept in which many legislators could see stakes for themselves. Although it was not included in the measure brought forth in 1966, it was discussed widely as the kind of program that might be encouraged if there was more backing for oceanography by the White House. This had the effect of enlarging the constituency for the oceanography bill of 1966.

Thus, the bill was relatively weak, but the legislative backing was strong. There was no opposition of any significance in Congress. For these reasons alone, Johnson might have been expected to give it his support, but there was also a third, more personal reason: friendship. After the bill was passed, it lay on Johnson's desk awaiting an adoption that the president was obviously reluctant to give. Kennedy had vetoed an oceanography bill; Johnson might do the same. Proponents of oceanography became nervous. Given the advice that Johnson was getting from BOB and the science adviser, they had good reason to be.

At this juncture, Johnson happened to attend a Washington cocktail party where he was approached by the wife of Warren Magnuson, the principal backer of the bill in the Senate. The Johnsons and Magnusons were friends. Their relationship went back a long way. Mrs. Magnuson reminded Johnson that her husband had worked extremely hard getting the bill to the point where all that remained for adoption was a presidential signature. She said that she sincerely hoped that Johnson would not disappoint Senator Magnuson by scuttling his measure at the last moment. Johnson listened, and the conversation ended with the president declaring, "Honey, for you, I'll sign it."[2]

Thus, there was presidential acquiescence. It came reluctantly, but it came. Johnson initially resisted a bill that was more a product of Congress than of his own administration. It would add another advocate to the many he already had in his executive office. It was not a bill that he had wished to adopt. The bill's passage indicates ingredients that may be conditions for presidential acquiescence: a weakening of the bill's threat to fundamental presidential prerogative; a strong, growing congressional constituency; and a personal touch such as an appeal on the basis of obligation, or simply friendship.

Partnership

Partnership is another mode of adoption. It reflects a relatively equal balance of power between the political estates of the president and Congress with respect to a particular issue. The action of one party stimulates the other toward adoption. An example of presidential adoption in partnership with Congress is the 200-BEV nuclear accelerator. In this instance, Congress was an active participant with the technoscience presidency throughout.

One reason that a partnership was possible was the nature of the program. The stakes were high; the 200-BEV was a scientific and political prize. It was the largest, most advanced, most expensive accelerator ($300 million) built anywhere in the world during the decade. It was the epitome of big science. There was national prestige in having it, and there was regional prestige within the United States in getting it. Many legislators wanted this prize for their districts and states. Thus, the politics surrounding the choice mattered to both the president and Congress.

Another reason for the partnership style of presidential adoption in this instance was the influence of the Joint Committee on Atomic Energy. JCAE was one of the most powerful congressional committees ever created. Although it was eventually terminated and its function was absorbed by a number of committees in the mid-1970s as atomic energy became part of a broader energy mission, JCAE was still very influential in the 1960s. With an able staff and committee members of considerable experience, legislative skill, and seniority, JCAE's decisions invariably were endorsed by Congress as a whole. Many joint committees are study committees. In contrast, this one was deeply involved in legislation and had the advantage of being highly cohesive. The president could not play one chamber against the other. JCAE presented a common front vis-à-vis the executive branch and Johnson.

To some extent, Johnson must have been happy to share authority with Congress and JCAE in adopting the 200-BEV. The locational politics concerning it were unusually fierce. Johnson had taken criticism for an earlier nuclear accelerator decision. He was content to let JCAE push decision making along while he retained his own prerogatives in the adoption process.

Finally, there was presidential partnership with Congress on this decision because an interest group outside both institutions pressed hard for the 200-BEV and provided a common base of information concerning the technology. The high energy physics community lobbied as hard with Congress as it did with its allies in the technoscience presidency. It thus helped to bind the two institutions and keep them moving toward the ultimate goal.

For these reasons, presidential-congressional decisions were sequential and interactive: one side made one move, the other side countered by making a move of its own; the first side responded to this action, and so forth. The partnership was not so much concurrent as it was reciprocal and reactive. In the case of the 200-BEV,

Johnson was especially critical at the beginning and at the end of the
adoption process. In between, Congress and actors within the subpresidency maneuvered and tried to control events. Particularly important was a base of continuing inside support reflecting the desire
of the outside scientific community, consisting of Hornig, the science adviser, and Seaborg, the administrator and scientist.

Johnson began presidential adoption of the 200-BEV by *not* ap-
proving another nuclear accelerator proposal. This was a proposal
from the Midwestern Universities Research Association for a $120
million accelerator. More will be said of this decision in a later chapter. Suffice it to say here that Johnson rejected a proposal that
MURA took quite seriously. He had to justify that decision to a
number of irate legislators, and one of the justifications constituted a
first step in the adoption of the 200-BEV.

This peculiar circumstance followed from the advice rendered
by leading scientific experts. Under Kennedy, a special joint panel
had been established by PSAC and AEC. Chaired by Norman Ramsey
of Harvard, the panel's charge was to make recommendations as to
the optimal long-term nuclear accelerator program for the nation. It
had given priority to a 200-BEV machine being proposed by a group
at the Lawrence Radiation Laboratory of the University of California. It had also recommended building a second machine at MURA,
provided that constructing this machine did not detract from the
commitment to the 200-BEV. This reservation became a rationale announced in Johnson's decision to kill the MURA machine in late
1963. However, whether or not the president intended it to be interpreted in that way, this same rationale could be seen as a decision for
200-BEV. As the *OST Administrative History* notes, "This was the
first implicit commitment to build the 200-BEV because it would be
hard to give for the reason not to build a cheaper, low priority accelerator that a higher priority one was more important, if you did not
intend to build the higher priority machine."[3]

The MURA cancellation had another impact: it united the high
energy physics community behind 200-BEV. This machine became
not just *top* priority, it became *the* priority. Throughout 1964, leaders of the high energy physics community pressed hard, and the science adviser and his staff were made fully aware of the intensity of
this community's feeling. Together with Seaborg of AEC, Hornig became a catalyst for more overt and explicit presidential adoption.
Thus, there was a core of support within the technoscience presidency's scientific and administrative estates. This would help to sustain momentum over the years. The problem was to obtain the political decisions necessary for adoption.

Observing the presidential scene and annoyed with cutbacks in technological programs that it favored, JCAE demanded a straightforward statement from Johnson on national policy for high energy physics, including the 200-BEV. JCAE warned that, otherwise, it might not support some of the expensive basic research programs coming up for a decision. It declared, "The committee does not believe it should approve, or participate in setting the stage for such massive increases in funds without a clearly defined national policy on high-energy physics research. A position must be taken by the Executive branch as to the long-range, technical goals and plans for this program."[4] By speaking negatively, JCAE had a positive effect in getting the subpresidential alliance of Seaborg and Hornig to push more urgently for a presidential statement signaling adoption.

A statement on national policy for high energy physics prepared for Congress by OST, BOB, and AEC was submitted to Johnson on March 27, 1964. Among other provisions, the statement called for design studies for constructing 200-BEV. Hornig noted that, while the statement gave JCAE assurance that it was not contemplated that expensive design studies would be put on the shelf once completed, the policy statement stopped short of a commitment to construct. That would "necessarily depend on the outcome of the design studies, the state of advance in this field, the overall national science program, and the fiscal situation at the time the decision [was] to be made."[5] Special Assistant for National Security McGeorge Bundy received the draft letter at the Johnson ranch in Texas and suggested certain changes before sending it to the president. A key recommendation by Bundy was that Hornig, not Johnson, sign the statement. This would presumably protect the president from foreclosing future options.[6]

JCAE was unhappy that Johnson's signature was not on the statement. However, it did not contest the point, but requested AEC, as a next step, to prepare a more detailed national policy plan for submission to Congress (and the president) the following year. In the latter part of 1964, the AEC report was written. It was ready to go to Congress in January 1965; however, the issue was the degree of presidential endorsement in the transmittal letter. As an aide to the budget director noted:

We think the Presidential endorsement of the report of the sort visualized by AEC and possibly by Dr. Hornig, even if qualified as being subject to the final situation, would be undesirable. Once the projects and their timetables have presidential endorsement, we are concerned that *the burden of proof would be on the Bureau* to demonstrate why they should not be built at a particular time. There are two ways of overcoming the problem. One is to attempt to persuade AEC to change the report. We do not especially favor this course. The other, which we recommend, is to allow the report to go to the Joint Committee essentially in its present form but without Presidential endorsement or with only a non-committal Presidential "blessing." It is not at all clear, in light of the Joint Committee's request, that the request need be transmitted to the Committee by the President himself, although both AEC and Dr. Hornig prefer this.[7]

As written by OST and AEC, the transmittal letter concluded with Johnson stating, "I endorse the AEC report. . . ."[8] As rewritten following the BOB negotiation, this was changed to "I believe that the AEC report provides a useful guideline for decision making in the development of high energy physics." Thus was the OST/AEC's strong "endorsement" changed to BOB's weaker "blessing."[9]

In sending the AEC report, "Policy for National Action in the Field of High Energy Physics," and the letter of transmittal to the president on January 25, 1965, Hornig noted that it had been reviewed by the president's science and technology staff as well as by BOB. All had agreed with its content; and Hornig noted that "like all planning documents, all expect the plans to be reassessed in light of progress in the field." Hornig emphasized that the suggested letter of transmittal did not commit the president to a "program in detail," but did reaffirm the president's "general support for an area of science." He called the report a "useful guideline for decision." He noted that the location was not mentioned, since the issue had not been resolved, and that a national consortium was being discussed as a way to operate the facility wherever it was eventually located.[10]

The transmittal letter kept open the president's options. It also helped BOB in its power position within the subpresidency. The alliance of Hornig and Seaborg would have to negotiate with BOB before achieving the "brass ring" of presidential adoption. However, each presidential interaction with Congress over the 200-BEV was reducing BOB's leeway. Presidential endorsements (and adoptions) can be quick and front-ended, as was the case with Kennedy's decision to go to the moon; they can also come incrementally and along the way, as was proving to be the case for Johnson and the 200-BEV. Momentum was nevertheless building. Wholly aside from the president's transmittal letter, there was the report itself. It recommended "construction of a high-energy proton accelerator of approximately

200 billion electron volts, in accordance with technical specifications developed by the Lawrence Radiation Laboratory, to be operated as a national facility."[11]

JCAE held four days of hearings on national policy in high energy physics in March 1965. The question of *whether* there should be a 200-BEV was fading. The discussion was now more about *how* a national facility would be managed and *where* it would be placed. The shift in emphasis arose from the fact that the location issue was opened up by Johnson. The Ramsey Panel had wanted the Lawrence Radiation Laboratory to build the machine, and this laboratory was at the University of California at Berkeley. It assumed, therefore, that the accelerator would be built in California. However, Johnson instructed Seaborg to search the country for the best possible site. Once the site question was opened, a vast competition unfolded in 1965 and 1966. Congressional, state, and local pressures began to build. AEC asked the National Academy of Sciences (NAS) to assist in judging the proposals. There were eighty-five detailed proposals from every state except North Dakota and Massachusetts. Visiting teams of scientists inspected all of the sites and found themselves greeted by members of Congress and local dignitaries.[12] The site selection procedures were elaborate and lengthy: "[They] . . . served to continue to keep the accelerator in the public mind and to make it more difficult not to fund it if a suitable site could be chosen and if design showed that, in fact, the machine could be built for the price contemplated."[13]

Throughout, there was heavy lobbying, particularly in the Midwest. The science adviser and BOB were not strongly involved in the choice of the site. This was a technical and political decision. The technical aspects of location were in the hands of NAS and Seaborg, and the politics of location were beyond BOB and Hornig at this point. Hornig was concerned that anything he said would be attributed to the White House and that he would "end up making one friend and five enemies for the President in the process."[14] BOB continued to be concerned with holding back what now seemed the inevitable adoption of a machine that it judged would cost $300 million to build and $60 million a year to operate. Director Schultze of BOB wrote Johnson on August 31, 1965, "The site location [decision process] has been scheduled with the hope that you would approve this for the 1967 budget review. We have talked with Chairman Seaborg and urged him to avoid any implication in the press release or otherwise that this program has been approved for the 1967 budget. In fact, we plan to raise this as one of the major issues with AEC in our fall budget review."[15]

Meanwhile, Califano advised the president on his various options, emphasizing how politically controversial the decision would be and that anything he said might leak and cause him problems. He even advised Johnson to be guarded in speaking with Seaborg. He noted on March 14, 1966, "I am not sure you realize, however, that anything you say to Seaborg will be transmitted to the other Commissioners of the AEC, if my experience with him is any indication. It will also be transmitted to the Hill through one or more of the Commissioners and into the staff of the AEC."[16] He also argued against undue urgency in presidential adoption. In the same March memorandum, he noted that Hornig wanted "to move forward as rapidly as possible." Califano said that his own inclination "would be not to choose a specific place until after November." He also stated that Hornig asked him whether the committee that was reviewing sites should recommend a single site or several. "I told him they should recommend several and leave some flexibility in the AEC."[17] This also left flexibility for Johnson, should he choose to involve himself. The president was under great pressure on site selection from Congress, such as JCAE members and various representatives of particular states. Senator Paul Douglas of Illinois, an old legislative friend who was retiring, was especially active on behalf of his state.[18]

Ultimately, in spring 1966, the National Academy of Sciences submitted a list of six possibilities to AEC. All were acceptable from a technical standpoint. These included Brookhaven National Laboratory, Long Island, New York; Ann Arbor, Michigan; Denver, Colorado; Madison, Wisconsin; Sacramento, California; and Batavia, in the vicinity of Chicago, Illinois.[19] From outside government, it appeared that AEC was making the decision, with Johnson agreeing; but, according to David Robinson (then of OST), "the AEC sent proposals from six finalists to the President, and Johnson personally picked a site in Batavia, Illinois, outside Chicago. The decision was made in November [1966] just *after* the elections."[20]

As the primary OST staff person working with AEC on the 200-BEV, Robinson certainly was in a position to know about the president's involvement. In any event, it was extremely unlikely that AEC (i.e., Seaborg) would make a decision not acceptable to Johnson. Given the Midwest's complaints over Johnson's MURA decision, the politics of presidential decision certainly favored a Midwest site, as long as it was technically adequate—which it was.

On December 16, 1966, AEC made the formal announcement. Adoption moved to the next phase. Funding for 200-BEV was included in Johnson's FY 1968 budget request submitted to Congress in early 1967. This would carry the project beyond the design and planning stage to actual construction. However, during 1967, Johnson cut back this request and asked that more time be given to design and planning, before moving to construction. The committees in Congress that appropriated money were different in orientation from those that authorized new programs. The momentum for adoption was beginning to be interrupted, as even the design phase funding came under fire. On July 16, 1967, the *New York Times* editorialized against going ahead with a "scientific luxury" at a time when there were riots in the nation's cities and "a bloody war in Vietnam." In Congress, debate centered around the open housing issue and the failure of the relevant Illinois and local authorities to provide adequate assurance that blacks would be able to get housing on a par with whites in the neighborhood of the giant machine. The debate was intense, but the proponents of design funding for 200-BEV won. Senator Dirksen of Illinois was an important force in the outcome.[21]

Now the scene shifted back to the presidency. Construction funds were an issue in the FY 1969 budget debate. BOB Director Schultze contested with Hornig and Seaborg over how many and how fast commitments should be made for the next year. Schultze wanted to keep 200-BEV in the less expensive design phase and further delay construction funding.[22] He had denied AEC construction funds. On December 8, 1967, Hornig wrote Schultze:

> I wish to register my strong support of the AEC appeal for restoration of construction funds for the 200-BEV accelerator. In my view, at least enough should be provided to proceed into the next phase. This project is of the highest importance to the development of high-energy physics and to American science as-a-whole.
>
> The near unanimous view of scientists is that particle energy is the single most important parameter governing the pace of discovery in high-energy physics. Panels of the PSAC, the AEC, and the National Academy of Science have all stressed this point. The U.S. has seen no advance in particle energy since 1961 when the 33 BEV AGS at Brookhaven came into operation. Most of the important new discoveries of the last three years have been made on this machine or its twin at CERN in Switzerland. The USSR began the successful operation of its 76 BEV proton accelerator at Serpukhov in September 1967. With this machine, which apparently is a good one, the Soviets will be able to work in an energy region inaccessible to U.S. scientists. I believe it would be a serious mistake to delay exces-

sively the construction of a facility which will regain a position of world leadership for this country in high-energy physics.[23]

Calling 200-BEV an item of "the highest priority," Hornig said, "Other research construction sought by the AEC should be deferred, if necessary, in order to keep construction of the 200-BEV accelerator."[24]

The issue went to Johnson for final decision. The president opted for proceeding, and the FY 1968 budget included a $25 million item for starting construction on the 200-BEV. Congressional approval was ultimately forthcoming; and the machine began moving slowly toward completion.

The story of the 200-BEV illustrates presidential adoption in a partnership mode. Neither the president nor Congress took charge, but each took year-to-year actions that caused the other to take further action. Authoritative decision followed, all leading to what seems in retrospect to have been an irreversible choice to adopt (i.e., to legitimate and allocate funds for building the 200-BEV). Adoption was not inevitable, however. There had to be constant pressure for incremental actions from advocates of the machine.

Within the subpresidency, the alliance of Hornig and Seaborg never waivered from its course. Schultze, the budgeteer, and Califano, the principal, leavened these proponent pressures in accordance with their somewhat different perspectives. But the dominant force on Johnson for adoption was an outside force, Congress. Within Congress, most of the pressure came from the midwestern legislators, some of whom were on JCAE and in other congressional leadership positions, who saw the 200-BEV as their region's best hope of winning the kind of spectacular, big-science resource that always seemed previously to go somewhere else. There were a large number of proponents of the 200-BEV and few ardent opponents. Those against it came into the contest late. There were many constituents for adoption and few for rejection. Almost imperceptibly, the partnership between the presidency and Congress phased from discussing "whether" to the issue of "where." Decisions were shaped and, over years, made.

Arbitration

Another model of adoption is arbitration. Here issues relate not only to whether, or how fast, but also to "who does what." The president judges, or arbitrates rival bureaucratic and congressional claims to jurisdiction in the process of adopting.

Consider the case of Johnson's arbitration of the Manned Orbital Laboratory (MOL) dispute. This was a large-scale technology program that was terminated by Nixon after it had been adopted by Johnson in an era when space concerns were at their height as a national interest.

Largely forgotten as a program, MOL has some lasting significance in illustrating a certain type of presidential adoption process. MOL was a manned satellite that would provide a platform in space from which scientists or the military could conduct observations and surveillance of the earth below. Eventually, a combination of technology and politics would lead to the conclusion that unmanned satellites could adequately perform the tasks conceived for MOL; but, in the 1960s, the human role was deemed essential. The issue was not a manned vs. unmanned laboratory, but whether it would be under the authority of NASA or the Air Force. What was done with MOL depended upon whether NASA or the Air Force would develop and operate it. The space committees in Congress favored their agency; the military committees preferred the Air Force. Secretary of Defense Robert McNamara did not stand in the way of his agency, the Air Force, pressing its case. James Webb, the administrator of NASA, represented the civilian space interest. This was a classic case in which there was a spirited contest for control of a new program and adoption of the policy establishing the program required presidential arbitration. It was also a case in which military reconnaissance missions of a classified nature were hidden behind much of the public debate.

The situation with which Johnson was confronted had evolved slowly. Under Eisenhower, the decision had been made to have both a civilian *and* a military space program. After Kennedy made his Apollo decision in 1961, the NASA program surged forward and became dominant. The Air Force did retain one space program of significance, called Dynasoar. This was a manned space glider. However, McNamara took a dim view of Dynasoar and canceled it later in 1963. The cancellation made the Air Force fight all the harder for adoption of an alternative program, MOL. McNamara was apparently sensitive to the argument that some manned military space capability was desirable. He was also willing in this instance to defer to the judgment of the Air Force secretary, Harold Brown, himself a scientist.

During the Kennedy administration, the Air Force and NASA discussed a cooperative MOL program. By the time Johnson became president, the Air Force was set on a course for an independent program, a direction perhaps influenced by McNamara's decision on Dynasoar. NASA viewed the Air Force action with alarm. While

NASA's post-Apollo plans were extremely uncertain in 1964, as we shall later discuss, it was important to Webb that NASA retain the MOL option. As Senator Clinton Anderson, chairman of the Senate Aeronautical and Space Sciences Committee, argued, "Air Force MOL [planning] funds could be applied more profitably to the development of an Apollo [space] station, called Apollo X, because it has a greater potential. . . ."[25] Hornig agreed. He recommended that MOL be dropped because the Air Force concepts did not promise a system that would involve sufficient size or capability to represent a real step forward in the technology of space exploration.[26]

Considerable debate took place in 1964 among congressional proponents of the two sides. For example, Anderson not only talked with Johnson but also had analyses prepared by his staff and sent to BOB. This was an obvious effort on his part to strike an alliance with BOB in the contest for presidential decision. He wanted to make certain that the Air Force MOL program was aborted at the outset.[27] The executive secretary of the National Aeronautics and Space Council was in favor of MOL; Hornig was against it.[28]

One of the key issues in the debate was the utility of the major manned space technology in existence, developed for the Gemini program. This program, which placed two men in orbit, was a stage in the creation of the larger, more advanced Apollo system. If the Air Force moved toward a manned orbital laboratory, it could immediately make use of the Gemini technology. If NASA was placed in charge, such a laboratory would have to await the development of the more advanced Apollo. Where NASA was concerned, Apollo would always have to come first. It could not run two huge technological development programs simultaneously. Therefore, the issues were: should there be a MOL program? if so, when? If the answers were "yes" and "soon," this would mean a program run by the Air Force. The technological system to be put in space would be less advanced than that promised by NASA; however, it would work and have some measure of military significance. At the time (1964), all that Johnson was permitting was planning by both agencies; he had yet to decide on the issue of whether there should be a MOL program.

In the first half of 1965, Hornig was active in nudging the Air Force and NASA on behalf of the president to consider questions of redundance. McNamara cooperated by announcing that he would not commit funds for the program until after the planning studies were completed and various issues resolved. Webb was not displeased with the delay, since it was in NASA's interest, but was delay in the national interest? To "go early" with a Manned Orbital Laboratory meant developing the Air Force MOL. Decisions on "whether" and 'when" determined "who." Johnson had to judge if MOL was needed and, if so, how soon and which agency should have the developmental responsibility. The answers to those questions depended upon Johnson's own perception of the Cold War competition in space with the Soviet Union. Did the USSR constitute a military threat to the United States in space?

The House of Representatives Committee on Government Operations, Subcommittee on Military Operations, attempted at this point to influence the president's thinking in this respect. In June 1965, the subcommittee issued a report in which it declared, "The paramount mission of NASA at this time is to land a man on the moon before the Russians do. The urgent need for MOL is to catch up with the Russians in technology which may have more military significance."[29]

In August 1965, the Senate Appropriations Committee took another step that increased pressure for a decision favorable to the Air Force MOL. It wrote language into the DOD appropriations bill that precluded McNamara from reprogramming MOL funds for any purpose other than MOL. These events did not necessarily tip the congressional scale, however. NASA had equally formidable supporters in Congress. As indicated, Clinton Anderson on the Senate space committee was a major advocate of the civilian space agency. Johnson continued to hear from him and others on NASA's behalf.

The question was whether Johnson would arbitrate among the competing claims or let decisions slip more. Johnson chose to decide. On August 25, 1965, he declared that there was a national interest in having a Manned Orbital Laboratory as soon as possible. He ordered the Air Force to move ahead immediately with MOL's development. The cost was estimated at $1.5 billion at that time.[30]

The president had thus arbitrated among competing technological, bureaucratic, and congressional interests. He had plenty of advice and pressure; but, on space, Johnson had considerable expertise and self-confidence. He decided that there should be a Manned Orbital Laboratory; it should be developed as soon as possible; and the Air Force should be in charge. Thus, he made MOL the top space priority for the Air Force for the remainder of the decade.

On August 30, 1965, Johnson received a letter from the former Air Force chief of staff, General Thomas White, thanking him for the decision: "I am happy that one who has been in authority in the American space program since its beginning is now our Chief Executive and has such a deep understanding of the military implications of space."[31] In responding, Johnson called his decision "vital" and thanked White for his counsel in making it.

NASA was injured by the decision, and its post-Apollo planning with respect to possible laboratories in space was constrained. If it was to include a MOL-type concept in its own plans, it would have to do so in spite of the Air Force program.

Preemption

On the other side of the continuum from presidential acquiescence and one large step beyond arbitration is presidential preemption. Preemption is a style of adoption in which the presidency makes decisions and imposes them on Congress. It is not so much that the presidency excludes Congress as that it minimizes and selects/controls congressional input. There is no sense of partnership; nor is there a need for arbitration, since preemption takes place in a context in which administrative or congressional rivalry is deliberately contained. A major method of containment is through limiting information about adoption to those with a need to know. Many scientific and technological decisions involving national security have been of a preemptive kind. In the era of President Johnson, there were certain preemptive adoptions concerning new weapons to be introduced into the Vietnam War.

One example was weather modification (i.e., cloud seeding with silver iodide and other chemical agents to augment rainfall). As a technology, weather modification emerged dramatically in scientific credibility in the mid-1960s. Results in civilian applications caused considerable optimism on the part of certain scientists and administrators that precipitation could be significantly enhanced. The same technology that could be used to prevent harm could also be used as a weapon to inflict damage on an enemy. The fact that this was a weapon of uncertain capability did not deter advocates within DOD's scientific estate from proposing its use. Vietnam provided a real-world laboratory, and weather modification was introduced into Vietnam with a minimum of legitimation from Congress. Adoption was incomplete, in this sense; but this limitation did not present a barrier. The mode of presidential decision making was preemptive.

In 1966, while Congress was debating competing bills providing for the establishment of a new civilian program in weather modification, the Pentagon's top R&D office, that of the Director of Defense Research and Engineering, was active in launching a military weather modification effort. It proposed using cloud-seeding techniques in Southeast Asia as a means of inhibiting the movement of enemy troops and supplies. In October 1966, there followed a series of experimental tests authorized by McNamara and conducted in the

Laos panhandle by the Naval Weapons Center, which had been developing the technology for some time. In November 1966, on the basis of these tests, Admiral Ulysses S. Grant Sharp, Jr., then commander in chief of the U.S. Pacific Fleet, concluded that rainmaking could be used as a valuable tactical weapon. The Joint Chiefs of Staff agreed. In February 1967, the Joint Chiefs recommended to Johnson a program applying rainmaking techniques on an operational basis. A memorandum to the president included the wording: "Laos Operations . . . Authorization required to implement operational phase of weather modification process previously successfully tested and evaluated in the area." The necessary legitimation was provided by Johnson, and the operational phase of the program was in action by March 1967.[32] (Ironically, while this was taking place, the proposed new civilian program in weather modification was not getting started because the two bills mentioned above nullified one another. Neither one had enough support to pass. The president chose not to get involved in this highly visible civilian debate, partly because he had been asked not to by the sponsor of one of the legislative proposals.)[33]

From 1967 to 1972, covert operational seeding took place in an attempt to slow the movement of North Vietnamese troops and supplies through the Ho Chi Minh Trail network. A total of $3.6 million per year was spent. The list of those with a need to know was very small and included only very carefully selected top officials of the Department of Defense, the Department of State, the Central Intelligence Agency, and the White House staff. Among the few on the White House staff who were privy were key national security aides, the science adviser,[34] and the Vietnam panel of PSAC. There was some debate within PSAC. There was concern that use of weather modification should be restrained, that it should not be deliberately used to cause flooding.

As for Congress, the chairmen of the House and Senate Appropriations and Armed Services committees were informed. The Thai government was not told; nor was the Laotian government given information other than that a general interdiction campaign was being fought. No one at the Arms Control and Disarmament Agency was informed. Presidents changed, and the secrecy continued. Not even Melvin Laird, whom Nixon appointed as secretary of defense, was briefed until after he suffered the embarrassment of denying before Congress that such seeding had taken place.[35]

Another case of presidential preemption in the technoscience policy adoption process was that of the electronic barrier. This was envisioned as a forty-seven-mile-long barrier across Vietnam, capable of preventing the movement of enemy troops from the north. It was a complex combination of barbed wire, mines, sensors, and de-tectors; and it would use the very latest technology to smell, hear, see, locate, and kill the enemy.

Information concerning the barrier was not as well contained as in weather modification (a program that did not come to light until after Johnson had left), but it nevertheless also constituted presidential preemption. It was adopted with only minimal congressional participation. In such cases as weather modification and the electronic barrier, secrecy and dispatch were regarded by the president and his advisers as vital.

In the case of weather modification, the Joint Chiefs of Staff appear to have been the prime forces influencing Johnson's decision to adopt. In the case of the electronic barrier, it was NcNamara. Indeed, the electronic barrier came to be known in some circles as "the McNamara line."[36] During the summer of 1966, McNamara drew together a group of scientific experts and asked them to study the technological aspects of the war to see if they could suggest new and better ways in which the United States' purposes might be achieved. The experts were an ad hoc group; they were advisers to McNamara, not to the president. Among the new ideas that these scientists examined was that of the electronic barrier.

They did so in a context of dissatisfaction with the primary means being used to interdict enemy infiltration into South Vietnam from the north: massive bombing. In their view, the bombing had not been very effective; moreover, it was worse than ineffective because it was creating a negative reaction to the policy within the United States. These scientific experts recommended the electronic barrier as an alternative that would be better in all respects in stopping the infiltration without causing potentially vast and indiscriminate destruction as the bombing was seen as doing.

McNamara liked the electronic barrier idea, although he was not sure about the desirability of using it in place of bombing. In his role as adviser to Johnson, however, he decided to recommend the barrier's adoption. He prepared a memorandum dated October 14, 1966, that included a proposal for an electronic barrier as a new means of fighting the enemy.[37] He also raised the possibility in the same memorandum that the bombing policy might ultimately have to be abandoned if it did not prove more effective. Johnson also received advice from the Joint Chiefs of Staff. They did not oppose the barrier as long as it was not used as a means of stopping the bombing. They regarded the bombing as being more effective than did McNamara's science advisers and other critics of the war.[38] National Security Adviser Walt Rostow also was not sanguine about the effectiveness of the electronic barrier; it smacked too much of "Maginot Line thinking." Nevertheless, he saw the barrier as providing a stimulus for accelerating and proving out a variety of potentially useful new electronic and other military technologies.[39]

Johnson's decision was to adopt the electronic barrier while continuing the conventional technology, the heavy bombing campaign known as "rolling thunder." Like weather modification, the electronic barrier was one more, new technological counter on the U.S. side to throw against the enemy. There was always the hope that just a little more force, or perhaps a new type of force, would bring the enemy down.

While the chairmen of relevant military committees in Congress were no doubt informed, it is equally clear that intentional efforts were made to restrict the circle of those with a need to know to the smallest possible number. The coalition for presidential adoption was kept small and concentrated; that for congressional acquiescence was kept smaller still. As actual construction of the barrier began in Vietnam, however, evidence that something new and large was being built began to make its way from the field back to the United States.

In June 1967, Lieutenant General Marvin L. McNickle, the second highest official in the Office of the Director of Defense Research and Engineering, responded to an inquiry from Senator Carl T. Curtis concerning reports of an electronic barrier. The general said that the idea was interesting and worthy of study, but not an option for the time being. He declared, "Reallocation of effort to construction of the barrier in this very difficult terrain would seriously penalize military and pacification actions in more immediately threatened areas."[40] This comment did not end the rumors, leaks, and even observations by correspondents in Vietnam that something novel was being constructed. Unlike weather modification, which was amenable to exceedingly clandestine operations, constructing a forty-seven-mile-long electronic barrier, which involved displacing people and clearing jungle, could not be accomplished entirely without notice.

On September 7, 1967, McNamara called a press conference and announced that the electronic barrier was being built. He said little more than that, declaring, "The more the enemy knows about our plans, the more ready he could be to defeat the system once it is installed." It was not until 1970, long after the electronic barrier had been adopted and partially implemented,[41] that the Senate formed a special subcommittee to investigate this and related technical aspects of the war. This gap between presidential adoption and congressional discussion (and quasi legitimation) points up the preemptive character of the original decision by Johnson.[42]

Conclusion

Four modes of presidential adoption in technoscience policy have been discussed: acquiescence, partnership, arbitration, and preemption. These approaches have been highlighted through studies of oceanography, the 200-BEV, MOL, weather modification, and the electronic barrier.

Adoption can happen after an issue gets on the presidential agenda, but it does not have to take place. There has to be a mix of pressures, internal and external to the presidency, to make it possible. Sometimes, the pressures are more external than internal. In either event, the technoscience presidency does not adopt alone. Adoption entails legitimacy: some degree of congressional assent is required to legitimate what the president adopts as policy. Even in preemptive presidential adoption, some legislators are usually involved, such as those who chair the key authorizing and appropriating committees in the relevant substantive area. The more congressional involvement, the more complete or authoritative is presidential adoption.[43] Sometimes, however, a president will risk legitimacy to gain a policy closer to his liking.

Adoption processes can take many years or be concluded virtually overnight. When the technoscience presidency acquiesces, it usually bargains for the policy least threatening to its interest in maintaining decision control, as in the case of oceanography. In this instance, Johnson and his aides placed a "sunset" or termination provision on what they adopted. When the presidency preempts, as in weather modification and the electronic barrier, it moves as quickly as possible, often racing into implementation before making the program widely known to Congress. Therefore, Congress is placed in the difficult position of stopping an ongoing effort rather than preventing a program from being adopted in the first place. Having executive power is an advantage in adoption. Presidents can preempt, but Congress really cannot. It needs presidential acceptance to get any kind of programmatic action. The best that Congress can do is to exert pressure on the president for a decision. The president, for his part, can act in such ways as to greatly restrict congressional participation in adoption.

Lyndon Johnson was adept at maximizing presidential advantage in his dealings with Congress. Even where he did not lead, he made certain that his losses were minimal. In partnership modes, he extracted room for maneuver so that he could back away from a decision that he thought was unwise, or he could continue to work for a decision that made sense to him. In the 200-BEV decision, for example, he kept options open as long as possible. The opportunity to pull back from total commitment was retained, although that opportunity grew smaller and smaller as time went on. In an arbitrating mode of adoption, the conflicts within the bureaucracy and Congress are such as to push decisions up to (and from) the president. The Air Force and NASA could not both have MOL. The president had to decide which agency should have control in making an adoption decision.

Of course, the president does not have to arbitrate. Adoption does not have to take place. He can let Congress debate an issue and decide or prevent adoption through its indecision and/or internal conflict. This is what happened in civilian weather modification. In this instance, the president did not intervene, and adoption failed to take place. This is not what happened in the military weather modification and electronic barrier cases. There the president did not permit congressional ventilation of the issues. He allowed the relevant estates to bring the matter to him, and he made the choice to move ahead and to preempt decision making through a strategy of quick decision and minimal involvement of Congress. Those involved were likely to be favorably disposed to what he was doing in terms of the war's conduct.

Adoption, no less than agenda setting, requires advocacy, alliances, and the building of coalitions among subpresidential aides. In oceanography, the key advocate was the vice-president, a member of the political estate, aided by scientists and other professionals from the Marine Council staff. In 200-BEV, an alliance was struck between Hornig and Seaborg, thus creating a strong axis between the science adviser and an administrator who was also a scientist.

MOL revealed advocacy derived from competing alliances of agencies and congressional committees. Achieving adoption often begins with alliances of like-minded individuals in each of the two bodies (presidency and Congress) which then bring together the larger units. Weather modification's dominant advocates were the military professionals, the Joint Chiefs of Staff. In the case of the electronic barrier, McNamara, an administrator, took the lead.

Both the Joint Chiefs of Staff and McNamara had linkages with scientists; these alliances, however, were not with the president's scientific advisers but with their own experts. Adoption decisions varied as to which subpresidential officials were involved. All, of course, required the president's support. In MOL, weather modification, and the electronic barrier, the advocacy coalition was small, deliberately so in the latter two instances. The nonmilitary adoptions required greater support or at least acceptance. The 200-BEV involved aides such as Califano and the director of BOB in ways that affected timing, if not ultimate choice.

Important as they might be, relationships among presidential actors are usually not enough for adoption. This is a critical difference between agenda setting and adoption. Congress does not have to be involved in the setting of the president's technoscience agenda, although it may be and it was, graphically, in oceanography. But Congress is supposed to be involved in adoption; otherwise, adoption lacks complete legitimacy. Hence, even in the preemptive decisions discussed, there was token informing of at least some members of Congress. The "rules of the game" in American government seem to require at least a symbolic legislative involvement. The president adopts alone at his own peril.

4. Implementing the New

The technoscience presidency is involved in the implementation of two kinds of policies: those that it has adopted itself and those that it has inherited from a previous administration. Those that it has adopted are newer and, thus, reflect the issues of early implementation: getting a policy reduced to an organized program of action that can be carried out in a reasonably systematic way. Those that it inherits, usually relatively further along in implementation, are embodied in programs that are capable of being evaluated. They present different kinds of problems, often those associated with making changes in a program that is ongoing. This may be because the policy is not being implemented well or because a president dislikes the policy (and program) that he has inherited. This chapter focuses on the first kinds of implementation problems. The following chapter deals with the second variety.

There are a number of managerial stances that the technoscience presidency can take toward the implementation problems of newly adopted policies and programs. Which unit actually takes the lead in implementing the president's decision depends upon the chief executive's preferences as well as upon who is the most interested in a particular task and whose jurisdiction is affected. The following presidential approaches to implementation are highlighted: *protection*, *monitoring*, *coordination*, *structuring*, and *displacement*. They cover a continuum of strategies: from those providing maximum support and minimum intervention to those in which the perspective from the top is critical and the resulting intervention is far-reaching.

The first approach is one in which the presidency protects an agency in carrying out a program. Such protection provides a minimum of actual interference and a maximum of help for the administrative unit. This may be because the program is more closely identified with the policy system of the presidency than with that of the bureaucracy. Monitoring is supportive, but there are more elements of control. It provides for some periodic reports back to the presidential oversight unit and may yield a presidential commendation or complaint, depending upon the feedback on an agency's activities. Third is coordination. Here the effort to control is more overt. Coordination entails getting two or more agencies to work together on a common program or, at least, not in opposition to one another in carrying out a particular effort. In such cases, a presidential estate is often needed, although interagency committees frequently are used, mostly without success.

Structuring can also be applied as a strategy by various components of the technoscience presidency. This is an organizational strategy similar to that demonstrated in the agenda setting case featuring oceanography. However, whereas in agenda setting Congress was pushing its perspectives into the presidency, in implementation the presidency seeks to penetrate the bureaucracy with its perspective through structural techniques. This can entail reorganization of an agency charged with undertaking a presidential priority or staffing an agency in a particular way conducive to the presidency's interests. Structuring is a heavier-handed implementation strategy than the ones previously mentioned. Sometimes it is called "capacity building" by those who are engaged in its imposition; however, those whose capacities are being built do not necessarily always like the way in which they are being improved.

"Displacement" connotes an even greater intervention in an agency's way of doing business. The term is used here to refer to those cases in which the technoscience presidency takes on (or is assigned) work that is usually expected of the line agency. This means that a White House component above the agency goes beyond coordination and even beyond structuring the work of the agency to assuming some of its functions. The technoscience presidency may call for the creation of a new agency. This is ordinarily done when it is perceived that the agency is unwilling or unable to move in a direction in which the presidency believes it should go.

Such implementation modes run the gamut in possible presidency-bureaucracy relations. They extend from the softest (protection) to the hardest (displacement). They can involve any of several estates of the technoscience presidency, from an administrator protecting a program on behalf of the president to a member of the White House staff (or even the president) intervening in the operations of a program by displacing the agency in order to impose a policy direction.

A number of cases illustrate these various implementation processes. For protection, we have the electronic barrier. For monitoring, there is the "New Centers of Excellence" university program.

Coordination is illustrated by the case of nuclear desalting. Structuring is seen in the effort to build a science and technology capability in the Department of Housing and Urban Development; and displacement is demonstrated in the attempt by the science adviser and his associates to place science and technology at a higher priority in the nation's mechanisms for dealing with the developing nations of the world than was the inclination of the Agency for International Development (AID).

Protection

Many presidential policies that are adopted derive from plans put forth by agencies. Most policies probably are the result of such maneuvers; however, some of the most important and innovative policies derive from a source outside the bureaucracy. The presidency, including the administrator running the agency, may be perceived as an outsider by career bureaucrats inside. Programs that come from outside-initiated policies may therefore need special attention, protection, and freedom from normal administrative processes. Otherwise, they may be defeated by bureaucratic indifference or hostility, as in the case of the electronic barrier.

As noted earlier, the electronic barrier was not conceived by military professionals. It came largely from a segment of the scientific estate that McNamara had gathered from outside the Pentagon to advise him. However McNamara may have viewed himself, he was surely seen as an outsider by the military. Hence, the electronic barrier adopted by Johnson in response to a McNamara memorandum of October 14, 1966, was seen as an innovation by McNamara, not by the military. The estimated cost was $1 billion, but money was the least of the problems where Vietnam was concerned. The problem (for the military) was the McNamara connection.

Thus, the electronic barrier needed protection not only from congressional carping (solved by Johnson's preemptive approach) but also from the military bureaucracy. McNamara's initial intent was to keep the program close to himself, where he could keep track of it and could give it special attention until the merit of the idea could be proved to the military professionals. On September 15, 1966, in anticipation of Johnson's later formal approval, McNamara had appointed Lieutenant General Alfred Starbird, a highly regarded, uniformed, technical manager, to head up the Joint Task 728 in DDR&E, the R&D unit reporting directly to the secretary of defense. The Starbird group would work under the secretary and would concentrate on a "high-priority, top secret, and low profile" program.

This implementing group was called the Defense Communications Planning Group (DCPG).[1]

With direct access to the secretary of defense for broad policy and funding decisions, DCPG had freedom to contact any part of the military up to and including the joint chiefs: ". . . the right to jump immediately to the 'head of the line' for materials, facilities, and contractors; the freedom to tap scientific help in government agencies outside the Defense Department; and virtually unlimited funding."[2] Normal personnel rules were waived or ignored as the most qualified technical people available were brought together from the military, civil service, and high-technology organizations close to government. "In scientific and engineering terms," one of those who participated commented, "what was created in a very few weeks was a new community, the sensing community."[3]

For its initial goal, DCPG chose to develop an air-delivered, predominantly antivehicular barrier, listed by the scientists who were originally convened by McNamara as one of the two key components of the overall electronic barrier's system. Within ten months, the first prototype was ready for testing. Other technologies followed, many of them newly invented. The development of the electronic barrier by DCPG produced an array of technological components employing acoustic, seismic, magnetic, and infrared sensors to detect the enemy.[4]

DCPG worked feverishly and productively. Rather than having interference from above, it had relative autonomy plus protection, as needed. Consequently, the atmosphere within the unit was described by one who worked there as follows:

> As an engineer, it is what you dream about. You count yourself
> as extremely lucky if something like it comes along just once
> in your lifetime. It allowed you to be in on the birth of an idea
> and see it move through all its stages—design, development,
> prototype, testing, production—and into combat in Vietnam in
> just about the fastest possible time, which was less than a year
> in most cases. This is an amazing thing because, in most military projects, the cycles take at least seven years, and the men
> there at the beginning are seldom around for its application.
> But that's just one point, everything else about it was exhilarating. For instance, everything was streamlined, and there wasn't
> a lot of paperwork, red tape, and running around getting approval for every little thing. You could work your own hours;
> and, if you felt that you had to go to Europe, California, Vietnam, or wherever, to get you work done, you'd just get on the
> next plane. What a wonderful experience it was![5]

The role of units of the technoscience presidency, other than the secretary of defense, was minimal in any management sense. The secretary had been the key person in the presidential advisory system in getting adoption, and he was key in the presidential implementation system. There was a PSAC Panel on Vietnam that suggested a number of technological innovations which were sent to the Pentagon. Hornig met regularly with McNamara and served as a broker between the presidential scientists and the scientists at the Pentagon. There was no shortage of ideas from White House–related sources. Briefings were arranged, chiefly by Starbird, so that Rostow, Rusk, and other key national security officials could be kept informed. However, the secretary of defense was in charge, and DCPG was free to use or not use the suggestions as it saw fit.

DCPG was created primarily to implement McNamara's electronic barrier. The barrier's components could be developed in the laboratory, but they had to be assembled in the field, and this took time. Once deployment actually commenced, McNamara's ability to protect and insulate the barrier concept from bureaucratic incursions broke down. There was no avoiding a further delegation of control over the electronic barrier and the electronic and sensing technology associated therewith. Some military field commanders, who had originally resisted the electronic barrier as a possible Trojan Horse whose hidden aim was to halt the bombing, became persuaded that the components of the electronic barrier, but not the barrier per se, might be useful. They began to adapt certain technology of the electronic barrier to their purposes, and the technology began to be used on various separate fronts in specific battles. Its use was justified on the basis of urgent need to help save American lives.

A few days before McNamara left as secretary of defense, a member of Congress asked him whatever had become of the electronic barrier, or as the legislator referred to it, "the McNamara line." The use of this term was indicative of the degree to which it was still seen as the personal program of McNamara. The secretary responded, "The McNamara line is no longer referred to as that because it is successful."[6] What he could have said more precisely was, "The line is no longer a line; and, for that reason, it has been successful in the sense of being widely utilized in the field." The military field commanders had reinvented the concept and redeployed the technology to their purposes. The price of the electronic barrier's success for the military was the loss of the original objective set by the administrator and, through him, the technoscience presidency as a whole. The electronic barrier, as such, was never finished.

Thus, subpresidential protection (by McNamara) had been sufficient to secure the barrier at the outset of implementation. The

R&D organization established to develop the technology was given all of the resources, including autonomy from regular service pressure, that it needed to accomplish its task. However, the electronic barrier experience also points up some of the limits of oversight. Once out of development and into an applications arena, the technology came more under the control of the military commanders in the field, who began to adapt the technology to their own needs as they saw them. Ultimately, the electronic barrier per se was redeployed; in its wake, a broader concept, the electronic battlefield, was born. This was the application of advanced electronics and sensing to military operations in general, often in a highly scattered and decentralized mode, rather than concentrated along a single line at one place.

Monitoring

Monitoring involves observing, receiving reports, and keeping informed. It is basic to all implementation strategies carried out by the technoscience presidency. Often it is part of a broader process such as coordination or a prelude to administrative strategies that entail intervention in the bureaucracy.

While it is a relatively soft managerial device, monitoring does permit the presidency to know what is happening, and this in itself can be important in keeping control of a program. However, as seen in the case of the electronic barrier, there are limits to control and even to monitoring. In the electronic barrier case, the point of overview was the secretary of defense; in the case of the New Centers of Excellence program, the presidential component responsible for monitoring was the science adviser assisted by the subcabinet-level Federal Council for Science and Technology.

Johnson adopted his New Centers of Excellence program on September 13, 1965. The program did not have an official name. The phrase "New Centers of Excellence" captures the key Johnsonian thrust with which agencies were expected to comply. This was a time when basic science, particularly university science, was regarded very highly in political circles. The R&D budget of the government was continuing to rise. Universities were seen as being important to the nation because science and higher education were regarded as important. They were also seen as being significant for economic development. For example, the outstanding research facilities of Harvard University and the Massachusetts Institute of Technology had attracted many high-technology firms to the area, along Massachusetts Route 128. "Route 128" was perceived as a model of what could be done elsewhere. Around such universities would grow high-technology firms that would develop from ideas and graduates spun off from the universities. The creation of Route 128s in other parts of the country could give life to regions badly in need of economic growth. This notion was part of the conventional wisdom in the mid-1960s, and Johnson was receptive to the idea of little Route 128s throughout the nation. Basic to such a populist strategy was the creation of New Centers of Excellence in university science; hence, there emerged the idea of spreading the wealth in federally funded scientific research.

As a venture of the technoscience presidency, the policy was broached by Science Adviser Hornig in a speech at Temple University on March 21, 1964, in which he said, "What we need as a nation is to maintain excellence where it now exists and to develop more sources of excellence where we can."[7]

In July 1964, Johnson had one of his infrequent meetings with PSAC. He was "especially interested in the subject of geographical distribution of federal R&D funds."[8] On August 28, 1964, Hornig wrote Johnson that there was a problem: "The midwestern states receive less than one-third the funds one would expect from population figures." He asked to have the opportunity to discuss this issue with Johnson.[9] Hornig obviously wanted to take the initiative on this issue before it was placed in the hands of someone else.

On May 19, 1965, Leland Haworth, director of the National Science Foundation, wrote Hornig in the latter's role as FCST chairman suggesting that FCST adopt a policy stressing the responsibility of each federal agency for strengthening the capabilities of colleges and universities in all parts of the country for research and education.[10] The emphasis in the policy proposal of Haworth was on strengthening university science and on geographical spread. This would protect the scientific values while recognizing the salience of political interests. During summer 1965, OST, BOB, and NSF worked on a statement embodying Haworth's concept that could be forwarded to FCST. Late in August, Hornig sent a draft to the president for his information, with the recommendation that he endorse it.[11] Johnson liked what he read and called Hornig on the telephone to say that he wanted to make the policy his own rather than endorse one that belonged to FCST.[12]

Following this telephone call, the policy statement was redrafted to reflect more strongly the president's particular point of view. As adopted by Johnson on September 13, 1965, and subsequently announced by him at a cabinet meeting that day, the policy statement embraced the following principles:

(1) Federal research funds should strengthen academic institutions and increase the number of institutions capable of performing research of high quality;

(2) Quality should be maintained where it exists and contribute to the improvement of potentially strong institutions; and

(3) Federal agencies should act in concert to a greater degree in making decisions.

The policy seemed simple and inclusive, one that was good for the "haves" as well as for the "have-nots" of academic science. Johnson said, "I want to be sure that all practical measures are taken to strengthen the institutions where research now goes on and to help additional institutions to become more effective centers for teaching and research."[13]

The policy statement was given considerable publicity by the technoscience presidency, and the geographical distribution aspects were seen as the new Johnsonian flavor of the policy. In the course of being transfigured from an FCST statement, based on the Hornig draft, to a Johnsonian statement, there was also a change in terms of the way the policy was to be administered. Initially, there was to be merely an FCST policy statement and some general overview by the members of FCST, who of course represented the biases of their various agencies. It was, in effect, to be a policy enunciated and administered by equals. Now there was to be presidential monitoring (formalized oversight) of how the policy was to be carried out. Johnson had specifically indicated in his policy statement that the president's science adviser would receive monthly reports on how well the program was progressing. He, in turn, would provide monthly reports to the president. Johnson made it clear that he wanted compliance with his policy. Horace Busby of the White House staff underlined Johnson's concern to Hornig: "I know the President is deeply interested in this. I hope you will seek out opportunities to follow through with him on it."[14]

To strengthen his capacity to monitor the policy on behalf of the president, Hornig set up a standing Committee on Academic Science in FCST. The committee would provide an opportunity for one agency to keep the others informed. They would learn from one another as they implemented the president's policy.

The first report to Johnson came in late September 1965 and dealt exclusively with Hornig's perceptions of reactions to the policy. He told the president that Congress was favorable but that some elements of the scientific community feared that the policy meant redistributing funds from the centers of existing strength to those that were seeking to become New Centers of Excellence. He felt that their fears were groundless and that implementation of the policy would prove this to be the case.[15] Hornig took the occasion of an address at the National Academy of Sciences Symposium on Universities and Federal Science Policies, on October 11, 1965, to assuage the concerns of the scientific elite. He defended the past system based on "talent and on the merit of individuals" and said that there was no intention of abandoning the merit system. He proceeded to discuss the president's directives, the flexibility to be developed in expending federal funds, and the intent to strengthen less-developed institutions.[16]

In the months that followed, regular memoranda reported on what the various agencies were doing. In many cases, there were programs on "developing universities" in being or in the planning stage. The president's statement had the effect of getting existing federal programs enlarged and incipient programs started.

An example of an older program that was augmented was NASA's Sustaining University Program (SUP), established in 1962. An example of a new program that was started in response to the policy was DOD's Project Themis. Themis was scheduled to cost $25 million per year and was specifically aimed at universities that had not been significantly engaged in performing work for DOD. Between the former NASA program and the new DOD program were those of NSF, NIH, and other agencies. These were also programs that had been under way when the president issued his statement. The president's views bolstered such programs and made their proponents hopeful of more dollars in ensuing years.

While these enterprises varied in specifics, they reflected Johnson's overriding desire for geographical spread as a concrete and visible purpose.[17] The monitoring was friendly, since it was performed by FCST and Hornig. The monitoring also had the effect of maintaining the programs as "affected with a presidential interest," a source of status and a degree of autonomy within host agencies.

Monitoring had some rewards for those agencies that performed well. Johnson seldom thought much about NSF, for example; but when NSF started to develop universities in the hinterlands, Johnson took note. Informed by Hornig of NSF's activities, Johnson wrote the director of NSF on March 15, 1966. The letter was written for him by Hornig. As Hornig explained, the letter would "let the NSF and other agencies know that agency action on the September 13 policy is continuing to be watched; to encourage NSF to continue in its present policy direction; and to help NSF with the congressional appropriations process."[18] In the letter, Johnson praised the agency for its responsiveness to his policy.

Thus, monitoring was a presidential implementation tool; but it was also a vehicle for getting political support for certain university policies that the director of NSF, Hornig, and various federal science administrators favored. True, they had to give Johnson his geographical spread; but, in response, they got legitimation for new programs providing for the health of the institution: institutional grants that would supplement (not displace) the individual project awards. Monitoring carried a *quid pro quo* in the hierarchical politics of the executive branch. The president got his geographical principle; Haworth and Hornig got their principle of institutional grants. They also made certain that they had a strong hand in shaping the policy.

Under the impetus of the president's policy, much else was attempted. Through FCST, efforts were made by Hornig and others to get agencies to work more closely in making decisions affecting how they dealt with the same institution. There were also attempts—favored by Johnson—to have agencies eliminate unnecessary paperwork in applications, reporting, and accounting practices.[19]

The monitoring strategy was carried forth for several months. As 1966 wore on, however, Hornig decided that monthly reports were too frequent, given the actual activities of implementing various grant programs.[20] The agencies had been very responsive to the president's policy; and, according to *Science*, the Johnson directive was "beginning to show some effects."[21] Presumably, implementation would continue indefinitely. The president agreed with a suggestion from Hornig that monitoring through monthly reports be ended.

What happened to the programs depended now on more normal presidential management procedures, particularly the budgetary process. The removal of monitoring may have eliminated a special presidential quality-control device from these university programs. It also removed a special security that they had had. Where programs established by an incumbent president were concerned, monitoring had meant nurturing. With such nurturing, it was assumed that much wealth would be shared. However, in the latter Johnson years, when budgets became tight, the newer starts had a difficult time.

Coordination

Nuclear desalting illustrates presidential coordination. In this instance, the president asked the science adviser to do more than monitor. A large-scale technological development program was tied to concrete presidential goals. However, two strong line agencies were also involved, and they had interests of their own; each would rather coordinate than be coordinated. Coordination entailed more than a representative of the scientific estate trying to move line administrative agencies in a coherent direction. That direction ultimately depended upon the perspective of the president. What if that perspective was part of the coordination problem? What if the president's point of view was not always realistic? And what if there were many interests within and outside the technoscience presidency seeking to influence presidential perspective? The answers to those questions are suggested by the case of nuclear desalting. This sequence of events points up the limits, not the potentialities, of coordination by a subpresidential aide.

Nuclear desalting might be said to be a program that was adopted, implemented, and largely terminated under Johnson. There was already a desalting program in effect, under the auspices of the Department of Interior, Office of Saline Water (OSW), but the linkage of nuclear power and the Atomic Energy Commission was new to this effort. This linkage changed the nature and scale of the existing enterprise into something not only new but considerably more impressive. Our focus will be on implementation and the science adviser's role as Johnson's coordinator in the implementation process.

The notion of linking nuclear power with desalting derived, in part, from studies at AEC's Oak Ridge National Laboratory (ORNL) in the early 1960s. Those findings pointed to considerable potential for economic desalting, given sufficient scale-up of some of the reactors then being developed. Alvin Weinberg, director of Oak Ridge National Laboratory, had been a member of PSAC under President Kennedy and had persuaded Science Adviser Wiesner to evaluate the ORNL work. Wiesner had OST organize an ad hoc study to do so. In March 1964, with Johnson and Hornig now in office, that study was completed.[22] It concluded that, by 1975, a high-level R&D program could develop combined nuclear energy, salt water conversion plants that would be capable of producing 500 to 800 million gallons of water per day for 20 to 25 cents per 1,000 gallons, plus delivery costs. This would make converted salt water competitive with fresh water for municipal water supplies in many areas. It would still be too costly for irrigation, but there was optimism for the future.

Johnson was extremely interested in nuclear desalting. It combined two long-standing interests, atomic energy and water supply, in a way that fit his Great Society notions. He wanted to leave a technological legacy, one that would "make the deserts bloom." At least, he wanted to get started. Almost immediately, in his conversations with visiting heads of state, he moved to common problems such as water. Arrangements were discussed for applying nuclear desalting to the water problems of many impoverished nations and for sharing technology with more developed countries, including Israel and the Soviet Union. As far as Johnson was concerned, there had been a breakthrough in nuclear desalting, and he said as much in a June 10 address at Holy Cross University.[23]

Hornig was concerned. On July 9, 1964, he wrote the president and later met with him in the oval office. He pointed out that the government (i.e., Johnson) was offering to share U.S. technology internationally on the basis of the favorable prognosis in the OST report; and, in particular, it had committed itself to cooperation with Israel. "We are about to enter discussions with the Soviet Union. Yet, we have no clear internal commitment to proceed down the road toward large-scale desalting plants." Hornig argued that there had to be a development program before there could be one of application or transfer; the technology was not ready. It could be made ready, but the president should realize that nuclear technology was ahead of desalting technology. He urged, "in general terms, we do commit ourselves to such a development and . . . AEC and DOI [should] be instructed to prepare an imaginative plan to do so." Hornig said that he would "play whatever role" Johnson wanted him to in this field.[24]

Johnson asked Hornig to get together with Director Kermit Gordon of the Bureau of the Budget and draw up an order calling upon AEC and DOI to produce "a bold and imaginative plan for a development program leading to large-scale desalting units immediately and for inclusion in the fall budget." He said that he considered the program to be "as important as space."[25]

Johnson did not give Hornig a role at this point, but it quickly became clear that some role above the two agencies might be necessary. As AEC and DOI planned their joint program, there were differences and tensions. In a sense, it was a forced alliance; but only through such an alliance could nuclear desalting be accomplished. The problem was who would be dominant in the relationship. DOI was the user; AEC supplied the means. In theory, DOI would lead; but, from a technical standpoint, DOI relied on its Office of Saline Water, and OSW was no match for AEC with its national laboratory backup and JCAE support.[26] There was a danger that the "tail would wag the dog." An aide to Budget Director Gordon commented on the problem on July 31, 1964:

> Interior representatives privately express with some justification some fear of the size of AEC ambitions in this field. . . .
> The effect of this fear may be useful to the extent it keeps

Interior on the ball to maintain its leadership role, but it may
also inhibit close cooperation and the most effective utilization
of all resources. . . . AEC, as expected, needed very little
encouragement to initiate a major effort. Our problem in
the future will be to keep the AEC effort within reasonable
bounds. . . . It is not clear that AEC has accepted the notion
that the program is focused primarily on water, not on nuclear
power, and that Interior is to take the lead. There are several
hints that AEC intends to play at least a coequal, if not primary, leadership role . . . some care will be necessary to insure
that AEC does not run away with the program.[27]

AEC and DOI produced a plan of action in September. The report was not well received by Hornig and Gordon. Hornig, for example, thought that the two agencies made a very poor case for a
large-scale desalting program.[28] Their reservations notwithstanding,
the science adviser and budget director sent the report to the president on October 19, recommending acceptance and release but not
endorsement.[29]

On the assumption that acceptance and release could be interpreted as a form of presidential adoption (albeit not the strongest
form), AEC and DOI moved forward (on their own as much as possible) to implementation.[30] The key line administrators for AEC
were Glenn Seaborg, the chairman, and James Ramey, a commissioner who took a special interest in nuclear desalting. For DOI, it
was Secretary Stuart Udall. Udall was very positive, but his operating agency, OSW, was not. The idea of a *nuclear* desalting program
had been imposed on OSW, and it held back. In January 1965, a new
director of OSW was appointed who would, presumably, cooperate
better with AEC. As an extra measure to assure that presidential perspectives would be implemented in a joint program, Johnson made
Hornig the "federal desalting coordinator" as of July 22, 1965.[31]

Congressional involvement in the adoption process came in August 1965. On the eleventh of that month, Johnson signed a bill authorizing $185 million to DOI to accelerate its desalting effort over a
five-year period. Johnson made it clear that he wanted action soon
and said that he might or might not be the most optimistic person in
America about the progress we could make on desalting the seas.
"But I am—and I intend to remain—the most determined that we
shall make the great breakthroughs before the calendar turns to
1970." He declared that Congress had sent to his desk some truly
historic legislation and added, "It is my own studied and considered
judgment that this bill may well be the most historic of all: not for

what it provides, but for what it promises; not for what it accomplishes, but for what it symbolizes."[32] AEC needed no new authority. It was already embarked on a mission to promote what Chairman Seaborg called "the proliferation of the peaceful atom."[33]

As the federal desalting coordinator, Hornig was at the center of the technoscience presidency where nuclear desalting was concerned, but being at the center did not constitute influence over the administrators or the president himself. Hornig and others in leadership positions were painfully aware that Johnson's goals were ambitious and that "getting there" by his deadline of 1970 would be difficult indeed. A major nuclear desalting prototype demonstration plant would have to be built. There was no guarantee that this would be successful. Hornig wanted Johnson to control his rhetoric and his promises to foreign nations.

Hornig feared that political pressures might force the United States to build nuclear desalting plants abroad before the technology was ready. On September 14, 1965, he told Jack Valenti, a Johnson assistant, that the United States might be transferring "white elephants" or "lemons" if the administration was not careful.[34] With the first International Desalination Conference coming up in Washington in October, Hornig grew apprehensive. He persuaded White House aide Douglass Cater to write Johnson on behalf of Schultze, Valenti, and himself, asking the president not to say anything at the conference. Their view was that the United States should make a breakthrough on the domestic front before making concrete proposals to an international audience.[35]

Hornig was only partially successful. "Coordination" was for others, not for Johnson. While the president did not attend the conference (words of presidential welcome were read by Hornig), he did, on October 7, address the foreign delegates at the White House. His words then were reminiscent of Eisenhower's 1953 "Atoms for Peace" address. The difference was that Johnson called for "Water for Peace." Proclaiming the need for "an international crash program to deal with world water resources," Johnson pledged that, by 1970, America would have new prototype desalting plants constructed.[36]

The president had spoken (or, more accurately, had continued to speak). Now it was up to Hornig and the agencies to deliver. Hornig favored a nuclear desalting demonstration in the Los Angeles area, as did most of the others involved in the program. AEC Commissioner Ramey was taking the lead in trying to work out a prototype project in Southern California, and discussions had been under way for some time. Meanwhile, other states with water problems became interested. New York was suffering from a drought. Governor Nelson

Rockefeller, like the president, had a long-standing interest in nuclear energy. He even had a state agency that was concerned with atomic energy. In summer and fall 1965, Rockefeller made a strong effort to get a federal-state nuclear desalting prototype project for New York.

The political nature of this proposal raised it to the president almost immediately. Johnson told AEC and DOI, which had received the Rockefeller request, to "call it as they saw it."[37] They indicated they would probably reject it. Lee White, a member of the Johnson staff at this time, was concerned that rejecting during a drought would be "a political problem." He indicated that Johnson might instruct AEC-DOI to approve, or disapprove, or delay decision on the project, and advised, "it seems to me that the idea of holding it open is most desirable. This might get us to a time when the water shortage problem will have eased and could afford a better opportunity to define the weaknesses of the technological aspects of the proposal." Johnson "checked" the option on the White letter: "Take a pessimistic attitude but hold the door open."[38] By the turn of the year, White again brought the Rockefeller matter to Johnson's attention, saying AEC and DOI were ready, on technical grounds, to reject the New York request "unless you indicate to the contrary."[39] Johnson let the rejection take place.

Meanwhile, various subpresidential aides were concentrating on the demonstration they wanted in Southern California. By fall 1966, what was known as the Bolsa Island Project was entering the final planning stage. This project would involve two nuclear reactors plus a desalting plant with an ultimate capacity of 150 million gallons per day. The project would be sited on an artificial island (Bolsa Island), one-half mile from Huntington Beach south of Los Angeles. The cost would be $72 million. Various California organizations would work with the federal government in building the prototype plant.

The various estates of presidential technoscience were elated as plans for Bolsa Island moved to completion. Hornig said that this was a "fine" project. It was the "only good sensible candidate available." Seaborg concurred "very, very enthusiastically." He believed that it would "be a good project." Schultze found "no problem on this project."[40]

In May 1967, Johnson signed legislation authorizing the project and declared, "This plant alone will not suddenly and overnight make our deserts bloom. But more than anything that we have done yet, it does point to the day when lands now dry and empty will sustain life and will feed the people of the world."[41]

At long last, it appeared that nuclear desalting had a focus and direction and that Hornig's effort to contain Johnson's foreign-policy/ technology-transfer aims until the technology was ready was succeeding. It seemed that there was a consensus within the technoscience presidency about priorities. Then, in June 1967, came the Six-Day War in the Middle East and some unexpected outside intervention in the nuclear desalting program.

The "outsiders" were none other than Lewis Strauss, the chairman of the Atomic Energy Commission under President Eisenhower, and Eisenhower himself. In July 1967, they proposed a plan for building two huge nuclear desalting plants in the Middle East as a technological solution to some of that region's festering problems. Their plan would embrace electric power, water, and irrigation. As Eisenhower noted to Johnson on July 28, the proposed plants would also alleviate the refugee problem: "Obviously, the building of plants, as well as power and water distributing systems, in an operation of this size would give employment to a large number of refugees. The thousands of productive acres thus made out of land, now nothing but desert, would permanently aid their resettlement."[42]

Strauss indicated to Hornig that the plan was to have been kept secret until Johnson had had time to consider it his own, but it had somehow "leaked." Johnson was annoyed; and, in his response to a letter from Eisenhower explaining the idea, he made the point that his administration had also thought of it.[43] However, now the proposal was visible, and various Republicans in the Senate were supporting it, including Minority Leader Everett Dirksen. Udall pressed Johnson to try to regain the initiative, complaining, "The Republicans are 'stealing our clothes' on this issue."[44]

The resulting publicity brought about considerable review beyond the technoscience presidency. Various officials examined the proposal from a national security perspective. The more it could be seen in national security terms, the less economics would matter. This was important, since the technology was clearly not yet viable in an economic sense. Hornig was concerned that consideration was being given to a major announcement by Johnson of a program to counter that proposed by Strauss and Eisenhower. Hornig once again turned to a presidential principal he hoped would translate his concerns into words the president would follow. He asked Califano to exclude the subject altogether or at least to let Hornig "put this 'dream of the future' in perspective."[45]

Hornig worried needlessly. The Strauss-Eisenhower Middle East plan died as the problems in that region proved too volatile to permit consideration of the vast effort proposed. Also, the Bolsa Island prototype project was providing a reality test to dull the dreams of politicians and former and present presidents. On August 25, 1967, Hornig wrote Seaborg and expressed concern with the safety and licensing aspects of the site selected.[46] In 1968, a whole series of technical, economic, and political problems began to bedevil the Bolsa Island project. Concerns were raised about the proximity of the plant to population centers and earthquake faults. Moreover, BOB became restive as costs soared well beyond the original estimates.[47] The nuclear technology, which in the early 1960s was a political asset in the desalting project, now was viewed increasingly as an albatross. The Bolsa Island project collapsed as the Johnson administration came to an end. In his role as coordinator, Hornig could do little but watch as Johnson's nuclear desalting program fell as abruptly as it had risen.

Structuring

One step beyond coordinating agencies is actually shaping the agencies themselves. As a presidential scientific and technological strategy, structuring was used in connection with attempts to reorganize an R&D capacity in agencies already possessing such competence. For example, a PSAC panel on antisubmarine warfare worked closely with McNamara and the Navy in restructuring the R&D work and units in that field to make them operate most effectively.

There were other examples of structural strategies supplied by the technoscience presidency to certain agencies aimed at making those agencies more efficient originators, hosts, and managers for programs desired by Johnson. One of the most significant illustrations of the structural approach to technoscience implementation was the effort to build capacity for science and technology in HUD. HUD had been created in 1965 under Johnson's sponsorship as a centerpiece of his Great Society. It was born chiefly by elevating the old Housing and Home Finance Agency (HHFA).

Neither HHFA nor any of the other components that made up HUD had had much experience in managing large-scale R&D. The science adviser thought it natural that HUD should gain such a capability; there were precedents. No sooner had science and technology come to the White House after Sputnik than the scientific estate moved to establish beachheads at the highest levels in the various agencies. By the time Hornig arrived, there were numerous assistant secretaries for science and technology, science advisers, or their equivalents in the agencies of the bureaucracy. Now, in 1965, with the creation of HUD, Hornig decided that this was another opportunity for technoscience proselytization. He did not move quickly or effectively enough, however, and the legislation establishing HUD had little scientific and technological input. While there were provisions in the legislation for research, there was no special structure or focal point established for science and technology. Hornig believed that such a focus at the highest level was essential. On November 4, 1965, he wrote the president:

> Science and technology has a potential role to play in a substantial number of the problems which affect the livability of our cities. . . . Now that the Department of Housing and Urban Development has come into being, it seems to me to be an opportune time to assure that the new Secretary is properly equipped to face these problems. I would suggest that it might be helpful to him to have a science advisor on his staff who could assist him with these problems at the earliest possible stage, before the new department's plans, programs, and organization are completely jelled. If you so desire, I would be glad to assist in locating appropriate candidates for such a position and in providing any further assistance I can in getting on with the job.[48]

Whatever Johnson may have thought, he did not act immediately on the Hornig memorandum. Hornig continued to seek to persuade the president as well as BOB and Califano that HUD's capacity for dealing with science and technology had to be upgraded. Hornig gradually made some headway; meanwhile, his OST staff worked with HUD trying to sensitize officials in the agency to the fact that science and technology represented relevant tools in implementing the various programs that Johnson had set in motion with HUD's founding. There were allies and skeptics within the agency. Some of the skeptics were individuals who had seen many an urban innovation supported by the federal government only to collapse from resistance at the local level. Others were program officers who feared any centralizing trend in the department that might impinge on their prerogatives. Still others, agreeing as to the relevance of science and technology, nevertheless questioned the status Hornig sought. Hornig kept pressing. On February 6, 1966, he wrote the new secretary of HUD, Robert Weaver, encouraging him to appoint an assistant secretary for R&D.[49]

The most that Hornig could get was a decision by HUD jointly to sponsor with OST a study conference in summer 1966 on "Science and the City." This conference brought together authorities from government, industry, and the university to discuss possible connections between science and technology and urban America. It was a positive conference, one that yielded a menu of many possible opportunities that could keep HUD busy on the R&D front for years. Hornig informed Johnson of the conference and said that OST "will work closely with HUD to formulate a comprehensive R&D and demonstration program for that agency which will incorporate many of the summer recommendations."[50] From the perspective of OST, however, HUD was slow to move.

In Hornig's view, the ideas generated by the study conference would remain in the realm of the potential until the scientific estate was better represented in HUD's top management. Therefore, Hornig continued to lobby for a science adviser or an assistant secretary of science and technology for HUD. In 1967, he won support from various subpresidential components in making this item one element of a three-pronged strategy for better linking HUD with R&D. A second component was a think-tank, modeled after the RAND Corporation, that would provide policy analysis for HUD, embracing nontechnological as well as technological factors. A third was an increase in HUD's R&D budget from a minuscule $500,000 to a more respectable $20 million. With the backing of HUD Undersecretary Robert Wood, legislation was prepared incorporating these elements. Johnson announced the increase in HUD R&D as well as the new position of assistant secretary of HUD for R&D in a message on the cities, delivered on March 8, 1967.[51]

By the time the proposed legislation made it through Congress in 1968, however, there had been some compromises. The position of assistant secretary was no longer designated for science and technology per se. HUD was to be given a new assistant secretary, but was provided with the option of making or not making this a position of science and technology. This option, provided by Congress, no doubt came at the behest of the skeptics within HUD. The think-tank was authorized and became known as the Urban Institute. The HUD request for R&D was cut in half, to $10 million. Given the fact that the technoscience presidency was seeking structural change, combined with budgetary growth for R&D in an era of curtailment, a great deal had been gained. But what was achieved was short of what was wanted.

For example, on the structural front, the secretary of HUD, Robert Weaver, created an Office of Urban Technology and Research, at a status lower than that of the assistant secretary. This may have been acceptable to Weaver, but it was not good enough for Hornig. The science adviser also was concerned about the budget and content of the R&D program of HUD and wrote Weaver on September

17, 1968, of his intent "to allocate a good share of my own time during the next few months to the study of research and experimentation proposals advanced by HUD in order to make sure that the budget requests submitted to Congress are both adequate and defendable and to satisfy myself that these programs will be effectively implemented."[52] HUD had legislation that required it to build 1,000 units of 5 prototypes of industrialized housing a year for 5 years (a total of 25,000 units) to determine if costs could be substantially lowered by mass production and industrialized methods. This was a major effort in housing technology. There were other urban programs (e.g., model cities) of great interest to Johnson which Hornig believed would benefit from scientific and technological advice at the highest levels of HUD. In one of the last memoranda that he wrote as science adviser, Hornig told Lee DuBridge of the California Institute of Technology, the man who would take his place, that he regarded the structuring of HUD for science and technology as unfinished business. He noted that Undersecretary Robert Wood was positive toward a top management position for R&D but that there were "a number of forces in the department, mostly staff, [who] would like to see the post allocated to other administrative tasks."[53] In the succeeding years, the other points of view prevailed, and science and technology did not achieve a strong position in HUD.

Displacement

Structuring involves the arranging of components within an agency with the hope of yielding a better (or different) administrative output. As a presidential strategy for implementation, structuring reorganizes existing capacity or attempts to infuse a new capacity into an agency. Sometimes it works, sometimes it does not. Sometimes the technoscience presidency gives up on the structuring strategy and opts instead for carrying out the activity itself. It goes beyond policy supervision or overview to performance of operating tasks. There was a hint of displacement in the HUD case when OST jointly sponsored a study conference to assemble an urban R&D agenda for HUD. There was more than a hint in certain aspects of technical assistance to less-developed countries, as managed by the Agency for International Development.

The fundamental problem was that Johnson's scientific estate and AID disagreed about the relative priority of science and technology in providing help to developing nations. The president himself was favorably disposed toward giving science and technology a high priority in developmental assistance, but perhaps not as high a priority as Hornig and his associates would have preferred. He would not adopt a general policy on science and technology as it related to AID's work with the developing nations. Rather, he adopted, ad hoc, specific policies for specific countries. Quite often, however, these were policies advocated by his White House science adviser, and Hornig and OST played a major role in carrying them out, at least through their initial implementation stages. The policy advisers became policy implementers.

One of the first incursions by Johnson's technoscience presidency upon AID's domain took place in May 1965. At that time, President Chung Hee Park of South Korea was coming to Washington to confer with Johnson. The Korean president "was about to undertake a statesmanlike but unpopular move of restoring normal relations with Japan; and he was eager to obtain a gesture from the United States which would reaffirm the interest and concern of the United States in Korean affairs."[54] What could the United States do to show its support for Korea? What could it do that would be worthwhile and, at the same time, noncontroversial? The question emanated from Johnson, and numerous suggestions came back from staff and agency sources.

Of all the ideas he received, Johnson liked the one from Hornig most. The science adviser proposed establishing an Institute of Industrial Technology and Applied Science in Korea. He pointed out that such an institute would help Korea to retain highly trained scientists and engineers who otherwise would be lost in a "braindrain" to industrialized nations. It would also serve to engage the talents of the best of Korean youth in helping that nation to develop its economy.[55] Not only did Johnson like the idea, but Park was equally enthusiastic. The idea was a "ten-strike," Horace Busby, a White House aide who was relatively close to Johnson, told Hornig.[56] In fact, Johnson himself wrote Hornig on May 19 praising the idea's show of "originality and imagination." Johnson told him that the State Department thought the idea was "the best thing contributed for the visit."[57]

In early July, Johnson sent Hornig to Korea to work out details. When Hornig returned, Busby recommended to Johnson that he have "an appropriate discussion" with Hornig about the Korean and other foreign science initiatives, including another recent one involving Japan. Busby said, "The 'language of science' is most persuasive language in establishing rapport and understanding between the United States and other countries. I have no original ideas about how to embody this in a program. But I do believe we should give some deep thought to a much broader and more imaginative use of exchanges of this sort."[58]

On August 4, Hornig sent Johnson a report on his trip, along

with recommendations for implementing the Korean plan. He requested that Johnson ask David Bell, administrator of AID, "to take
necessary action, in consultation with me [Hornig], to assist the
Koreans in setting up as rapidly as possible along the lines proposed
in our report." He further asked Johnson to "ask AID to give the proposal full support and keep you [Johnson] informed through me
[Hornig] on progress."[59]

Hornig met with Johnson the following day. Johnson approved
his requests. Adoption of the Hornig Korean proposal came officially
on the same day when Johnson directed AID "to proceed as rapidly
as possible with concrete steps" to set up the institute.[60] AID followed where Hornig had led.

Johnson believed that science and technology was a useful instrument in his dealings with developing countries. The United
States was perceived as being the world's leading nation in science
and technology; developing countries wanted to be in a position to
utilize whatever science and technology the United States had to
offer. However, AID had relegated technical assistance to a role in
support of capital assistance. The scientific estate worked as a pressure group within the presidency to change that balance, to upgrade
the priority of science and technology vis-à-vis capital assistance. In
going to foreign countries, Hornig went beyond policy advising to
policy implementation. Thus, when Johnson asked AID to carry out
the Korean program, he told it to stay in touch with Hornig's office.[61]
Hornig dealt not only with AID but also with a country's ambassador.[62] The Korean experience became a precedent not only for what
was done abroad but also for the scientific estate in attempting to
displace AID's funding priorities with its own.

The pattern became familiar. A head of state would visit Johnson.
Johnson would ask for ideas from various sources on what the United
States could offer to indicate support. Hornig would make a scientific and technological suggestion of one kind or another. Johnson
and the foreign head of state would agree to pursue the idea. Hornig
or his designees would go to the foreign country and work out ways
to put the idea into initial practice. AID would find itself carried
along by the momentum and paying the bill. Thus, on December 13,
1965, on the occasion of a visit from the president of Pakistan,
Hornig suggested the United States:

(1) Cooperate with them in improvement of their medical
    schools, especially by establishing full-time facilities
    which could act as centers, not only for medical educa-
    tion but for developing new approaches to rural medi-
    cine and public health. . . .

(2) In order to help the Pakistanis to help themselves to increase their farm productivity, it is proposed that I lead a team of agricultural scientists drawn from AID, USDA, universities, and industry to work with appropriate Pakistan officials in exploring steps that might be taken cooperatively to strengthen the science and technology base for Pakistan's growth and development.[63]

As the Johnson administration continued, the president utilized Hornig in various personal diplomatic ways. Hornig was able to travel around the world on behalf of the president, promoting science and technology as a major means of helping developing nations. Among the places that Hornig visited as Johnson's technoscience ambassador were Taiwan, Pakistan, India, Libya, and Latin America. Everywhere he went, he talked about technical assistance and building an in-country capacity for using science and technology. He and his OST staff were giving the emphasis to technical assistance that AID did not. Johnson found it useful to let Hornig "show the flag" through science and technology. A number of new institutes and programs thereby were established in developing nations at the urging of the technoscience presidency. Hornig kept Johnson informed of progress in getting the various science and technology institutes established. He kept an eye on the further implementation of these ventures by AID. On February 27, 1967, Hornig wrote William Gaud, Bell's successor as administrator of AID, complaining of the lack of progress on the institute being set up in Pakistan. AID had to listen; at least on this issue, Hornig had the ear of the president.[64]

On April 3, 1967, Hornig responded to a request from Johnson for bold and creative new ideas for an upcoming Summit of Inter-American Nations at Punta del Este. He recommended the establishment of an Inter-American Foundation for Science and Technology. He specifically stated that this would fill a function not performed by AID.[65] Shortly before, he had told Sol Linowitz, a U.S. Representative to the Council, Organization for American States (OAS), ". . . the resources devoted to science and technology as weapons for development have been inadequate in Latin America, and . . . there exists no present agency (including AID) which provides a critical mass of competence adequate to deal with the problem." He raised the notion of the Inter-American Foundation for Science and Technology and said that the model would be somewhat like the National Science Foundation and associated with the Organization for American States.[66] Once again, Johnson liked the Hornig suggestion and made the proposal at the summit meeting.

This role brought Hornig increasingly into disagreement with

AID. In the latter part of 1967, on behalf of Johnson, he went to Taiwan. When he came back, he prepared a report to the president dated November 16, 1967, in which he said, "The central issue raised is the nature of our relations with a country after the termination of assistance."[67] He complained to Budget Director Schultze:

> What is involved is a refusal by AID to take the lead within the U.S. government for arranging U.S. technical assistance with Taiwan in the post-AID period. . . . The problem is aggravated by the disorder within the institutional development programs of AID which is supposed to help prepare countries for successful transition to a post-AID status. . . . [The government] should find an agency to take the lead in arranging post-AID technical cooperation with AID graduates, if AID will not do so.[68]

Hornig made essentially the same points to AID directly.[69] He even asked a member of the OST staff in early 1968 to visit David Bell, the former administrator of AID, now with the Ford Foundation, to discuss "the AID problem" with him.[70]

In September 1966, Hornig had set up a PSAC Panel on Technical Assistance to study, in part, how better to organize the United States' effort and thus deal with this problem. The panel filed its report in February 1968. PSAC criticized AID's science and technology record. It concluded that, for a variety of reasons both internal and external to the agency, AID's efforts to combine capital and technical assistance had not worked and had resulted in "AID being inadequate to that basic kind of technical assistance whose purpose is to produce the indigenous scientific and technological base necessary for self-sustaining economic and social development."[71] The report pursued the displacement strategy to its logical conclusion: it called for the establishment of "a new, separate, and independent agency of the federal government to formulate and execute projects of technical assistance with respect to the less-developed countries."[72] Before PSAC could press its view upon the president, however, AID ran into extreme difficulty with Congress, and its very survival as an agency became jeopardized. Under the circumstances, PSAC recommended that the report be kept on the shelf until such time as it might usefully be considered. An appropriate time never quite came.[73]

At the end of the Johnson administration, in discussing unfinished business with DuBridge, the Nixon appointee as science adviser, Hornig mentioned AID as a problem, much as he had done with HUD. The difference was that he believed that more drastic remedies were needed in the case of AID. It was not so much a question of getting rid of AID; the issue was how to extricate science and technology from an agency that either could not or would not appreciate what it could do for the developing nations. Referring to the PSAC report, he wrote DuBridge on December 30, 1968, "If it were feasible to establish a foreign technical assistance agency under qualified direction, I am confident that it could be highly effective in furthering our foreign policy objective at a relatively modest cost."[74] He went on to note, "Our recent pilot program in Taiwan demonstrates what can be done." He suggested that the beginning of a new administration might be an opportune time to consider placing technical assistance in a separate agency outside AID, under technical leadership.[75] As with HUD, the AID unfinished business went unfinished.

Conclusion

In implementation, the presidential and bureaucratic policy systems meet. In asserting its claims, the technoscience presidency uses a range of strategies. Those discussed include protection, monitoring, coordination, structuring, and displacement. They run from a maximum of top-level support to the relevant operating agencies to a maximum of intervention in certain aspects of their administrative activities. Strategies reflect the relative convergence and divergence of presidential and bureaucratic goals. As the literature makes clear, a great deal of policy can be remade in the process of "carrying out" policy.[76]

Different elements of the technoscience presidency were revealed in the processes associated with these presidential implementation strategies. In the case of protection, the electronic barrier showed McNamara to be in charge on behalf of the president. He provided protection for the research and development unit of DOD that was responsible for developing the electronic barrier program and also served to contain outside knowledge of its activities. Thus, protection had multiple purposes: to make a technically effective program; to secure the program from critics and rivals within the operating agency; and to suppress information about the program from those outside who did not have a need to know. Given the relationship of McNamara and the president, the defense secretary was the appropriate element of the technoscience presidency to preside over and protect the implementation of this innovation in its earliest stages.

Monitoring was carried out by the science adviser with the help of FCST. As the president's basic policy favoring New Centers of Excellence in "have-not" regions of the country came to be incorporated into agency practices, the method of overview, monthly progress statements, was abandoned. Once set up, the multiagency program entailed thousands of separate grant decisions. A measure of monitoring agency procedures through interagency (FCST) discussions was deemed appropriate. Beyond that, the technoscience presidency chose to do little. Implementation was up to the agencies and would take place through many discrete grant award decisions over a long period of time.

Monitoring involves elements of the protection strategy. Any new presidential program, including one coming from the technoscience presidency, needs to be watched lest it be emasculated by those who are against it or indifferent to it in the agencies. Not even McNamara could prevent his electronic barrier from being ultimately diverted from its original goals by the operating commanders in the field. (The McNamara line became military-controlled and ceased to be a "line.") Thus, top-level protection is required to secure the technoscience presidency's goals in agency administration. Protection requires monitoring. As the electronic barrier case shows, however, there are limits to protection and monitoring. Eventually, McNamara left DOD, and the military professionals remained. Protection can last only so long, and monitoring can reach only so far. This is especially the case when a program is as dispersed and decentralized as the effort to create New Centers of Excellence.

As in monitoring, the science adviser was in charge of coordinating the nuclear desalting program. The nature of what was being managed was quite different, and the variations were substantial. Large-scale technology was an issue in nuclear desalting, not a myriad of small grants. Results were expected soon by the president and others. The problem was that the technology had to be developed. For development, there had to be cooperation between two major agencies, DOI and AEC. DOI had desalting expertise, and AEC had knowledge concerning atomic energy. Linking the two technologies (the goal of the technoscience presidency) meant linking the two agencies. This was easier said than done. Coordination implies someone coordinating and someone else being coordinated.[77] DOI and AEC had their own lines to the White House and were not easily moved. The levers Hornig had for making them work together were few.

Complicating Hornig's (horizontal) coordinating role was the vertical problem that he had with Johnson. Johnson wanted bold action. He wanted to mount a "Water for Peace" program on the model of Eisenhower's "Atoms for Peace" idea. Hornig argued that a domestic technology had to be developed before you could apply and transfer it to other nations. He pressed for less rhetoric and more cooperative action in technological development. He found himself having to coordinate not only the two line agencies but also the president. It took a long time to provide a focus for the work through a prototype project, and the project was really a creation of AEC, not the coordinator. Under such circumstances, further exacerbated by the Strauss-Eisenhower initiative, coordination proved impossible.

In nuclear desalting, the science adviser was dealing with a strong set of actors. Structuring and displacement, more potent control strategies than coordination, were used in connection with agencies that were weaker both in a technical and in a political sense. Such agencies as HUD and AID were faced with top-level intervention in their implementation efforts which stronger agencies could circumvent through their political alliances.

The scientific estate's strategies differed vis-à-vis HUD and AID because the agencies that were their targets differed. HUD was a new agency; its policies and practices were still in the making. It could be helped if it could be changed so that it had more capacity in science and technology at the highest levels of agency management. The fight for an assistant secretary for science and technology became a symbolic struggle for the status of technoscience in a social agency. The dominant view within HUD was not in favor of an assistant secretary specifically for science and technology. Here, apparently, the science adviser and administrator differed. Congress created the necessary position but allowed HUD to resolve how it would be designated. The HUD secretary made a place for science and technology in HUD, but it was not at the top, where the scientific estate wanted it. The status of HUD technoscience suffered; so did its influence.

As structuring was a strategy targeted at HUD, displacement was sought in connection with AID. For AID, the scientific estate felt that there was little hope. Here was an old agency that would never learn, never change its ways. As opportunities arose to insert their interest into presidential initiatives with developing nations, the science adviser and his associates did so. Thus, an institute was established here, a program was set up there. It was an ad hoc and fragmented form of displacement strategy in which the science adviser was an initial implementer as well as a proposer of ideas. The president's scientists displaced AID's priorities with their own whenever they could by gaining the president's attention for advice and his backing for execution. The scientific estate was successful in partial displacement, but it wanted a stronger displacement strategy. It determined that a proper role for science and technology in development could not be left to AID to implement.

When Hornig wrote DuBridge, "Our recent pilot program in Taiwan demonstrated what can be done," he revealed two key notions: first, when he said "our" program, he meant a program designed and put into being by the technoscience presidency; second, in calling this a "pilot program," he suggested that a broader and sustained effort in implementing a proven concept was in order. To have such a program carried out on an operational basis, to diffuse the concept and the philosophy behind it, would require an agency that was more hospitable to science and technology than AID. The remedy? Displace AID with another agency, one managed by individuals who would understand the priority of science and technology as an instrument to help the developing countries.

All of these strategies and others were used by the technoscience presidency (or elements within it). They were possible to the extent that Johnson provided those under him with legitimacy and a measure of support. When the president took an active part in decision making with respect to these strategies, there was a special force behind the actions of particular individuals or groups within the presidency that were engaged in carrying out a strategy. When he did not, the individuals or groups usually had many more problems in achieving their goals. This was particularly the case with the more interventionist strategies, such as structuring and displacement. Often there were efforts without results. When the president interfered with his own strategy (e.g., coordinating nuclear desalting), there was little that the individual in charge of implementing the strategy could do. To manage a bureaucracy, the technoscience presidency needed to cohere; and this presented difficulties, given differing points of view within it. But the ultimate limit on the *Johnson* technoscience presidency lay in the fact that it did not last beyond 1969. Agenda setting and adoption are possible within the span of a given president's tenure; implementation usually is not. The fate of the programs that Johnson began depended considerably upon what his successors would do. Similarly, what Johnson did with the programs that had been passed on to him from his predecessors determined their success or failure to a substantial degree. This is the subject of the next chapter.

5. Carrying Out the Old

The technoscience presidency inherits programs established by predecessor administrations. It can change these programs so much that they represent changes in kind rather than in degree. In effect, it creates new programs on top of the old. The novelty implicit in the action is most evident in those cases in which a new agency is brought into being to manage the program. Alternatively, an agency not previously associated with a program is given the mission to manage (or co-manage) it specifically to add a new president's imprint. This latter situation was seen in the decision to add nuclear power and the Atomic Energy Commission to the desalting program of Interior—Office of Saline Water. This represented a change in kind, not just of degree. Nuclear desalting was an initiative of the Johnson technoscience presidency. It went beyond building on what had gone before to produce discontinuous change—in effect, a wholly new program.

Most programs inherited from predecessor administrations are not so radically transfigured, however. They continue under the same administrative agency and pursue the same basic goals they had before. They have bureaucratic momentum that is not easily interrupted. The new chief executive and his associates in the technoscience presidency are more likely to modify inherited programs than to transfigure them radically. To curtail a program—wholly or partially—entails a great deal of trouble, as we will note in the succeeding chapter. So new presidents generally either accelerate or decelerate an existing program. Sometimes their changes are so modest that they can be said simply to be maintaining the previous president's commitment. Occasionally, they try to reorient an effort slightly, continuing support, but moving it in a somewhat different direction.

This chapter reviews how the Johnson presidency carried out a number of programs inherited from Kennedy, indicating how it attempted to 1. *maintain* Apollo; 2. *reorient* the National Institutes of Health's basic research toward a more applied effort; 3. *escalate* Victnam defoliation; and 4. *decelerate* the supersonic transport. These programs illuminate a range of administrative stances. The programs themselves are different. NIH involves scientific research; Apollo and SST entail technological development; and Vietnam defoliation represents a technological applications program. What they have in common is that they were all initiated prior to Johnson's becoming president. He inherited them and had to make decisions in regard to their continued implementation. In doing so, he sought varying degrees of continuity and change.

"Carrying out the old" does raise somewhat different issues of presidential management than "implementing the new." These arise from the fact that the presidential policy that is being managed is at a later stage of its own evolution. This means that the problems (in contrast to the opportunities) of a particular policy stance are more likely to be evident. In the case of large-scale technological programs, this is sometimes painfully evident. Given the sequential nature of the science and technology process and also presidential decision making, "carrying out the old" presents the possibility of a dual mismatch: the president in office is carrying out a policy he did not adopt; and he is in office at a later stage of the science and technology process than he might like in order to put his stamp on a program, or correct an error.

Maintaining

John F. Kennedy was the president who made the historic decision that launched the Apollo program to send Americans to the moon. Lyndon Johnson was the president who largely implemented that decision. Presidential implementers are not accorded the credit they deserve by historians. As the cases treated in this study suggest, it is often easier to launch new programs than to carry them out. This is especially the situation where one president is policy adopter and the other is policy implementer. Perhaps one reason Johnson was such a devoted implementer of Apollo was that he had been vice-president and chairman of the National Aeronautics and Space Council under Kennedy. In the latter capacity, he had been a policy adviser to the president on space. He had coordinated the subpresidential effort that led ultimately to the Apollo decision. It was a decision he personally advocated. Prior to that, as Senate majority leader, he had been one of the strongest voices calling for America to overtake and surpass the Russians in space. He had sponsored the bill that created NASA.

Now, as president, he had to make sure that the Apollo decision was carried out. The man appointed by Kennedy to lead NASA was James Webb, whom Johnson had recommended for the role. In his book *The Vantage Point*, Johnson would later write, "The choice of Webb as administrator of NASA was one of the best selections I ever made."[1]

Thus, while Johnson inherited space policies and programs, they were not an unfamiliar activity. He felt a sense of fatherhood in NASA and Apollo, and he believed he actually knew a great deal about the subject matter. In implementing Apollo, Johnson worked with Webb, and Webb with Johnson, and seldom did anyone get between, including other components of the technoscience presidency. This was especially true of Apollo; it was not true of post-Apollo programs, which required crucial adoption decisions during Johnson's administration.

Johnson declared his support for the Apollo goal shortly after becoming president. In his first State of the Union Message, delivered in early 1964, Johnson said, ". . . we must assure our preeminence in the peaceful exploration of outer space, focusing on an expedition to the moon in this decade—in cooperation with other powers, if possible, alone if necessary." Then, in his budget message, shortly thereafter, he declared:

> Our plan to place a man on the moon in this decade remains unchanged. It is an ambitious and important goal. In addition to providing great scientific benefits, it will demonstrate that our capability in space is second to no other nation's. However, it is clear that no matter how brilliant our planners and managers, or how frugal our administrators and contracting personnel, we cannot reach this goal without sufficient funds. There is no second-class ticket to space. Appropriations enacted for 1964 for the National Aeronautics and Space Administration were $600 million below the amount requested. As a result, major development programs leading to the manned lunar landing have fallen behind schedule. . . . Even so, more funds are needed in 1964, and I am therefore recommending a supplemental appropriation of $141 million for this year.[2]

On November 23, 1964, the director of the Bureau of the Budget asked each agency for a statement "of desirable reforms in ongoing programs" that would help "to free funds" in FY 1966 and later years for urgent programs. Webb's reaction was to write Johnson on November 30 that "what this vigorous agency needs is not reform or reduced resources but increased support. Both of these, in my view, are essential to the kind of efficiency which you seek in the execution of the public business."[3] To a considerable extent, Johnson agreed with Webb, at least where Apollo was concerned. In 1965 came another White House public endorsement, and a comment from Vice-President Humphrey that Johnson was the "father" of the space program:[4] "He has put his heart into it, his spirit into it, his hand into it, and his mind into it. And the fact that he was the author of the Space Act and not only authored it, but shepherded it to success and then nourished it into fulfillment is, I think, the real strength, the real underpinning of the program."[5]

However, there were increasing pressures on Johnson to let Apollo "slip," and thus save money. To a large extent, Johnson created the programmatic competition for Apollo when he started building the Great Society. In making the problems of urban America an increasing priority, he gave rise to expectations on the part of mayors and various local interest groups that could not be met given budget constraints. In 1966, James Cavanaugh, mayor of Detroit, expressed a view shared by many of his colleagues that there was a budgetary conflict between space and the cities. He stated that a delay in the Apollo program "for only a few weeks" would save enough money to restore cuts made in urban programs in low-income housing, poverty, and education.[6] But Johnson would not be moved. On March 16, 1966, he accepted the Robert H. Goddard Trophy from the National Space Club and said, "We intend to land the first man on the surface of the moon and we intend to do this in the decade of the sixties."[7]

It was not just the trade-off between Apollo and the cities that bothered some critics. There were also important trade-offs within the overall NASA budget. In 1967, Charles Schultze, director of BOB, warned Johnson that Apollo was causing too many cuts elsewhere in NASA's budget and that a degree of slippage of Apollo into the 1970s might permit a better post-Apollo program to get under way.[8]

Johnson remained adamant. He wanted the decision that John Kennedy made and that he favored carried out. He regretted the cuts in urban programs, as well as the squeeze Apollo exacted on other NASA endeavors. He was sympathetic to those who wanted more for social programs. But he was also determined to stay on course and place a man on the moon within the decade.

The supreme test of Johnson's policy to maintain the Apollo goal came on January 27, 1967. On this date, a fire ignited in the Apollo capsule. Three astronauts in training within the capsule lost their lives. For the first time, the credibility of Webb and NASA's management of Apollo was widely questioned. The whole space program was disrupted.

Congress launched an investigation. It became known that, in 1965, Major General Samuel Phillips, the director of the Apollo program, had found the North American Aviation Corporation, prime contractor, lax in certain of its quality-control responsibilities. When Webb indicated reluctance in making the "Phillips Report" available, he personally came under severe criticism. Some asked whether Webb might be trying to hide something.

Should Johnson call for an investigation of the space agency by a group independent of NASA? The president did not move in this direction. He was supportive of Webb, and did not want to add to NASA's woes. Webb spoke to Johnson and indicated that, while he would accept an outside inquiry, he felt that he could be trusted to conduct an investigation himself. He would take whatever actions were necessary, based on the findings. He needed no outside evaluation. NASA could evaluate itself. Moreover, Webb pointed out to the president that investigations sometimes got out of hand and turned into witch hunts. He noted that there were those in Washington who were already beginning to link Johnson to some alleged improprieties surrounding the North American contract award through one Bobby Baker, former Johnson Senate aide.[9]

Johnson listened to what Webb had to say and decided that NASA should conduct the Apollo fire inquiry on behalf of the executive branch. Johnson thus reaffirmed his confidence in Webb, and steadfastly backed the Apollo program budgetarily and in other ways, to maintain the lunar goal. Webb, NASA, and Johnson rode out the criticisms. After several months of postponements due to NASA and congressional investigations, changes were made to tighten management both in North American Aviation and in NASA. There was some reshuffling of personnel under Webb and reorganization of offices. But the delays and changes were not permitted to become so severe as to threaten the Kennedy (and Johnson) goal.[10]

On Christmas Eve, 1968, just a matter of weeks before Johnson left the White House, American astronauts circled the moon. The culmination of Apollo was now clearly within reach. The last step to fulfill the goal remained to be taken by Johnson's successor. "People frequently refer to our program to reach the moon during the 1960s as a national commitment," Johnson later wrote. "It was not. There was no commitment on succeeding Congresses to supply funds on a continuing basis. The program had to be justified, and money appropriated year after year."[11]

Kennedy had adopted Apollo; Nixon would complete the program. But it was Lyndon Johnson who maintained Apollo and largely implemented America's journey to the moon. To the extent there was a national commitment, it was embodied in Johnson himself. It was demonstrated in the cohesive alliance between the chief executive and the administrator, an alliance that protected NASA from other estates within the presidency, as well as from critics outside.

Reorienting

As a man who had once suffered a heart attack, Johnson had personal experience as a basis of his interest in health research. The federal government's billion-dollar effort in health science, funneled largely through NIH, was not one Johnson—or his presidential predecessors—controlled to any great extent. The health research programs had grown over the years largely as an enterprise run by a triumvirate of interests: NIH itself, the health appropriations subcommittees in Congress, and assorted biomedical research–oriented pressure groups. Not even presidential budgets were levers of control. Every year, Congress gave NIH more funds than the president requested. It was good politics to be for health.[12] John Kennedy had not attempted to buck the health research system.

Johnson took a different stance. He was certainly for health and for research. What he saw, however, was an agency out of presidential control, continually generating new knowledge, but somewhat uninterested in getting that knowledge utilized. It was an agency that did not reflect his philosophy. This was revealed strikingly in early 1964, when he appointed a panel to study heart disease, cancer, and stroke. The primary charge to the committee was finding ways to facilitate the flow of knowledge of research discoveries in these areas to the people and to speed up the actual implementation of new knowledge.[13] Johnson was interested in the application of science. With the ensuing formulation of the health policies of his Great Society, such as Medicare and the Regional Medical Program, it became even more obvious where Johnson's interest lay. NIH, however, continued with its traditional approach. Mary Lasker, a wealthy philanthropist, friend of the Johnson family, and long-time proponent of a more applied NIH research stance, did not hesitate to suggest that a reorientation strategy was in order.[14] On June 14, 1966, she wrote the president as follows:

> Saturday night I made a suggestion to you to meet with the Director of the National Institutes of Health and the nine heads of the individual Institutes.
> I urge you to ask them to review with you their plans for reducing deaths and disabilities and prolonging the prime of life of the American people during your Administration. . . .[15]

The next day, June 15, 1966, Johnson called a meeting at the White House for the purpose of announcing the beginning of Medicare. In the course of the meeting, the president addressed the need to reorient the NIH health research program. He told the assembled medical and hospital leaders:

> Now actually, a great deal of basic research has been done. I have been participating in the appropriations for years in this field. But I think the time has come to zero in on the targets by trying to get this knowledge fully applied. There are hundreds of millions of dollars that have been spent on laboratory research that may be made useful to human beings here, if large-scale trials on patients are initiated in promising areas. Now Presidents, in my judgment, need to show more interest in what the specific results of medical research are during their lifetime, during their administration. I am going to show an interest in the results. Whether we get any or not, I am going to show an interest in them.[16]

He went on to say that he was calling a meeting of the director of the National Institutes of Health and the directors of the individual institutes, as well as the surgeon general of the Public Health Service. He stated, "I am asking them to come here to meet with me for the purpose of hearing what plans, if any, they have for reducing deaths and for reducing disabilities and for extending research in that direction."[17] He also stated that he was serving notice on John Gardner, secretary of HEW, of his intent, publicly, because he did not want him to object privately.[18]

On June 27, 1966, the announced meeting took place. Gardner was there, along with virtually all top NIH officials. Johnson spoke strongly, demanding to know where the payoff was for all the years of lavish support. He said that he was "keenly interested to learn not only what knowledge this buys but what the payoffs [were] in terms of healthy lives for our citizens." Johnson cited statistics showing the relatively poor standing of the United States in many health areas. He berated the administrators at length and concluded by asking whether "too much energy was being spent on basic research and not enough on translating laboratory findings into tangible benefits for the American people." He asked NIH to review priorities and, if necessary, to reshape them in order to get maximum results from existing programs.[19]

The reaction was immediate, intense, and vocal. As Strickland described it:

. . . the President's words fell like a bombshell on NIH officials. They were shaken, and so were their friends to whom the word was quickly passed. The President's initiative . . . caused an explosion among the scientists and in the universities. They took it to mean that the Lasker forces were in the saddle; that support for applied research and development was to be substituted for support for basic research by an anti-intellectual, unsophisticated President who could never understand such things.[20]

NIH decided, as one response, to prepare a detailed report identifying research on specific diseases and directed research programs. Friends of NIH, in Congress and in the biomedical community, used other ways to react. They complained, vehemently, to subpresidential officials presumed to be close to Johnson. Among these were Gardner, the administrator, and Douglass Cater, the member of the White House staff whose portfolio included health policy.

Cater asked Irving Lewis, the chief of the Health and Welfare Division, BOB, "to make some informal inquiries as to whether NIH was stirring up the scientific community to protest against the President's desire for some tangible results from the heavy federal investment in biomedical research." Lewis reported that because of the general uneasiness among scientists concerning "the Administration's support for basic science, we doubt that NIH had to take any specific actions, overt or covert, to stir up the concern of the scientific community further." He noted that Johnson's meeting with NIH was but the most recent of a number of signals the biomedical community had been perceiving suggesting "a sharp reorientation of federal policies." He went on to say that "while NIH itself as yet has done little to correct any misimpressions, . . . Secretary Gardner is seeking a number of speaking engagements where he can clarify the Administration's intents and soothe any ruffled feathers."[21]

On August 23, 1966, at a meeting of all NIH consultants in Bethesda, Maryland, Gardner began the process of "clarification." He denied that the government was retreating from its concern for basic biological and medical research.[22] He argued that the commitment was still there.

Gardner's efforts were only partially successful. Cater was concerned about the damage to Johnson's image. In June 1967, he and Hornig discussed "the deep suspicion that exists within the scientific community—not only the biomedical community, but the general community as well—that the administration does not understand the importance of basic research and would like to increase applications at the expense of basic research."[23]

Meanwhile, the report that NIH had begun preparing after the president's address was being completed. It made the case that medical research and health services were not incompatible. In fact, one was the goose that laid the golden egg. "They are a continuing sequence essential to the progress and well-being of man." In essence, the report recommended that, with minor adjustments, the present NIH arrangement would work well: no reorientation was necessary.[24]

The impact of the report on the president was expected to be small even though presidential staff members were working on the wording of the report. Far more important was the continuing reaction to the Johnson statement. Cater and Gardner argued that Johnson had to blunt the political implications of his increasingly negative image. They concluded that only Johnson himself could repair the damage. It was decided that because Johnson had made NIH officials come to him when he castigated them, he would now have to go to NIH in a show of support to basic research. A visit was scheduled and carefully arranged by Cater, Gardner, and NIH. Various NIH officials would make the case verbally that was being made in the written report. At the same time, Johnson would have a chance to save face in backing off from his earlier statements.[25] Philip Lee, assistant secretary for Health and Scientific Affairs, HEW, said:

> We believe it would be very important for the President, in his statement, to voice his strong support of fundamental (basic) research and its importance to our long range goals—he should praise the contributions of the universities and the medical schools, and he should pay tribute to Dr. [James] Shannon's leadership [as director of NIH] and very fruitful relationship between the Federal government and the universities, as illustrated by the NIH programs.[26]

The meeting was set for July 21, 1967. Johnson had a helicopter fly him to the Bethesda, Maryland, campus of NIH, where he was given a tour of the facility. Following the tour, Johnson expressed satisfaction with the progress being made in the war against disease. He lauded the NIH directors, their staff, and their grantees for a "billion dollar success story." While noting his continued interest in research applications, he emphasized his support for basic biomedical research: "The government supports this creative exploration because we believe all knowledge is precious; because we know that all progress would halt without it."[27] The Johnson tour and words, of course, were covered by the press.

Whether Johnson's initial intervention had a major effect in reorienting NIH toward greater efforts in applying research is doubtful.

The pressure was certainly rewarded with at least some symbolic shifts. However, the fundamental character of the NIH program remained essentially as it was. It was left to Nixon and his "crusade against cancer" to increase the presidential pressure. The Johnson effort was significant more as a harbinger of what was to come than as a direct challenge itself. The impact of Johnson's decision was mitigated because the president, ever mindful of the politics of an action, pulled back when he was made aware of the damage to his image. Johnson, at this time, was trying to win friends in the academic community, not lose them. The attempt to reorient NIH was certainly handled clumsily; it is primarily significant as an example of the hazards of presidential intervention in ongoing programs with influential constituencies. In going along with the advice of an outsider (Mary Lasker), Johnson apparently did not seek the counsel of subpresidential insiders (Cater and Gardner). The second presidential meeting with NIH attests to the fact the insiders were persuasive, belatedly.

Escalating

It is a long way, both philosophically and geographically, from the campus of NIH to the jungles of Vietnam. But, as president, Lyndon Johnson had to concern himself with both. And while his science and technology policies for NIH aimed at extending and improving life, those for Vietnam unfortunately worked in the opposite direction.

As we have noted, the Vietnam War saw the introduction, under Johnson, of extremely sophisticated electronic technology (the electronic barrier) and of weather modification for military purposes. It also saw the accelerated use of certain technologies introduced by Kennedy. Perhaps the most notable example of a novel technological applications program that Johnson maintained and augmented in Vietnam was defoliation.

Chemical defoliation was, of course, not new to the world. What was new was its application to warfare. As a weapons innovation, defoliation chemicals were adapted to wartime purposes. They were applied in their strongest forms at levels of unprecedented intensity to denude trees of their leaves so that the enemy could be better seen. They were also used to destroy crops on which the enemy fed, crops grown by Vietnam civilian farmers. One of the chemicals used was called Agent Orange, an exceptionally toxic herbicide deployed at a rate of application thirteen times greater than that used for civilian purposes. As a weapons program, defoliation worked well in terms of its immediate military purposes. Adopted by Kennedy, the program was largely implemented—and expanded—by Johnson. At its height, it involved 1,200 men in its operations.

The program was known as "Ranch Hand." It began officially in 1962. A high-level Pentagon official was later quoted as saying that three factors led to the decision to use defoliants in Vietnam. One was the need to conduct defoliation experiments in heavy jungle areas. A second was the need of the operating military personnel, who viewed defoliation as a means to avoid or end ambushes and, perhaps, starve out the Vietcong; and a third was the sheer promotional effort of the Army Chemical Corps.[28]

The decision was not uncontested. Not long after the program started, in a very small way, a high-ranking State Department official, Roger Hilsman, journeyed to South Vietnam and observed the effort. Whatever its military virtues, there were political drawbacks, in his view. As he later wrote:

> Defoliants . . . were new. They were chemical weed killers which had been highly developed in the United States. . . . The military headquarters in Saigon thought that the defoliants would be ideal for clearing the underbrush along the sides of roads where the Vietcong laid their ambushes and for destroying crops in areas under Vietcong domination, and General Taylor [ambassador to South Vietnam] and the Joint Chiefs of Staff agreed. The State Department view, on the other hand, was that the political repercussions would outweigh any possible gains. Defoliation was just too reminiscent of gas warfare. It would cost us international political support, and the Vietcong would use it to good propaganda advantage as an example of the Americans making war on the peasants. . . . The National Security Council spent tense sessions debating the matter.[29]

In this case, the ambassador to Vietnam and the Joint Chiefs of Staff prevailed over the State Department. The actual management of Ranch Hand was delegated to levels well below the presidency by the time Johnson reached the White House. Authority for the use of defoliants to remove tree-cover was lodged in the commander of U.S. Forces in Vietnam and the American ambassador. Authority for their use to destroy crops required somewhat higher approvals in the State and Defense departments. By the time Johnson became president, the program was well under way. As he escalated the war, there were pressures from the field to escalate the technologies already being used to fight the war. Those involved in the field operations as well as their administrative superiors wanted to accelerate and enlarge the defoliation effort. Neither McNamara nor Johnson denied them the authority to proceed.

Over time, Johnson came in for a great deal of criticism over the program. In escalating the war in general, he also augmented the application of defoliants. Not until very late in his administration did reduction occur. Until then, the policy behind the program was acceleration and expansion.

Thus, in 1963, 24,700 acres were sprayed. In 1964, Johnson's first full year in office, this number tripled.[30] In 1965, the target area went up again, to 155,610 acres. Crop destruction had been relatively restrained to that time, with the bulk of defoliation aimed at removing tree-cover. Now, in 1965, the restraints were loosened and the crop destruction became more "systematic." By 1966, it "had become an important phase of counter guerrilla activity."[31]

Unlike weather modification and other Vietnam science and technology programs, the use of chemical defoliation was known in the United States, at least among war critics and the scientific community. As the program expanded, awareness and protests grew apace. From the beginning, the most vocal critics of this aspect of the war were members of the scientific estate. For the most part, scientific protests against defoliation came from outside the presidency, however.

In 1964, the Federation of American Scientists released a statement expressing concern with reports from Vietnam relating to the deployment of chemical weapons. It questioned whether the United States was using Vietnam as "a proving ground" for new weapons.[32] Hornig, who received the statement from the Federation, responded that the "President seeks to preserve American military power and undertake those measures whose implementation will advance the cause of peace and arms control."[33] In 1965, protests mounted, and in 1966, they began to be widely reported. In that year, John Edsall, professor of biochemistry at Harvard, led a group of twenty-nine students in the Boston area, appealing to Johnson to proclaim publicly that the use of chemical weapons by our armed forces was forbidden and to oppose their use by the South Vietnamese or any of our allies.[34]

Later in 1966, twelve universities and seven Nobel Laureates were represented in a protest letter written by twenty-two scientists and addressed to Johnson. Both lists contained the names of Edsall, Matthew Meselson, Keith Porter, and George Wald. In 1967, the defoliation campaign continued to expand. Johnson again received petitions against Ranch Hand from the scientists. On February 14,

Meselson, Edsall, and Paul Doty of Harvard and Irwin Cy Gunsalus of the University of Illinois went to Washington with a petition of protest for the president. They had gathered 5,000 signatures. The scientists went to their point of access to Johnson, science adviser Donald Hornig, himself a chemist.[35]

Hornig tried to explain the president's position. The visitors were particularly appalled at the use of defoliants to kill crops and deprive people of food. Hornig explained that the target was not really crops per se. Rather, it was the people who grew and consumed them. The motive for destroying food was to force people to move. He pointed out that when the United States found a Vietcong-supporting area, it was faced with the alternatives of bombing, bull-dozing, attacking, or dropping leaflets telling the people to move be-cause the defoliants were coming. "It's all geared to moving people," Hornig stressed.[36]

The scientists were not persuaded by Hornig's articulation of the president's policy. Hornig, caught in the middle, delivered the pe-tition to Johnson. The president was equally unpersuaded by the sci-entists' view that the policy should be changed. He was increasingly familiar with the debate surrounding Ranch Hand. He was aware that there were those who felt defoliation was counter-productive and was losing the United States and its allies support in Vietnam among civilians who were adversely affected. He was aware that many scientists feared for the long-term ecological damage to Viet-nam and its people wrought by defoliation. On the other hand, the Joint Chiefs continued to urge that it was needed. Johnson chose to let the defoliation campaign continue and even grow.

Meanwhile, it was left to Hornig to deal with the scientific crit-ics. He made it clear, in a letter to Meselson, dated March 13, 1967, that the president was aware of their point of view and that the matter of defoliation and related issues had "been the subject of con-tinuing study within the government."[37] In contacts with National Security Adviser Rostow, he urged restraint. Beyond actions of this kind, Hornig could say or do little. He was far removed from the locus of authority for technological applications affecting Vietnam.

Throughout 1967, the area sprayed was augmented to 1,486,446 acres. One-sixth of the defoliants were for crop destruction. More than 100,000 tons of food were destroyed, of which two-thirds was rice.[38]

Having failed with Hornig and Johnson, scientific critics sought to influence change through Robert McNamara, generally regarded as at least accessible to members of their estate. During the course of 1967, the largest professional association of scientists, the American Association for the Advancement of Science (AAAS), sought McNamara's support. All it wanted, it said, was the Pentagon's cooperation in establishing the facts concerning the long-term consequences of the highly toxic chemical agents being used in Vietnam.

In February 1968, with McNamara leaving the Pentagon for the presidency of the World Bank, the director of Defense Research and Engineering, John Foster, responded to the AAAS proposal. He stated, "Qualified scientists, both inside and outside our government, and in the governments of other nations, have judged that seriously adverse consequences will not occur. Unless we had confidence in these judgments, we would not continue to employ these materials."[39]

Nevertheless, Foster continued, he would ask an independent, nonprofit organization, the Midwest Research Institute, to make a study of the matter and have the National Academy of Sciences set up a group to review the study.[40] The next month, Johnson announced his decision to partially halt the bombing in Vietnam and not to run for reelection. This decision, more than the Foster announcement of a formal evaluation of Ranch Hand, was the point from which the policy of escalation began giving way to one of deescalation.

As Nixon took power, there were widespread reports that children were being born in the defoliated areas of South Vietnam with serious and unexplained birth defects. There were further cutbacks of defoliation; in 1971, the program was terminated altogether. Years later, many American soldiers who had participated in Ranch Hand reported a high incidence of cancer and other dread afflictions. They claimed (but could not prove) that they too were casualties of the Vietnam war.

Decelerating

In 1961, the FAA, with President Kennedy's blessing, began probing the possibilities of building a civilian supersonic transport. By 1963, FAA (and others) had convinced Kennedy that such a plane was both feasible and desirable. FAA, by this time, had spent $31 million on SST studies. Also, the English and French were united in an effort to build their version of a plane (the Concorde), and the Soviet Union also had an SST program of its own under way. It seemed clear that there was going to be an SST. This being the case, the United States had to have one, and not be left behind, in the view of many presidential advisers. Presidential adoption seemed almost "natural," given the temper of the times in 1963, and Kennedy's own New Frontier philosophy.

On June 5, 1963, in an address at the Air Force Academy, Kennedy declared, "It is my judgment that the government should immediately commence a new program in partnership with private industry to develop at the earliest practical date the prototype of a commercially successful supersonic transport, superior to that being built in any other country in the world."[41]

As with Apollo, Johnson favored and promoted the decision Kennedy made. As vice-president and chairman of the National Aeronautics and Space Council, Johnson had headed an interdepartmental committee that advised Kennedy on the necessity of competing with the Russians and Anglo-French and producing a supersonic aircraft to vie with the ones they were building. The fact of international economic competition in an industry at the cutting edge of high technology moved FAA in 1961, and Kennedy in 1963, to act. There was perceived to be a national interest in accelerating the development and use of the SST beyond that which would have taken place had "the market" been left to decide. Paced in accord with the Concorde competition, SST was scheduled to be operational by 1967. Hence, what Johnson as president inherited looked like a military and space-style "crash program" to develop and deploy a new plane intended for civilian use.

Johnson's initial policy decisions relating to the implementation of the program, however, were such as to put SST on hold. This was quite uncharacteristic of Johnson, who generally favored high-technology projects. Why and how he slowed down SST constitutes an important chapter in the history of Johnson's science and technology policy. It should be emphasized that this policy was one of slowing down, in order to evaluate and strengthen, an ongoing program whose policy goal remained unchanged. There was never a presidential intent to kill or diminish the program. There was an intent to produce a product that would be commercially viable.

Johnson inherited more than an existing R&D program estimated to cost $1 billion over its lifetime. On December 19, 1963, the same day he signed a $60 million appropriation bill for SST, he received a report on SST from Eugene R. Black, former president of the World Bank, and Stanley de J. Osborne, chairman of the board of Olin Mathieson Chemical Corporation.

The report had been commissioned by Kennedy as an initial evaluation of the program. Black and Osborne recommended that the United States proceed with SST as a project in the national interest. However, they noted many reservations about the way the program was being planned and run. They warned against the technical and economic dangers inherent in "one of the basic philosophies of the current program, namely, of tying the United States' effort to Concorde." Despite an "almost unanimous view" by the airlines that the SST should be postponed for another decade, they found that the British-French program, now well under way, set the pace, posed other problems, and defined the competitive and technical necessities of the U.S. SST. "Never before will such vast sums have been invested in capital facilities, development costs, and production financing just to produce a commercial aircraft," said Black and Osborne. They went so far as to recommend dropping the program if the nation was not willing to face the issues "financially, technologically, or managerially."[42]

"The schedule," they pointed out, "which would have five production aircraft building as early as when the first production prototype flies, creates a financial and technical gamble of such proportions that we cannot possibly recommend it." They felt that the FAA's management approach was unrealistic. There would be a need for much testing and prototype flying in order to solve what they called the two biggest question marks involving the program: 1. the sonic boom; and 2. the economic viability of SST as a commercial operation. "Unless solutions to these important unknowns are found, the entire program could fail."[43]

Because of uncertainties and large costs, they recommended that the government absorb more of the risks of moving ahead, contributing ninety percent of development costs rather than seventy-five percent, as originally planned. However, they did not believe FAA was the right agency to lead the federal effort. They felt an independent authority led by an individual of great stature and ample power reporting to the president was needed. This recommendation reflected, in part, a widespread concern in industry and government that FAA was not up to the job. It had no experience in managing large-scale technological development programs such as SST.[44]

Johnson was undoubtedly aware of the Black-Osborne report when he approved a $60 million expenditure for SST. He was sufficiently concerned to ask BOB to lead a government-wide review of the report's implications. The management recommendations did not escape scrutiny. FAA's role was an issue. An outsider evaluation had indicated problems with the SST program. Johnson wanted his insiders, led by his Bureau of the Budget, to corroborate or deny the Black-Osborne findings, and to suggest what could be done about the real problems.

The administrator of FAA, Najeeb Halaby, was unhappy with the report. He had been close to Kennedy, and his agency had worked hard to make the program a viable one. Now, with a new president in power, problems were being raised. Moreover, Johnson apparently shared Black and Osborne's skepticism about FAA as a technological development organization. Halaby and his top aide for SST, Gordon Bain, deputy administrator for supersonic transport development, wrote Johnson separate letters defending their agency's management capacity. Bain complained of "misconceptions" in the Black-Osborne report in a letter to Johnson dated February 28, 1964.[45] Halaby, on March 4, said, "I believe that the agency [FAA] has demonstrated an ability to plan a program and faithfully meet its commitments."[46]

The BOB review, however, which included a survey of opinion of various agencies, turned up considerable support for some of the Black and Osborne administrative concerns. While it did not lead to the conclusion that an independent authority should run SST, it did suggest a possible need for a different managerial approach. One of the options being discussed was transferring the program to DOD, where McNamara, then at the height of his prestige as a big technology manager, could take charge.

Halaby, aware of the "solutions" being considered, looked for a compromise position that would retain the maximum control possible for FAA. In his March 5 memo to Johnson, he argued that any shift of jurisdiction over the program from his agency to DOD would not go well with Congress. However, he indicated willingness to accept a structure in which the president established an advisory committee and charged it with the task of "giving independent counsel with respect to policies and the management of the program."[47]

The Halaby "concept" was accepted in form. On April 1, 1964, Johnson asked McNamara to head up a special Presidential Advisory Committee on SST (PAC-SST). Included on this committee were Douglas Dillon, secretary of treasury; Luther Hodges, secretary of commerce; John A. McCone, director of the Central Intelligence Agency; James E. Webb, administrator of NASA; and Halaby. In addition, the president appointed Black and Osborne. However, in substance, there was a difference. This was to be more than a mere advisory committee. It was itself to be very involved in setting policies on pace and direction for the program. Johnson realized Halaby was unhappy with the turn of events. On April 23, 1964, he wrote Halaby to reaffirm his support for the program—and for Halaby. The president said he would look forward to the "recommendations from the [McNamara] committee and from you."[48]

On May 20, 1964, Johnson approved "the program recommended by the Advisory Committee on Supersonic Transport and the contractors proposed by the FAA administrator; the President directed appropriate federal agencies to implement the program immediately."

He declared he was "confident that this country will produce a supersonic transport that will continue to maintain American world leadership in the air."[49]

The program approved by Johnson inserted an extra phase into the development schedule of SST. Under Kennedy, the feasibility phase had been accomplished and the second phase of design competition launched. FAA had issued a request for proposals from industry and set forth requirements for the plane. Industry had submitted various proposals. FAA, under Johnson, was expecting to select an industry team to build the SST prototype. The agency was anxious to move from phase II to phase III, from design to construction. The McNamara Committee was not so anxious to move. It determined that more study of alternative approaches was needed before committing to one specific design for development. No potential contractor had been able to produce a configuration capable of meeting the requirements FAA had set. Hence, the McNamara Committee recommended, and Johnson accepted, an extension (phase IIA) of design competition, a "run-off" through contracts with two airframe manufacturers (Boeing Corporation and Lockheed Aircraft Corporation) and two engine manufacturers (General Electric Company and Pratt and Whitney Division of United Aircraft Corporation). At the same time, the McNamara Committee proposed and Johnson concurred that the Department of Commerce should conduct certain economic studies to judge the size and type of plane that would be most profitable. The program that Johnson accepted, and announced on May 20, also included an evaluation of the sonic boom problem to be conducted under the guidance of the National Academy of Sciences.

Under Kennedy, the SST had been launched, with the highest value being the technological race with Concorde and the Soviet SST, much in the manner of Apollo. Under Johnson, the frame of reference for the plane shifted. Johnson was very much for SST. The basic policy continued. The difference was in the implementation—the nature of the SST. In large part because of the Black-Osborne report, which Kennedy had commissioned, the concern was now more with the commercial and environmental realities of the plane. Simply developing Apollo technology was an end in itself—economics and noise pollution were not factors in decision making. But SST had to be used, as well as developed, and to be used commercially—and on earth, economics and noise did matter. Kennedy, with FAA pushing, had leaped; Johnson, with FAA held at arm's length, via the McNamara Committee, was looking. Hence, the implementation was decelerated, with the McNamara Committee being the mechanism to buffer the president from criticism.

Halaby had signed the committee report, but differences were made known to Johnson. For example, Halaby fought the assignment of the economic evaluation to commerce. He was also firm on a twenty-five percent industry sharing and was "very optimistic about the prospects for the development program." The McNamara Committee, of which he was, of course, a member, was "more cautious" or, as Moyers noted to Johnson, quoting McNamara, "more realistic." Johnson asked Moyers to get Halaby and McNamara together and reconcile their differences.[50] But the differences were really too basic.

The May 20, 1964, decision provided for a six-month phase II-A. This began June 1, upon signing of the contracts with the two competing industrial teams. FAA went along with the new phase, but differences of perspective continued. The president's May 20 directive stated that the "contracts should give the manufacturers the freedom to design airframes that they believed would be most profitable commercially, without restricting them to any particular design."[51] This latter statement was a signal to FAA that it should not prematurely substitute its technical judgment for that of industry. The Johnson technoscience presidency was coupling deceleration (a shift in timing) with substantive change (an improvement in the type of plane being developed).

FAA, which saw its "policy" authority diffusing under Johnson, did not wish to give up its "operating" control of contractors. In June, it made known the fact that it was going to issue "work plans" providing "minimum design objectives." BOB immediately complained. Budget Director Gordon told Halaby that this was not what the president had in mind. Setting forth such objectives might cause contractors to refine proposals already submitted, rather than presenting fresh ideas. New ideas were what Johnson and the McNamara Committee wanted, said Gordon.[52]

In October, BOB had to deal with what it regarded as yet another FAA attempt to avoid the implication of the president's decision. FAA was pressing for a substantial add-on of funds to its budget for prototype development. However, on October 30, Gordon reminded Halaby that there had as yet been no decision to move on this by the president, who would not act until he heard from the McNamara Committee.[53]

On November 24, the McNamara Committee concluded that prototype development was still not ready. It could not yet decide between the two design teams. There would have to be a further extension, a phase II-B. Halaby was annoyed and frustrated. From the FAA perspective, the Boeing/General Electric design was clearly better, and there was no point in spending additional money on Lockheed/

Pratt and Whitney. He told Gordon on November 28 that it would take a direct order from Johnson to make him extend the design competition again.[54]

On December 2, Johnson sent Halaby a memorandum, drafted by BOB. He stated, "I authorize you to contract with the engine and aircraft manufacturers to continue the work they have been doing during the past six months at a funding rate not in excess of the funding rate from the contracts they have been performing for the past six months."[55]

This meant at least a six-month extension of Lockheed/Pratt and Whitney. Johnson indicated that such an extension was necessary because evaluations by the Commerce Department and the National Academy of Sciences were not yet in. Nor had he heard from the McNamara Committee. If Halaby needed any further evidence as to who was running SST, Johnson provided it, saying, "I shall await the recommendations of my Advisory Committee on the Supersonic Transport before I make any further decisions concerning the SST program."[56]

On December 22, Johnson and Halaby met at the president's Texas ranch. Halaby explained that under FAA supervision, a technical evaluation team "had found the Boeing/General Electric studies and design proposal acceptable, and rated the Lockheed/Pratt and Whitney work unacceptable." Johnson asked for a memo from Halaby stating his intent, nevertheless, to extend contracts with both teams. Halaby supplied the requested memo on December 23, writing, ". . . we will continue all four companies at work on the supersonic transport program, adding a task for Lockheed to carry along with its own proposal, and thereby maintaining the advantage of competition and giving you and your advisers the range of alternatives to consider. I am proceeding in full compliance with your memorandum, even though it has been necessary to overrule the Government Evaluation Team in the process."[57]

As the end of this six-month phase II-B approached, the McNamara Committee concluded that still another extension of the design competition involving the two contractor teams would be necessary. On June 30, 1965, Johnson announced that there would be a phase II-C. This would continue the design competition an additional eighteen months. Thus, a decision to commence actual prototype construction would not be made until the end of 1966. Halaby, however, would not be around to participate in that decision. As the extension was announced, it was also made known that Halaby was leaving FAA. Halaby and Johnson parted amicably, but it was obvious that Halaby was frustrated. He was replaced by General W. F. "Bozo" McKee, formerly of DOD and NASA. In asking McKee to take the job, Johnson told him to "get yourself a good deputy administrator to run the FAA." His main task, the president said, was to take over the SST program.[58]

Why the further delay? There was a widespread rumor at this time that the Department of Commerce study had produced a 150-page "non-public" document that indicated the original FAA request for proposals would have led to an "economically impossible" airplane.[59] Reports on the sonic boom were no better. NAS had originally been given the assignment to assess the sonic boom, but it was making slow progress. Even slower was the contractors' progress in finding "technological fixes" for the boom.

McKee was barely on the job as FAA administrator before he requested a meeting with Johnson. On August 3, 1965, Califano told the president that McKee wanted to see him to recommend SST "be turned over to Defense on or about October 1. McKee feels that the FAA does not have the capability to handle the program." Califano, in mid-1965, had just come over from DOD to the White House as Johnson's special assistant for domestic affairs. As an aide to McNamara, he had worked on the SST program. He discussed the possible SST move with McNamara and told Johnson, "McNamara's main objection to taking the program is that he does not want to appear to be an empire builder. He is, however, willing to accept it if this objection can be met." Califano said he regarded defense as "the best place from which to run the program." However, he noted that there had been controversy over the McKee appointment: ". . . after the flap on making an Air Force general FAA Administrator, any transfer to Defense should be done carefully."[60] Johnson apparently decided the politics of the change precluded any transfer, for the reassignment issue did not surface again. For better or worse, SST stayed with FAA.

As time went on, the sonic boom was seen more and more as a problem. In August 1965, McNamara and Hornig agreed that Hornig should take over leadership for the sonic boom evaluation from NAS. In November, Hornig organized an OST Coordinating Committee for Sonic Boom Studies. This group included both governmental and NAS expertise.[61] In addition to utilizing existing data, Hornig wanted the Air Force to make a series of overflights of selected sites in order to evaluate sonic boom characteristics and public reactions to different noise levels. Two series of overflights were discussed. The first would be a series of overflights at Edwards Air Force Base by various high-speed aircraft "to analyze in depth various aspects of the physical propagation and effects of the sonic boom and to discover if it was possible to correlate the effects of booms generated by smaller aircraft with the effects of booms generated by

the much larger SST." The second type discussed was "a series of ir-
regular and frequent supersonic community overflights in a corridor
extending from Louisville to Indianapolis ninety days after the Edwards tests ended."⁶² The site of the community overflights was
chosen on strictly technical grounds.

There was little or no opposition to the Edwards tests. There was,
however, considerable conflict over the community overflights.⁶³
Hornig and Budget Director Schultze were in favor of going ahead as
soon as possible. Hornig wrote the president on April 23, 1966, arguing strongly for community overflights. He said, "There are no technical reasons for delay. The planning is as complete as is profitable
on the present schedule. . . . The present decision, therefore, is
whether a delay is justified on political grounds."⁶⁴ Schultze said, in
a memo also sent to the president on April 23, "We need to know
quickly what kind of restrictions, if any, will have to be placed on
the SST because of boom problems. Knowledge of these restrictions
*will help determine the specific design and characteristics of the
plane.*"⁶⁵

McKee was against the tests. On April 21, he sent Johnson a
memo detailing technical reasons why the community overflights
could be delayed. At the same time, he wrote Marvin Watson, an aide
close to the president, giving political reasons for not going ahead,
especially before the election. He enclosed a list of senators and representatives whose constituents would be affected. As he wrote,
"Any way you cut it most of the people will feel that they are being
used as guinea pigs. We can expect a considerable uproar and opposition. This could well result in an attempt by certain members of
Congress to delay appropriating money for the prototype program
until after the conclusion of the tests."

Such a cutoff of funds would be intolerable, in McKee's view. He
went on to say that the principal backer of the SST in the Senate,
Warren Magnuson, shared his reservations about the community
overflight tests.⁶⁶

Califano assembled these memos and summarized them for
Johnson. In a cover memo, dated April 27, 1966, Califano stated that
he and McNamara "believe that sonic boom tests over civilian communities are essential and failure to have them could leave serious
gaps and lead to wrong decisions in the sonic boom program." They
recommended that Johnson "approve sonic boom tests over civilian
communities right after the election in November, so that they can
be run for the most part while Congress is at home and as far away
from the 1968 election as possible."⁶⁷

McKee was sufficiently concerned that he went to the White
House directly on this issue. Ultimately, Johnson gave approval to

begin the Edwards Air Force Base tests. He did not do so for the community overflights. Hornig would have to make the best of whatever data he could get.[68]

By July 1966, the Edwards Air Force Base tests were under way. On September 8, 1966, Hornig was able to make initial conclusions on the sonic boom known to the president. The most important conclusion was that because of the sonic boom, for which no technological answer had been found, preliminary analysis indicated it was "extremely unlikely that either of the designs in the present competition can be flown over the continental U.S. in regular service without severe public reaction."[69] Later, on November 1, he expressed these views more fully in a report to the McNamara Committee.[70]

On December 31, 1966, phase II-C came to an end. Since the initial exploratory work on SST in 1961, FAA had spent $511 million on the plane; industry had provided another $70 million. The major product thus far had been studies. The hardware phase had been postponed again and again by the president on advice from the McNamara Committee. The time had come for another presidential decision. Hornig did not think either design would work across overland routes due to sonic boom, and a restriction to overseas routes surely would weaken an already shaky economic position. Johnson was aware of all the problems, including those of further postponement. He decided the United States had to move forward, as best it could, to the next phase. Significantly, however, *he* did not make the announcement, thereby permitting himself some leeway for the future. The announcement was delegated to FAA Administrator McKee, who made it known that the long design competition was at last at an end: the SST prototype would be built by Boeing and General Electric.

But first, contracts had to be negotiated, and this cost more time. There was haggling between the government and industry over financing. The original seventy-five/twenty-five percent split of the Kennedy era had given way to the ninety/ten percent formula recommended by Black and Osborne. But there were other problems concerning responsibilities for overruns, slippages in schedules, and so forth. Also, Johnson wanted to wait until he was sure that there were the necessary votes in Congress. Over the years, legislative opposition to SST, in part a result of the growing environmental movement, had increased. On March 24, 1967, when Budget Director Schultze sent the president a letter to sign directing FAA to execute the contracts, Johnson responded angrily:

> I'm not going to sign this until I get the positive position of
> every Senator—and the airlines ought to get after every senator

this weekend. Tell Boyd [Alan Boyd, secretary of the newly established Department of Transportation], McKee, Trippe [Juan Terry Trippe, chairman and chief executive officer of Pan American Airlines] that they ought to be contacting every one of the 100 senators and, particularly, the liberal ones, like the two Kennedys and Clark. I'm not going to have them demagoging and saying that I'm denying children milk to build big planes. Get the position of everyone—especially Magnuson, Jackson, and Monroney—and I want a special report on the leadership—Mansfield, Dirksen, Kuchel, Long, and Smith, Byrd—and of the Committee . . .[71]

The congressional information was assembled. It was not until April 29, 1967, that Johnson felt ready to give the "final" and official presidential decision "to go." He stated:

Today, I am pleased to announce that the nation is taking a major step forward in the field of commercial aviation. I am authorizing the Secretary of Transportation to sign the contracts for the prototype construction of a supersonic transport. I am also sending to Congress on Monday a request for the $198 million to finance the government's share of the next phase of the development of the transport aircraft. . . .[72]

It had been three years and four months since Johnson had received the Black and Osborne report. The report had triggered a process that had led to a conscious "decelerated implementation" of SST. Implementation moved forward, but at a slower pace than had originally been intended. In this period of slowed-down progress, a great deal of money had been spent, and a vast number of personnel-hours utilized in attempting to improve the design of the plane. Now a decision had been made, for better or worse, to put a prototype together. It was 1967, the year FAA had originally expected to have supersonic transports in commercial operation. The notion of a crash program to win an SST race had long since been abandoned. There was a debate in Congress on the SST decision, but, in the end, Congress went along with Johnson.

The presidential decision notwithstanding, SST continued to have problems. The Department of Transportation was chiefly responsible for dealing with these problems. DOT had been created in 1966. When Johnson moved the SST from a design to a prototype phase, he also ended the McNamara Committee and assigned SST management to DOT. He no doubt had hoped that he could extricate himself more from the thicket of SST problems. He made it clear to everyone that he fully backed the SST. He had given SST a top national priority for obtaining scarce equipment and materials. In view of the war and Apollo, this was an important decision.

On February 14, 1968, DOT informed the president of the department's "tentative conclusion" that the design selected for a prototype SST still left too large a gap between it and the production aircraft that airlines would be asked to buy. Further research and development would be necessary. Thus, Johnson's last decision on SST had the same effect as his early ones: to let the program schedule slip. He ordered yet another year's delay for the purpose of working out difficulties with the prototype aircraft.[73]

When Nixon came to power in 1969, he faced a program in technical, economic, and—for the first time—truly serious political trouble. He wanted to accelerate the much-delayed SST program. He wanted to finish the prototype. Congress would not let him, however. In 1971, Congress did what Johnson and Nixon had refused to do: it terminated the program. Johnson's implementation strategy had kept the program alive, but had never really solved its basic difficulties. The Russian and British-French planes did fly. But the key problems that killed SST—economics and sonic boom—eventually also brought an end to Concorde production.

Conclusion

The technoscience presidency has been discussed in its role as manager of programs inherited from previous administrations. One presidential policy system takes over the management of programs launched by a predecessor system. A range of inherited programs were included: Apollo, NIH basic research, Ranch Hand, and SST. Two involved technological development (Apollo, SST), one scientific research (NIH), and the remaining one, Ranch Hand, was a major effort in technological applications. Managerial strategies included maintaining (Apollo); reorienting (NIH basic research); escalating (Ranch Hand); and decelerating (SST).

What were the goals of these programs as they were inherited from Kennedy? Did the Johnson technoscience presidency try to change the goals? How? Did it succeed in what it tried to do? Why or why not? The implementation literature discusses programs but gives relatively little attention to the impacts of presidents on those programs.

The goal of Apollo was to go to the moon. The Johnson technoscience presidency did not want to alter this goal. Its strategy of maintenance was geared to this goal. It protected the program from budgetary cutbacks even to the point of hurting future NASA missions and drawing the ire of Johnson's urban constituents. At the core of this management strategy was an alliance between Johnson and Webb. Johnson had advice from within as well as outside the presidency to let Apollo slip. He rejected such advice, and relied on Webb when it came to Apollo. At the point when the fulfillment of the goal was most greatly threatened—the Apollo fire—Johnson was most supportive and protective. There was no evaluation of NASA's handling of the program by a source within the technoscience presidency other than the administrator of NASA.

In contrast, the goal of the NIH research program, as inherited from Kennedy, was pure research, a goal the Johnson presidency wished to change somewhat. It was not against basic research. It was *for* applied research. Its management strategy was to reorient NIH along lines of thought that came from an alliance of the president and an interest outside the presidency, health lobbyist Mary Lasker. Lasker saw the change in presidents (Kennedy to Johnson) as an opportunity to redirect NIH. The line of communication went from one key element of the agency/committee/interest group system to an even more critical element of the presidency: Lasker to Johnson. The remainder of the policy systems of which they were a part were not pleased. Presidential policy insiders did not have an opportunity to make an input to the Johnson reorientation strategy or the way he announced it. Johnson moved ahead on his own. This resulted in words that appeared to imply a much greater reorientation in NIH research policy than subpresidential advisers regarded as wise or desirable. Moreover, the rhetorical assault on NIH brought such negative reactions that the other estates within the technoscience presidency sought to get Johnson to back off from the reorientation approach. The political costs to his image were not worth the gains. In effect, presidential policy insiders recaptured Johnson's attention and got him to publicly reverse himself. The Johnson technoscience presidency thus went from an attempt to reorient NIH to one where it had to reorient the president.

Kennedy had set Ranch Hand in motion, and Johnson speeded it up. The goal was to clear the tree-cover the enemy in Vietnam employed in its guerrilla activities and also to destroy food crops. Critics argued that the program might have hurt the civilian farmer population of South Vietnam more than it did the enemy soldiers. But Johnson escalated the program along with other military technologies in an effort to bring the enemy to the negotiating table. The key proponents in the technoscience presidency for Ranch Hand were the president's military advisers, the Joint Chiefs of Staff. There was opposition to the program under Kennedy, and this was also the case under Johnson. The most strident opponents were outside, in the scientific community. The role of the science adviser was more to explain and rationalize the enlargement of Ranch Hand to the scientific estate than to lobby the president to deescalate or stop the program. For the dominant advisers to Johnson on the war, defoliation was another regrettable, but necessary, means to the end they favored. They did not regard the arguments raised by scientific critics as sufficient to bring the program to a halt. Instead, they selected escalation as the strategy, at least until the war as a whole began winding down.

For an example of an ongoing program that was decelerated, we must look to SST. The technoscience presidency favored the program, but also slowed down its implementation. Johnson's early actions as president revealed his own dilemma. He signed an appropriation measure for SST; he also launched an inside reassessment of the program on the basis of a critical evaluation by outside consultants. While Johnson protected NASA in order to achieve the Apollo goal, he decided to allow FAA's authority to be weakened as part of the deceleration strategy. The FAA administrator was displaced as the leader, among subpresidential advisers, for SST. The McNamara Committee, in general, and McNamara, in particular, took his role. Thus, as a Johnson-Webb alliance stood behind the maintenance strategy for Apollo, so a Johnson-McNamara alliance became key to SST's deceleration.

The FAA's role was thus diminished—the crash effort it preferred, abandoned—so that a more viable SST program might be implemented. The technical problems, however, could not be solved. Johnson decided to forge ahead, anyway. In the end, the delays merely provided time for an opposition to grow and mobilize. This was not the president's purpose. But that was the result of his decision to decelerate.

Thus, the Johnson experience gives added weight from the presidential perspective to what students of implementation have been documenting from other points of view in recent years: implementation is an exceptionally complex and difficult part of the total policy process. The conditions for successful presidential policy management noted by Allison and Halperin (beginning with unambiguousness of presidential involvement, words, and authority) are rare,[74] certainly in science and technology policy. Even when they are present, those "below" have their own ways of nonimplementing. Bardach states that "implementation politics is distinguished from policy-adoption politics by the characteristic absence of coalitions and the characteristic presence of fragmented and isolated maneuvers and countermaneuvers."[75]

The presidency's maneuvers can become part of the implementation process. A change in presidents inevitably provides opportunities for changes in policy. A number of stratagems, presidential and bureaucratic, are played out in the implementation process.[76] Different elements seek to maximize their own organizational interests, sometimes in alliance with the president, sometimes against him.

Implementation has been called "a process of assembling the elements required to produce a particular programmatic outcome."[77] The presidency is one element in a total implementation network, perhaps the most important control element. But many aspects are either only loosely under a presidency's control or wholly out of control. And sometimes the very goals to which a presidentially guided implementation system is attuned prove, in retrospect, to have been in error.

In comparing presidential implementation of programs that are inherited versus those that bear a personal presidential stamp, it is interesting to note the difference between nuclear desalting, discussed in chapter 4, and SST, reviewed in this chapter. In implementing its nuclear desalting initiative, the Johnson presidency—especially the president—let perceived opportunity becloud scientific reality. In carrying out the SST program, the problems were so evident that not even Johnson, an enthusiast, could fail to see the difficulties. In the one instance, the Johnson presidency charged ahead; in the other, it was more circumspect. Perhaps the difference lay, in part, in the role of the outside evaluators, who warned Johnson that another president's decision (SST) might get him in trouble. Nuclear desalting, being his own initiative, was not given the same critical evaluation—at least not in a way that got to the president, or significantly changed his policy.

6. Curtailing Science and Technology

Some of the most critical decisions a presidency makes are those concerned with curtailment of science and technology programs. Curtailment goes beyond decelerating to actually diminishing a program. What is intended is cutback or cutout. Presidencies curtail at various stages of decision making. Programs they may want can be curtailed by Congress.

The particular strategic stance that the technoscience presidency takes with respect to curtailment often depends upon the degree of curtailment involved. Curtailments can be partial or complete. In either case, curtailment often arouses more controversy than adoption does. Adding programs brings joy to many interests. Subtracting programs brings pain.

This chapter discusses a continuum of curtailment processes from the most partial to the most complete. The role of the technoscience presidency as curtailer, rescuer, and bystander is highlighted. The presidency plays different roles, depending upon the range of internal and external forces focusing on the curtailment decision. The curtailment process may reflect what the presidency wishes to do, or it may mirror what can be done or must be done given the external pressures of the moment. The behavior of the technoscience presidency is ultimately a function of presidential decision making. The president decides. However, the decision is influenced by the interplay of subpresidential interests, forces outside, and the president's own personal perspective.

The minimal curtailment process is *arrestment*, which curtails the "next step" in a program. The program continues, and it is clear that the potential for growth remains a distinct possibility. But the desire of the arrester is to hold back the program. Arrestment thus contrasts with deceleration. The difference lies in policy intent. Arrestment reflects the desire to stop a program; deceleration provides a pause for possible improvement. While minimal in the context of curtailment strategies, arrestment still hurts. There are usually many who want to see the next step taken, just as there are others who would prefer that it not be. Arrestment may be the strongest curtailment strategy politically available to a president at a given time.

Another partial curtailment strategy is *reduction*. Here the budget for a particular program is reduced or cut back. As with arrestment, there is at least the feeling at the time of the decision that growth may come again, and that the cutback is temporary. But if growth does not resume and if one reduction year is followed by another and still another and if new starts are continually deferred, reduction-over-time becomes a more extreme activity: *retrenchment*. The program survives, but at a lesser national priority.

The above represent partial curtailment processes. They fall along a continuum of severity from a program proponent's point of view. There are also two complete curtailment processes a presidency may use or seek to oppose. One is *rejection*; the other is *termination*. Rejection represents the curtailment of a program at the front end of policy, at the point of possible adoption. Termination occurs in the implementation stage. Ordinarily, sunken costs make termination a strategy that is used only where a constituency behind a program is relatively weak or the terminators are especially strong.

Who are the curtailers? Who are the rescuers? Who wins and who loses in these contests for ultimate control of a program's fate. Why? The following cases shed light on these questions, in the context of the Johnson presidency. For arrestment, there is the antiballistic missile (ABM) controversy; for reduction, a situation that befell basic science in the National Science Foundation; for retrenchment, the post-Apollo program of NASA. For rejection, the MURA accelerator is a case in point. Finally, the Mohole program represents an example of termination. The strategies of the technoscience presidency varied in these processes, as did the roles played by the subpresidency, outsiders, and the president himself in shaping those strategies.

Arrestment

Arms control is a primary objective of most technoscience presidencies. In the Johnson years, the Nuclear Nonproliferation Treaty of 1968 was signed. This was an effort on the part of those nations that had the bomb to keep those that did not from obtaining it. There were also predecessor discussions to what became the Strategic Arms Limitation Talks (SALT) under Nixon. Then there was the case of ABM.

ABM represented one of Johnson's more important decisions involving science and technology. The ABM decision was made in

1967, relatively late in the science and technology policy process, at the point where a program moves from R&D to production, when what has been developed is about to be deployed and constructed on an operational basis. This is the application stage, when a technology is transferred from the control of those who develop it (the scientists, engineers, and technical managers) to the control of those who will use it (military professionals). The pace and direction of that transfer process can be influenced considerably by the technoscience presidency.

Major issues were raised in connection with ABM at the time of the deployment decision. The ABM program entailed having missiles of such extraordinary speed and sensing capacity as to be able to intercept all (or most) of the enemy's offensive missiles. Could ABM do this? Was it technically "ready"? Did the technology work "well enough" to move to the next stage, and thus be deployed? Aside from technical ripeness, there was another issue related to political desirability. Even if ABM worked, should it be deployed? Many feared the advent of a new arms race if it was. The principal protagonists were the Joint Chiefs of Staff and the secretary of defense. McNamara did not believe that ABM was technically or politically ready. In his view, the American nuclear weapons strategy had to be based on the deterrence of an overwhelmingly powerful offense, one that would obviate any possible defense. He believed that both the United States and the USSR had that kind of offense and that ABM deployment did not make sense. Moreover, he also believed that, once deployment commenced, it could not be held in check. In connection with the deployment of ABM, McNamara declared, "If a system works, and works well, there is a strong pressure from many directions to procure and deploy the weapon out of all proportion to the prudent level required."[1]

Under ordinary circumstances, Johnson would have agreed with his defense secretary on decisions affecting weapons innovation. As a former Johnson administration official stated, "The President took much less interest than had Kennedy in the specifics of the defense program: he tended to leave it to McNamara to choose between 'X' and 'Y' programs; he was less interested in the technical issues, and it just wasn't his 'bag' to second guess McNamara. He was much more interested in political problems."[2]

For a long time, ABM was not a political—congressional or electoral—problem for Johnson. It was political in a bureaucratic sense, however. It was fought intensely, year-in, year-out, within the Department of Defense. McNamara was able to contain ABM in the R&D stage. He was also able to contain ABM as essentially a defense decision, rather than a presidential decision. Money was allocated, but the decision to move forward toward deployment kept being postponed. As the technology improved, however, and as the power of the Joint Chiefs of Staff grew and that of McNamara declined under the pressures of Vietnam, the Joint Chiefs of Staff decided that they could begin pushing much harder for a presidential deployment decision. The technology was ripe, in their view, and so were the politics of presidential decision making.

The key confrontation between McNamara and the Joint Chiefs of Staff took place on December 6, 1966, "on the ninth floor of the federal building at Austin, Texas, as Johnson was arriving at final decisions on the FY 1968 budget." Given the "difference in perspective between McNamara and the Joint Chiefs," the president sought advice from others in his administration. From officials in the State Department, he got the prediction that any U.S. deployment would be matched by Soviet deployment. Johnson also wanted to know exactly "what" was being deployed. How viable was ABM as a system for defense? To get that answer, he communicated with Hornig.[3]

In early 1967, the decision came to a head. On January 4, 1967, a meeting was called at the White House, including Johnson, McNamara, the Joint Chiefs of Staff, all past and current special assistants to the president for science and technology (James R. Killian, Jr., George Kistiakowsky, Jerome B. Wiesner, and Donald F. Hornig), and all past and current directors of Defense Research and Engineering (Harold Brown, John S. Foster, Jr., and Herbert York).[4] As York recalled:

> We [the technical experts] were asked that simple kind of
> question which must be answered after all the complicated
> ifs and buts have been discussed: "Will it work and should it
> be deployed?" The answer in relation to defending our people
> against a Soviet missile attack was "No," and there was no dis-
> sent from that answer. The context, of course, was the Russian
> threat, as it was then interpreted and forecast, and the current
> and projected state of our ABM technology. There was also
> some discussion of this same question in relation to a hypo-
> thetical Red Chinese missile threat. In this latter case, there
> was some divergence of views, although the majority view (and
> my own) was still, "No."[5]

While it was up to the scientists to assess the technical readiness of ABM, Johnson felt that he could assess the political ripeness of the issue. In his view, there was a possibility that ABM could have an impact on his reelection chances. He saw moves by Republicans in Congress to label him with an "ABM gap." Such a gap could hurt him if he ran for reelection. After all, Kennedy and he had used the missile gap against the Republicans in 1960. There were already Republican rumblings in Congress about the Soviet Union's building an ABM system around Moscow.[6]

Thus, because of the push from the Joint Chiefs of Staff and the pull from Johnson, the locus of decision within the technoscience presidency shifted upward to the president. However, Johnson made the minimal change that he could from the McNamara arrestment policy. McNamara had held ABM in R&D, postponing deployment. Johnson decided to allocate funds for certain long-lead-time items in deployment, but he ordered that these funds not be spent, pending the outcome of a summit meeting with Soviet Premier Kosygin. If he could get the Soviet Union to agree to a joint decision to hold back deployment, he could dampen military and congressional pressures building in the United States and avoid a possible ABM-gap issue being used against him in a forthcoming election.

On June 23 and 25, Johnson and Kosygin met at Glassboro, New Jersey. ABM was a key matter on their agenda and was discussed at some length. There was no agreement, however. Kosygin was adamant that a Soviet ABM did not constitute a threat to the United States; it was merely protection for the Soviet Union.[7]

Shortly after the summit conference, Johnson informed McNamara that he wanted to go ahead with ABM. McNamara continued to advocate arresting the deployment as much as possible. At the January 4 White House meeting, there had been talk of anti-China and anti-USSR systems. The former might work technically; the latter probably would not. McNamara argued now that the "thin" anti-China system should be deployed, as the lesser of two evils.[8] The Joint Chiefs of Staff preferred the "thick" anti-USSR system but expected that it would come later, as a second step in decision making.[9] Johnson approved the thin system. McNamara announced Johnson's decision in an address delivered to the editors and publishers of United Press International on September 18, 1967, arguing against the arms race and ABM but ending with a decision to deploy.

However, the decision was also to contain and arrest. The importance of this fact was seen more clearly when the SALT talks began under Richard Nixon. The process of deployment was only barely under way, and those talks produced a treaty that had the effect of stopping ABM deployment where it stood at that time. There was only one ABM site in each country. By thus arresting ABM as much as possible, Johnson had made it easier for Nixon to fully terminate the deployment process later.

In arresting ABM, the key linkages for containment were between McNamara and the scientific estate both inside and outside the technoscience presidency. The military professionals, the Joint Chiefs of Staff, were allied with outside politicians in Congress in promoting the deployment of the maximum technological system. The president decided in favor of arresting the technology in the stage of minimum deployment. This became the position of the Johnson presidency, and it was accepted by Congress. On the basis of this decision, the Nixon administration began to forge its policy.

Reduction

Reduction is budget cutting. As a science and technology curtailment process, reducing may be relatively temporary and, in fact, a departure from a longer-term policy. Of course, this does not necessarily diminish the protests of those who are the defenders of the program. It may lead to ambiguity and ambivalence among those in the technoscience presidency who are responsible for administering budget cuts to programs formerly favored. Sometimes it leads to disagreement over the direction and intensity of the cuts. This is especially the case when reducing is a presidential management strategy that is being accompanied by congressional budget cutting. A congressional reduction strategy may be more extreme than that of the presidency. It may push the presidency to try to be both a reducer and a rescuer at the same time—an awkward stance, to say the least. Consider the situation of NSF's basic research program.

For most of the Johnson years, a strong policy established by Hornig and BOB attempted to insulate basic research from the budgetary vagaries of the moment. Whereas R&D had a ten percent rise over the Johnson period, basic research received a fifty percent boost. As part of this overall policy of presidential support, a policy often not perceived by the scientific community, NSF was given special attention within the technoscience presidency. Often it was also given special protection. Unlike NIH, NSF had no mission other than basic research and related educational support. This made it vulnerable to congressional attacks. Under Kennedy and also under Johnson, the presidency tended to be more friendly to NSF than Congress was. Within PSAC, there had even been advocacy in 1964 for setting a policy of a fifteen percent annual increase in federal support for academic science. Much of this increase would be reflected in the NSF budget. In 1965, a committee of the National Academy of Sciences recommended the fifteen percent figure to Congress. BOB did not necessarily accept the figure, but it was moving toward acceptance of a need for constant growth in basic research.[10]

However, whatever the budgeteers in BOB may have thought, the politicians in Congress were of a different mood in 1966. The president's FY 1967 budget requested more than a ten percent increase for academic research over FY 1966 appropriations; but the final result, after congressional appropriations, was only a six percent gain. Still, the presidency's policy was clearly one of support. As a presidential or congressional strategy, reduction was not thus far an issue. It became an issue in 1967 and 1968, however, and not only brought frictions between the White House and Congress but also revealed differences within the technoscience presidency itself.

On November 22, 1967, Hornig sent Schultze a copy of a memorandum that PSAC intended to send to the president. It spoke of the cuts that Congress had made in the president's budget and those that BOB was considering in the upcoming FY 1969 budget. It said these cuts threatened "to produce what increasingly looks like a 'catastrophic' situation in some labs and some universities in the country. I [Hornig] am particularly concerned that, whatever else we do, we do not bolster the widespread impression that R&D is a 'patsy' by cutting NSF, which is regarded as a symbol, too much."[11]

Schultze replied on December 4 that he did not think that sending the memorandum to Johnson was a good idea. He believed that the academic science problem should be brought to the president's attention in the context of immediate budget issues. He declared, "We will have this opportunity when we talk to the President about the NSF budget for FY 1969. We can then cover the overall academic science situation in both 1968 and 1969 and its relationship to our actions on the 1969 budget for the Foundation, and, at that time, you can bring up the special concerns of PSAC."[12]

Hornig disagreed and sent the PSAC message to the president anyway. In a cover memorandum, Hornig noted that the press had picked up on possible funding problems in science and that he had been stressing to reporters that these were temporary setbacks which in no way signified a retreat from Johnson's policy of strengthening graduate education and maintaining American leadership in science.[13] He emphasized what he had said to Schultze, namely, that NSF was being especially poorly treated in the budget cutting taking place: "I am distressed in reviewing the whole to realize that NSF, which we have tried to build up, has fared worse in the FY 1968 cutback than any other agency. They are too meek, and the meek suffer—unhappily, they are also the key supporter of science in the universities."[14]

The importuning of the scientific estate bore some fruit. Instead of the feared reduction, the president's FY 1969 budget called for a slight increase in NSF's budget from $495 million appropriated in FY 1968 to $500 million in FY 1969. Also, for various strategic reasons, it was decided within the technoscience presidency that the budgetary category of basic research would be replaced by a new category called "academic research." It was expected that this would protect NSF to some extent from congressional budget cutters who were focusing on basic research. Perhaps it would also help to persuade outsiders of Johnson's desire to protect universities even in a period of general budget cutting. It was intended that there would be a government-wide, thirteen percent increase in academic research over what it had been the previous year.

However, in September 1967, Johnson sought a tax increase. By summer 1968, strategically placed legislators were saying that, if Johnson wanted his tax, he would have to impose a $6 billion spending reduction over and above whatever cuts Congress made from the original FY 1969 budget request. One of the legislators pressuring Johnson was Wilbur Mills (D, Arkansas), chairman of the House Ways and Means Committee. He told the president that he would back him only if the tax increase was coupled with deep cuts in domestic spending.[15] This would be potentially traumatic for NSF. Congressional committee actions exacted a twenty percent reduction in the original NSF request. Hornig was alarmed. He began to hear from scientists in universities of the effects that cutbacks were already having.

Hornig began to speak out publicly on the matter, attempting to convey to the scientific community and others the seriousness of the situation. The presidential environment was growing harsh. On May 11, 1968, he sent Johnson a copy of a report, "A Public Policy for Graduate Education in the Sciences," prepared by the governing body of NSF, the National Science Board (NSB). The report proposed that the federal funding pattern (now largely research project grants and contracts) be expanded and made much more flexible, primarily through a system of institutional (block) grants to graduate schools and their separate departments. Hornig recommended submitting the report to Congress as a "useful stimulus to a healthy discussion of the issues."[16]

Califano received the NSB report and Hornig's cover memorandum and passed them to Johnson with his own recommendation that Johnson not send the report to Congress lest it be seen as an endorsement. "The recommendations are impractical and unrealistic in a time of a decline in the research budget." He suggested instead that the NSB send the report to Congress as an NSF report with no presidential linkage.[17] The report included ideas in line with Johnson's own philosophy; it stressed geographical spread and that every state and large metropolitan area should develop a graduate institution of high quality. Johnson had HEW Secretary Wilbur Cohen review the report. Within HEW, there were mixed comments, with NIH strongly opposed. On August 12, Califano wrote the president, noting the disagreements and indicating that he, Cohen, and Hornig favored release, but not by the White House. Johnson decided against releasing the report at all for the time being.[18]

In fall 1968, BOB clamped an expenditure limitation on the various agencies, including NSF. This threatened the possibility that NSF would have to go back on commitments that it had made to investigators who had previously received grants. The strains within the technoscience presidency, already great, were aggravated by this turn of events. Hornig was angry with what he perceived as the insensitivity of BOB and even some members of his own staff to the implications. On September 26, 1968, he wrote Charles Zwick, the director of the Bureau of the Budget, "I think it's time that both BOB and OST staff stop saying publicly that things look about as usual when there are so many problems developing. It makes us look either insensitive or foolish; I'm not sure which reaction predominates. In any case, bland comments will open a credibility gap with a community that already doesn't trust us."[19]

It was increasingly clear that there was a split among subpresidential aides over Johnson's budget strategies. Hornig was seeking to represent the interests of basic science as embodied in NSF. BOB and some of the OST staff were approaching the issue from a cutback strategy or, at least, from one that accepted the inevitability of reduction. They may not have liked the policy, but they were carrying it out; Hornig, on the other hand, was fighting it.

On October 3, 1968, he took his case to Johnson, stressing that NSF cutbacks that reached into existing grants placed in doubt the "good faith of the U.S. government." He recommended that other agencies be curtailed so as to provide additional money for NSF. "I will be glad to nominate candidates for a $40 million cut from other agencies," he declared.[20] However, Hornig's pleas were in vain. The FY 1969 budget for NSF was reduced to $400 million from the $500 million originally requested as a consequence of presidential-congressional action.

A battle had been lost. What of the war? BOB was already at work on the FY 1970 budget. It was considering a preliminary figure that was much too low in Hornig's view, one that seemed to accept lost ground in FY 1969. Hornig and his internal and external allies mobilized to fight this last budget contest of the Johnson administration. At stake was the difference between a presidential strategy of reduction and one of retrenchment. The NSF budget should be brought back up in FY 1970, argued Hornig. This would make it clear that the presidency was fighting Congress on the cutback issue, not acquiescing.

On October 25, 1968, the Association of American Universities, representing the presidents of forty-four major universities and colleges, wrote Johnson, pointing out that the expenditure ceilings had created a grave situation:

> Specifically, the decision to place expenditure ceilings on all National Science Foundation grants in force in the fiscal year 1969 has created, for a variety of reasons, a unique situation with respect to cutbacks in federal spending. Because of the timing and nature of these reductions, the net effect has been to curtail the central body of NSF work on our campuses by an amount far in excess of the gross figures imposed by the Foundation, in many cases by as much as 55 percent, forcing most universities to add to their deficits in meeting commitments made in good faith.[21]

The letter found its way to the desk of James Gaither, an assistant to Califano, who asked Hornig if the situation was accurately described. Hornig responded that it was. Further, he believed that the letter deserved "the attention of the President, even though BOB has already sent back a routine reply." "The point is basically," he continued, "that we have had to go back on commitments which in private circles would make us liable to suits."[22] Gaither informed Califano that the letter from the Association of American Universities was "accurate."[23]

Meanwhile, within BOB, there was skepticism that the situation was as bad as Hornig and the scientific community claimed. Hugh Loweth, a BOB official with responsibilities embracing NSF, told Budget Director Zwick on November 13 that he did not believe that cutting NSF's budget would damage the "good faith of the U.S. government." Loweth noted that universities could still hire faculty and continue construction.[24] On December 2, Loweth told Zwick that Philip Handler, chairman of the National Science Board, was sending a memorandum to Johnson, a letter that Loweth characterized as "worse than those from Hornig in the past—all emotionalism—not a good reasoned case."[25] Whatever BOB may have thought, the fact remained that the scientific estate was pressing hard with its case. PSAC sent Johnson a statement on preserving the health of U.S.

science. On December 2, Hornig wrote Johnson, making a final plea: "Mr. President, so much has been accomplished during your administration that I think it would be a mistake to allow your successor to take the role of 'Rescuer of Science' for what is peanuts in the total budget."[26]

Ultimately, Johnson agreed to a budgetary allocation of $500 million for NSF. This was the same figure that he had requested the previous year. It was much more than BOB had originally recommended. In the end, Congress granted $440 million in FY 1970. By going with a higher figure, the technoscience presidency lost less in the ensuing congressional bargaining. From the standpoint of the scientific estate, this was a kind of victory. Compared to FY 1969, NSF's budget was going back up again. Recovery would be slow, but retrenchment had been avoided.

Retrenchment

Budget reduction is a destiny that awaits many programs. The situation of NSF was not unique. Agencies bend with the winds of a given budget battle, bolstered by friends in and out of government. A good number recover and grow again. However, some are harder hit than others. They face repeated reductions year after year. Programs are postponed, delayed, and diminished, radically altering an agency's place in national life. There is survival at a lower priority. This is more than temporary reduction; this is reduction-over-time or retrenchment.

It is a supreme irony that one of the best examples of retrenchment undertaken by Johnson's presidency was in the field in which Johnson took such pride as a pioneer: space. He protected and preserved the manned lunar mission, but a cost of this decision was retrenchment in the early efforts to launch a post-Apollo program.

According to NASA Administrator James Webb, the retrenchment in post-Apollo started early. On September 30, 1968, Webb delivered a lecture at Harvard in which he charged that the cutbacks that NASA had sustained over the years constituted "in total what may be called a national decision." This national decision to retrench had "been in the making since 1964."[27]

The decision *not* to sustain the momentum of Apollo through an equally large-scale, follow-on effort had been made incrementally, year by year. It is indeed significant that Webb traced it back to 1964, for that was the year Johnson asked him to begin planning for the next major objective in space beyond Apollo. The occasion of the request that was made on January 30, 1964, was concern by the science

adviser that NASA was not adequately planning for future missions.[28] Hornig was worried about the inadequacy of NASA planning
for post-Apollo in general. He was aware that the space program
would phase down—and many scientists and engineers would be
laid off—unless NASA had new objectives on which the nation
could agree. While the science adviser drafted the Johnson request,
independently of BOB, there was equal concern on the part of the
budgeteers, but more for financial reasons. They were unhappy about
the lack of connection between certain expensive programs NASA
was proposing and any articulated future plans or justifications. Of
particular concern to the budgeteers was NERVA, a nuclear-powered
rocket, successor to the Saturn rocket that was being created for
Apollo. The problem for BOB was that there was no mission approved beyond the Apollo goal. For what purpose was the multi-
billion-dollar NERVA program?

NASA's view was that it had to begin early to develop technological capability and that the post-Apollo goals would be articulated when necessary. BOB questioned whether this was not placing
the cart before the horse and whether NASA's engineers were not
simply pushing the frontiers of technology for their own sake. BOB
raised this issue with Johnson.

The president had set September 1964 as the deadline for a report on NASA's future plans for space exploration. It was not until
January 1965 that NASA responded to Johnson's request by providing
a compendium of possible programs: short-range, intermediate, and
long-term. The NASA report did not give priorities, just options.
Webb explained that priorities (the NASA post-Apollo program)
would emerge from a process of national consensus formation. Hornig disagreed, calling the report a "shopping list."[29] He may well
have been right. Webb was not anxious to state explicitly, "This is
the next goal beyond the moon." As he later explained:

> First, the announcement by NASA in the mid-1960s of a
> long-term goal would make the agency vulnerable. It would
> provide ammunition to critics, who would be able to shoot
> down the proposed program as being too expensive or imprac-
> tical, thereby raising the possibility that long-range technology
> developments tied to the announced goal would be cut out. . . .
> Second, should NASA announce a long-term, post-Apollo
> goal, critics would claim that the lunar landing was simply an
> interim goal, subordinate to the new effort. . . .
> Third, the major effort required for planning, proposing,
> and defending a new long-range goal would tie up the ener-
> gies of top NASA leadership and key scientists and engineers,

diverting them from concentrating on making Apollo a success. . . .[30]

Hence, Webb felt that it was in NASA's interest not to finalize a post-Apollo program too soon. On the other hand, unless certain long-term capabilities were developed in the 1960s, NASA's options in the 1970s would be greatly constrained. Hornig and BOB pressed for specification as to goals, while Webb emphasized means, permitting options. Johnson wanted options, too, but he also wanted clarification as to goals. Webb wanted to get some sense of what was politically salable and, hence, wanted to keep Congress informed of the plans to some extent. However, Johnson saw Congress as possibly constraining his own options, including those to turn down NASA. Thus, he was reluctant to have NASA send its report on future programs to Congress or even a letter summarizing the report. As he stated at the time, "I think I would have more leeway and running room by saying nothing, which I would prefer."[31] The letter and report eventually went to Congress, but Johnson's hesitation pointed up the conflict between him and Webb when it came to options, as well as the general divergence of interests within the technoscience presidency, where post-Apollo was concerned.

The consequence was drift and frustration. NASA was hurt at this early point by the Manned Orbital Laboratory (MOL) decision, as has been seen. In 1964 and 1965, the Air Force seemed sure of what it wanted; NASA did not. MOL went to the Air Force in 1965, and this showed NASA that it could not take Johnson's support for granted. If NASA did not move quickly enough, the other agencies would. Also, once the MOL decision was made, there was a natural reluctance on Johnson's part to approve additional expensive manned programs. MOL and Apollo were very costly.

In 1966, for the first time since Sputnik moved space to center stage in national priorities, a president did not mention space in his State of the Union Message to Congress. No new starts were approved in NASA. Also, for the first time since its establishment, the NASA budget of FY 1967 called for a decline in overall space expenditures. It was not Apollo that suffered; rather, it was NASA's future. At the time, nobody talked of an overt policy of retrenchment. Deferral was taking place, but Webb could see how deferral could lead to retrenchment. As he explained to Congress in defending the president's budget for NASA, "The FY 1967 budget reflects the President's determination to hold open for another year the major decision on future programs—decisions on whether to make use of the space operational systems, space know-how, and facilities we have worked so hard to build up, or to begin their liquidation."[32]

While publicly going along with the president, Webb was privately arguing his case as strongly as possible with the president and with BOB. He wrote Johnson on May 16, 1966, "I have done my best to obtain support in Congress for the reductions you have had to make and to minimize any political risk to your Administration from the fact that we are operating substantially under what would be the most efficient program."[33] Webb called the next budget, FY 1968, then in preparation, "a major turning point." He wanted $6 billion.

In FY 1967, once Congress had completed its work on the president's submittal, he had slightly under $5 billion. The budget guidelines furnished by BOB for FY 1968 were not much better. Webb foresaw actual layoffs looming in the near future, as NASA scaled down its effort. Webb wrote Johnson on August 26, 1966, that unless the president intervened to change this state of affairs, "[NASA has] no choice but to accelerate the rate at which we are carrying on the liquidation of some of the capabilities which we have built up. Important options which we have been holding open will be foreclosed. . . . Struggle as I have to try to put myself in your place and see this from your point of view, I cannot avoid a strong feeling that this is not in the best interests of the country."[34]

Johnson was listening to Webb, but he also was listening to Budget Director Schultze. On September 1, Schultze wrote Johnson, commenting on the issues raised by Webb in his August 26 letter. Schultze emphasized BOB's support for manned space and said, "We must keep open several options for later choice—e.g., manned Mars landing, earth orbital stations, etc.—although we don't want to set a specific timetable yet." However, he went on to say that BOB did not believe that the level of the U.S. space effort should be determined:

- by how much we can do within the limits of technical capability. . . .
- by attempting to guarantee that we are ahead of the Russians in every conceivable sphere of space activity, plus continuing emphasis on the areas where we are already vastly superior. . . .
- by the peak level of industrial manpower attained during the development of the Apollo system. The space program is not a WPA [Works Progress Administration].[35]

Furthermore, Schultze did not believe that a $5 billion budget would "accelerate the rate at which we are carrying out on the liquidation of some of the capabilities we have built up." He did not see how such a budget level could be seen as showing a lack of support for the space program when the federal government was spending:

- only $2 billion a year on elementary and secondary education;
- only $200 million on water pollution control;
- only $25 million a year on our entire program for high-speed ground transportation. . . .

And finally, I don't believe that, in the context of continued fighting in Vietnam, we can afford to add another $600 million to $1 billion in the space program in [FY] 1968.[36]

Schultze said more, and offered some views on the Soviet competition, but it is clear from the above that he and Webb sharply disagreed on how much was enough for the space program. Since, as we have seen, Johnson was adamant about maintaining Apollo, debate centered on post-Apollo. While this debate affected all post-Apollo activities, two programs became the focal points of struggle within the technoscience presidency on the future of space.

One was NERVA; debate over NERVA had helped stimulate Johnson's concern for NASA's future planning in 1964. The other was called the Apollo Applications Program (AAP). This had arisen out of that planning activity and the encounter with the Air Force. AAP would make use of Apollo hardware in near-earth orbit. The one program provided a long-range capability upon which Mars exploration could later be built. The other kept NASA in the Manned Orbital Laboratory field and paved the way for a longer-range program to construct a permanent space station. Webb and Schultze contested over these two programs much of the fall and winter of 1966.

In mid-December, the administrator and budgeteer sent memoranda to Johnson laying out their respective positions on the upcoming NASA budget. Later, they saw Johnson. Schultze noted that they agreed on some points:

. . . that we must continue our manned space flight capability . . . that we shouldn't announce a major new goal—like sending a man to Mars; that we can mount, at a reasonable cost, a useful series of post-Apollo flights with modifications of equipment used in the manned lunar landing. There would be a number of important long-duration, earth-orbit experiments involved.[37]

Thus, they agreed "we cannot postpone decisions any longer," lest there be a gap in the space program after Apollo. Hence, they agreed that AAP had to be initiated. However, the two men disagreed over the scale of the program, a disagreement that translated into money: Schultze called for $445 million; Webb, for $637 million.

On the other program, NERVA, the two were far apart. Webb pressed for a decision to develop a NERVA II rocket. This was a larger, more advanced, more expensive version of the rocket on which NASA had been working. Schultze stated, "We have two choices: (1) go ahead with development of NERVA II. This would add a combined $90 million to the AEC and NASA budgets and cost $2 billion over the next ten years. (2) Phase down the program, continue research and studies, and be ready to resurrect the program if needed. . . ."[38] Webb favored the first option; Schultze, the second. Webb told Johnson, "I believe that it will be extremely important for you to be able to point to a continuing nuclear rocket program when the USSR unveils a launch vehicle larger than our Saturn V, which may be soon and may involve a nuclear stage."[39]

Johnson got other advice, from friends of the space program in Congress as well as from Hornig and PSAC. In December, the latter provided him a report, "The Post-Apollo Program," which stated that PSAC "did not see any urgency in proceeding to the development of a nuclear rocket stage (e.g., NERVA II) at this time."[40]

The president decided that he had to make decisions, but he wanted to commit himself as little as possible. On AAP, where there was some measure of consensus, Johnson chose to move. On NERVA, where there was disagreement, he again delayed. On AAP, he sided with Schultze. On January 21, 1967, he requested the $445 million for AAP which had been recommended by Schultze. He declared, "We have no alternative unless we wish to abandon the manned space capability we have created."[41] The same day, NASA's leaders held a press conference to announce the Apollo Applications Program and thereby make it clear that NASA would still be in business following the lunar landing.

NASA's officials hoped that they could now regain some momentum; but on January 27 came the Apollo capsule fire and the deaths of three astronauts. As we have noted, Johnson acted to support the space program. In February, he announced that he would request $90 million to begin development of a NERVA II rocket. Thus, he opted not only for NERVA but also to proceed directly to a larger, more advanced version of NERVA, rather than a smaller NERVA I. In this case, Webb got all he wanted. This was a considerable vote of confidence in Webb, NASA, and the space agency's future.

The problem was that, by this time, the congressional mood was drastically different. The legislative environment for post-Apollo decisions was set by Johnson's 1967 request for a ten percent tax increase. This put Congress in a cutback mood in 1967. As noted, key legislators demanded a budget cut as their price for adopting the tax increase. They expected that cut to include NASA.

With Apollo continuing to be secured, Congress took its toll of NASA's future. These were the programs whose missions were least clear and whose constituencies were unformed. In questioning Webb, the Senate Appropriations Committee tried to get him to state his priorities on post-Apollo, but Webb replied, "I don't want to give any aid and comfort to anyone to cut out a program."[42]

If Webb would not set priorities for cutting, then Congress would cut on its own. Thus, both AAP and NERVA were curtailed. Midway through the legislative process, after the authorizing committees had acted and before the appropriations committees had moved, there was some question as to whether Johnson might intervene on behalf of post-Apollo. After all, *his* decisions of January and February were being undermined by congressional action in summer 1967. Webb and Johnson discussed what the president should do. Webb was a strong advocate on behalf of NASA, but he was also very much Johnson's man. As Webb told a House appropriations subcommittee on August 15:

> The President has reviewed with me personally the "blackboard exercise" and his concern about the deficit that is indicated at $29 or $30 billion, his concern about the borrowing capacity of the nation, his concern about the necessity to reduce expenditures at the same time he is making an urgent request for tax increases, and he is asking me to do everything in my power to help him with these programs.[43]

Johnson was quite obviously appealing to Webb's loyalty, asking him to consider the president's problem, not just NASA's problem. Webb was trying to be a good soldier and was making it clear to those NASA officials under him that he expected them to do likewise, but it was not easy. It was even harder on August 21, 1967, when Johnson signed a congressional bill that reduced the Apollo Applications and NERVA programs. In effect, the president acquiesced to the decimation of his earlier decisions. He declared that, under normal circumstances, he would have opposed the drastic cuts at NASA. Johnson pointed out that these were difficult economic times:

> . . . conditions have greatly changed since I submitted my January budget request. . . . [This action does not] indicate that we

have lessened our resolve to maintain a strong program on space exploration, science and technology. . . . Because the times have placed more urgent demands upon our resources, we must now moderate our efforts in certain space projects. But our purpose still remains as constant as the heavens we seek to explore: to master the challenge of space.[44]

Johnson explained that he had to distinguish between the necessary and the desirable. He had regretfully concluded that much of post-Apollo was desirable but not necessary, at least for the present. Given the congressional politics of 1967, it was necessary to cut NASA. As Johnson later explained to Webb, privately, he did not "choose or prefer to take one dime from [his] budget for space appropriations this year and agreed to do so only because Ways and Means in effect forced [him] to agree to effect some reductions or lose the tax bill."[45]

Whatever the reasons, the fact remained that a critical moment in NASA's history had passed. The year 1967 was to be a transition from temporary reduction to long-term recovery. Such a transition required an upswing in NASA's budget; instead, NASA faced transition from reduction to retrenchment.

As a result of congressional action for FY 1968, while approved, AAP was cut by $300 million. NERVA II was downgraded to NERVA I. The prospects for FY 1969 looked no better. Johnson's public acceptance of a $500 million reduction in his proposed budget for space was having the effect of lessening support for NASA by its congressional friends. If Johnson would not fight the cuts made by legislative opponents, why should they? Webb wrote Califano on December 1, 1967, requesting an explicit statement of support by Johnson for his beleaguered agency, lest there "be serious further erosion of congressional support for even a reduced program."[46]

That Webb felt obliged to seek the aid of Califano was indicative of the change in his own relationship with Johnson, at least where post-Apollo was concerned. He was accustomed to being the principal aide to the president on space. But what was true of Apollo was not true of post-Apollo. Johnson treated Webb as an administrator with no special influence in the case of post-Apollo. The president listened equally to Schultze, his budget director. The role of presidential principal thus had its limits and could vary with the program that was at issue at the moment. In any event, Webb found that his own adjurations were not sufficient. Someone more in the inner circle was needed. So he turned to Califano for help in rescuing post-Apollo, but it was too late.

The presidential-congressional budgetary environment did not change. While NASA's FY 1969 budget was before Congress, legislators were also considering the combination ten percent tax surcharge on which they had not yet acted and the accompanying $6 billion spending cut that they had exacted from Johnson. Under the circumstances, there was little or no hope for presidential rescue. NASA's total final appropriation for FY 1969 was $3.9 billion, down considerably from what it had been the year before and far below the $6 billion budget that Webb had said in 1966 the agency needed to prevent the "liquidation" of the NASA capabilities built up to go to the moon. Since Apollo continued to be protected, the cuts had a most drastic impact on post-Apollo. For example, AAP received $150 million, although the presidential request was $439.6 million.

On September 16, 1968, Webb spoke with the president and then announced his decision to resign from NASA, effective October 7, 1968. In making his announcement, Webb said that the retrenchment meant that the United States would be in second place to the Soviet Union for years to come.

The media gave considerable attention to the Webb statement, causing Hornig to write Johnson charging Webb (and other NASA officials) with "a series of unconscionable statements." His view was that "we are at least one year ahead of the Soviets" in the technology necessary for a lunar landing. The United States was "first in space and not second." It is true that the Soviets are continuing to make investments, he said, "at a high level while the future level of support for our own program is being reduced. . . . Nevertheless, these circumstances do not justify the response that NASA has fostered in recent statements to the press." He suggested that the president might want PSAC to make "an independent judgment" of the United States vis-à-vis the Soviet Union in space. The president might wish to consider the PSAC report "for public release."[47]

Johnson's response was that Hornig should "drop the matter." In fact, Johnson was angered by the Hornig memorandum in a way that provided some insight into the dynamics of the technoscience presidency and Hornig's place vis-à-vis Webb when it came to space. Johnson said:

It is hard for me to believe that Jim Webb would make "unconscionable statements" or be "motivated" entirely by budgetary problems. During each of the past two budgetary preparation periods, he has carefully and responsibly arranged to have before me the intelligence estimates and data on which he based his serious concern regarding the USSR: the trend of the

Soviet program upward and the U.S. program downward that could produce for the Soviets a base of competence that would provide options they could take up and use to achieve both the image and reality of power and forward motion. I know he now feels they are beginning to take up these options.

Over the entire period of his service as Administrator of NASA, during both the Kennedy and Johnson Administrations, I have supported his strong desire to present to the Congress the importance of proceeding without stretch-out or delay with the Apollo and other important NASA programs. At the same time, he has always assured me that NASA was in [a] position to operate at lower levels under effective control should my budgets not receive full approval. I wanted him to succeed and it was only with great reluctance that for the past two years I have taken action to meet the overall fiscal require-ments laid down by a determined group in the Congress by accepting cuts made in the House Appropriations Committee.

I note with interest your statement that "a continuing vig-orous Soviet program coupled with a constrained U.S. pro-gram" could reverse the positions you believe now exist. This is very close to what I believe Webb has been saying.

As you know, I am always conscious of the importance of maintaining the value of the Office of Science Advisor in the functioning of the White House. It seems to me there is a dan-ger that even if your group should develop evidence to sustain your views, your report might be shortly followed by some tragic occurrence in the U.S. program or a major triumph in the Russian one. This would inevitably bring into question the judgment of your group in a way that might impair its usefulness.

All this raises questions as to why we should try to estab-lish a public record of the kind you suggest. Further, I have serious doubt that the public release of a report of the Science Advisory Committee would go unquestioned in this pre-election period when both Democratic and Republican presi-dential candidates have urged strong space programs.

When I begin to study the 1970 Budget needs in detail, I will be prepared to consider all factors related to the space bud-get and consider at that time whether the Science Advisory Committee should be asked for a special report.[48]

The situation for NASA did not improve in FY 1970. Johnson left, and Nixon took over. AAP evolved into the short-lived Skylab;

NERVA was canceled altogether. Only the Shuttle program, a space initiative by Nixon, saved manned space from virtual extinction. As the Shuttle advanced in the 1970s, NASA revived somewhat, but it was nevertheless a very different agency from what it had been at its height in the mid-1960s. It settled at a scale of operations approximately one half the level reached in its heroic days.

When did retrenchment begin? Webb traced it back to 1964, the year that Johnson asked the NASA administrator for a report on his post-Apollo goals. This inquiry was symbolic of a new attitude at the highest level and an initial attempt to distinguish between what Johnson later called the "necessary and desirable." Also, by losing to the Air Force on MOL in 1965, NASA lost what might have been a centerpiece for post-Apollo.

Rather than asking when retrenchment began, we might ask when recovery did not begin. This was in 1967. A combination of circumstances over which NASA had little control—the Apollo fire and the presidential drive for a tax increase—dampened the congressional environment for new starts in space. Then Johnson himself administered the crucial blow by public surrender to congressional cuts. The difference between reduction and retrenchment lies in the recovery stage: its presence, absence, or slowness in arriving. For NSF, recovery was relatively swift from the time of reduction. For NASA, recovery came much more slowly and was never complete. The Johnson technoscience presidency maintained Apollo, but presided over NASA's retrenchment in that which came after.

Rejection

Rejection is defined as the full curtailment of a program at the time it is being proposed for adoption. To discuss this strategy for science and technology, it is useful to go into greater detail concerning the MURA accelerator. The MURA accelerator has been noted above as the program that was rejected prior to adoption of the 200-BEV accelerator. Here we analyze the process that led to the rejection of the MURA machine.

MURA was strongly backed by the high energy physics community of the Midwest as well as by the elected officials, including congressional delegations, from that region. The accelerator was a symbol, a means by which the Midwest could rise in the status system of science in the United States. President Kennedy, from Massachusetts, was in the White House when an adoption decision was approached in fall 1963. It was placed on his agenda by AEC, which favored constructing the accelerator, as well as by various legislative champions of the machine. Given the political support for the MURA facility, this was not a routine matter; it was a required presidential decision. Kennedy came under heavy pressure. Senator William Proxmire, the long-time foe of unnecessary R&D spending and the provider of "Golden Fleece" awards for what he regarded as irrelevant research projects sponsored by NSF, was an active lobbyist on behalf of the MURA accelerator. The expectation was that the accelerator would be built in Wisconsin, and parts of Proxmire's constituency made it clear to him that this accelerator was an expenditure in Wisconsin's interest. Senator Hubert Humphrey of Minnesota was also a strong proponent. In fact, Humphrey had spoken with Kennedy about MURA and, in his view, had gotten Kennedy to promise that he would support the MURA machine. On August 6, 1963, Kennedy wrote Budget Director Gordon, "If you determine not to go ahead with this [the MURA accelerator], will you speak to me about it first?"[49] A possible presidential adoption was in the offing, or so some thought.

Then Kennedy was assassinated. Friends of the MURA machine did not view the accession of Johnson as a threat to their interests. A president from Texas would surely understand the hurt and humiliation that the Midwest had suffered in recent years when major science projects and facilities were awarded to California and the "eastern establishment" of universities. On December 3, an aide to Senator Humphrey informed Walter Jenkins of the Johnson staff of the Kennedy-Humphrey conversation and asked him "to retrieve this matter from wherever it may be lying and get it moving once again. I believe that it was last in the hands of the Bureau of the Budget in Kermit Gordon's office."[50]

However, Johnson had a higher priority, which created a very different presidential environment for MURA than under Kennedy. Johnson wanted to get a tax cut through Congress. To do that, he felt obligated to show a genuine seriousness in minimizing federal spending. An ominous point was approaching, however. Upon becoming president, the new budget he saw topped $100 billion. There would come a time when $100 billion in federal spending would appear small indeed, but this was not true in late 1963. Johnson saw that figure as symbolic. If he could keep the figure under $100 billion, he could prove to certain skeptical legislators whose vote he had to have on the Senate Finance Committee that he was a true fiscal conservative. If they believed this, they would let him have his tax cut.

Thus, Johnson approached the MURA decision from a perspective quite at variance from that of MURA advocates. This particular issue became hostage to a broader problem (in his mind) of politics

and policy. Indeed, his perspective was probably different from that
of Kennedy. Because he was from Texas and not from Massachusetts,
he could afford to kill a project being proposed by the Midwest more
easily than could his predecessor. He would not be accused of having
a bias against a region of the country other than the East or California.

Johnson told Budget Director Gordon to identify programs that
could be cut to keep the budget below $100 billion. On December 7,
1963, Gordon identified the MURA accelerator as an obvious candidate because: 1. BOB did not regard it highly; and 2. it had not yet
been adopted and was thus most vulnerable in having the fewest
sunken costs. To adopt would mean an addition to the budget that
was not necessary. Gordon told Jenkins that he was unaware of a
Kennedy "commitment" to Senator Humphrey. He noted the memorandum from Kennedy to talk to him about the machine if BOB recommended negatively, but "this opportunity did not arise."[51] In his
final days as science adviser before giving way to Hornig, Jerome
Wiesner thought that the MURA accelerator was supportable on scientific grounds but should not be supported at the cost of delaying
the 200-BEV. Glenn Seaborg, chairman of AEC, had essentially the
same view.[52]

Johnson asked Wiesner to prepare a memorandum on the arguments against MURA. The science adviser did so on December 19,
1963, in a memorandum that read as follows:

> Although the High Energy Physics Panel [a joint panel of
> PSAC and AEC's General Advisory Committee] has recom-
> mended that the machine be built, the Panel also indicated that
> it is not essential for continued and vigorous U.S. progress in
> the field of high energy physics. In fact, the Panel has made it
> clear that they would be opposed to the construction of the
> machine if undertaking it would lead to substantial delays in
> the construction of a much higher energy machine when its
> design is complete.
>
> High energy physics is one of the most expensive scien-
> tific fields; the FY 65 budget for the field amounts to $185
> million. According to our best estimates, the sum is inade-
> quate to fully support the groups already in existence. MURA
> would cost approximately 170 million dollars to build (includ-
> ing preconstruction research and development) and about 30
> million dollars per year thereafter to operate.
>
> Such expenditures are difficult to justify in light of the fact
> that it has been necessary to make substantial cuts in funds for
> fellowships, badly needed research buildings at universities,

the development of new academic centers of excellence, and support for basic research and equipment for thousands of research projects already supported by the Federal Government. Projects like MURA must be judged against the needs of hundreds of other activities, including the dozens of high energy physics groups already in existence and the more vital requirements for new activities in other fields such as oceanography, astronomy, mathematics, and chemistry, as well as the educational requirements previously mentioned.

One of the strongest arguments for building the MURA machine is that it is needed to strengthen high energy physics in the Midwest. While it may be true that efforts should be made to strengthen science in that area, it is not clear that this particular project is the best way to accomplish this. The Midwest already has one of the largest national laboratories supported by the AEC, the Argonne National Laboratory, in Chicago. One of the Nation's biggest high energy accelerators (the ZGS) has just been put into operation there. Among those operating today, only the accelerator at Brookhaven is more powerful and its intensity is lower than the ZGS.

So, the fact is the Midwest already has both a large national laboratory and one of the most modern accelerators. Consequently, although the MURA machine would be an important scientific tool and contribute in a substantial way to the research effort in the central part of the United States, it cannot be justified under present fiscal conditions. In fact, it appears to be of lower priority than many other scientific needs which are being deferred this year.[53]

On December 20, the president had a delegation of MURA advocates, including both academic officials and midwestern legislators, escorted into his office. The meeting was scheduled to last twenty minutes. Greenberg has provided the following account of what took place:

Johnson started the conference by describing himself as "the only man in government who wants to save money and here are all these people who want to spend money."

Referring to debates within the administration over cutting down plutonium production at the AEC's huge installation in Hanford, Washington, Johnson pointed to the AEC chairman and said, "There's Glenn Seaborg. He wants to run a nuclear bomb WPA out in the State of Washington to get [Senator Henry] 'Scoop' Jackson reelected. . . . Seaborg wants to buy votes. Nobody ever had to buy projects down in Texas to elect me. Not only that, he wants to build a nuclear rocket [i.e., the NASA-AEC program for NERVA] and he knows not who and he knows not where."

Johnson went on to say that he was "willing to support anything that science needs," but that the American people expected him to avoid unnecessary expenditures, and he was not persuaded that the MURA machine was needed.

[Elvis] Stahr [president of Indiana University and the Midwestern Universities Research Association] protested that the machine was indeed needed and that, while the ultimate construction cost was estimated at $170 million, all that was required in the fiscal 1965 budget was a mere $3.5 million for advanced design and architectural studies. Humphrey followed this with the exclamation, "Why, my God, the Midwest has been getting shortchanged." Wiesner responded that he had looked into the distribution of funds for academic research and had found no justification for this charge. Humphrey and Wiesner proceeded to talk at each other when the President interrupted with, "The twenty minutes are up. I've got a memo here that I'd like to read and I'd like you to tell me what you think of it." And he read the anti-MURA memorandum that Wiesner had prepared at his direction. Total silence fell upon the group as the president recited a prosecutor's case against MURA. At the conclusion, Johnson said, "What have you got to say about that?" Those who were present recall that a babble of responses broke out among the dozen or so persons in the President's office. At this point, Johnson abruptly left the room. . . .[54]

Many of those present assumed that Wiesner had written the memorandum, and they placed much of the blame for the Johnson decision on his prejudiced advice. Wiesner's imminent return to the Massachusetts Institute of Technology did not help appearances. Stahr was absolutely furious and wrote Humphrey:

First, the memo which he [Johnson] read at the end [of the meeting, and which they had no "opportunity to rebut"] was not a fair and balanced analysis, even from a scientific point of view, according to the two scientists who accompanied me. It omitted some highly relevant matters, and its prejudice showed on its face. . . .

Second, this project has four dimensions, not just one.

They are scientific (on which, I repeat, we had had no chance to dispel the doubts evidently planted in the President's mind by the author of the memo), and also economic, fiscal, political and higher educational. On none of these last four is the President's scientific adviser even supposed to be competent to advise. Yet all four are of major and proper concern to the President himself.[55]

Johnson was not a victim of his science adviser, as Stahr and others seemed to assume. Johnson had considered MURA from a presidential perspective and had found it wanting. If anything, the president used Wiesner as a ploy to deflect criticism. There are strategies to presidential rejection, and one is to let an underling take the blame for an unpopular decision. In this instance, the tactic worked only in part. Johnson had the responsibility, and Humphrey and his friends from the legislative estate made that clear to him. MURA was a "symbol," as Senator Birch Bayh of Indiana wrote Johnson on December 24. Rejection would "produce an intense and lingering bitterness in the Midwest."[56] However, the president stuck to his decision; he wrote Humphrey that it had been a difficult decision, one to which he had "devoted more personal time . . . than to any non-defense question that came up during the budget process." But it was a matter of priorities, and he had to say no on occasions when he might have preferred to "go along with a proposal."[57]

So the presidential decision stood, and Congress did not try to override the president's choice. However, rejection decisions do not necessarily have neat conclusions. The president was indeed concerned with the political repercussions and had some of his subpresidential aides look for ways to soothe the angry Midwest.

Two of the reasons given for rejecting the MURA machine had been: 1. "the Midwest already has one of the largest national laboratories supported by the AEC, the Argonne National Laboratory, in Chicago," and 2. "one of the nation's biggest high energy accelerators (the ZGS) has just been put into operation there." It became clear that these reasons were insensitive to a nonstated political problem in the Midwest: the University of Chicago, which ran Argonne on behalf of AEC, was seen by other midwestern universities (especially the big public institutions) as favoring its own scientists over scientists from other universities when it came to access to the most advanced Argonne technology.

It fell to Seaborg to take the lead in working out a new arrangement in the Midwest so that universities associated with the MURA proposal would have the option of more equitable use of Argonne and ZGS. In Johnson's memorandum to Humphrey explaining his decision and in a subsequent meeting of Humphrey, Seaborg, Wiesner, and Elmer Staats, the deputy director of BOB, this matter of assuring equity within the Midwest was stressed as one potentially positive outcome of the MURA decision.[58]

Seaborg did see to it, eventually, that organizational arrangements respecting Argonne were "broadened," but this was a small and unreliable consolation prize for the scientists and universities of the Midwestern Universities Research Association. They wanted a machine of their own. Moreover, the midwestern legislators were left dissatisfied by what, for them, was a political defeat. The real consequence of MURA's rejection was the approval of the 200-BEV. In 1965, the ultimate presidential soothing strategy came with the decision to locate the 200-BEV in the Midwest, specifically, in Illinois. Since, in 1963 and 1964, the president had explained his decision against MURA in part on the basis that he could not locate another national laboratory near Argonne, it was ironic that the choice for 200-BEV was a site just twenty-five miles from that very same laboratory.[59]

Termination

The MURA accelerator is a case of rejection. It came at the point of the adoption decision. The president himself decided not to adopt (i.e., to reject). Mohole is a case of termination. It came at a point well into implementation. In other cases, we have examined curtailment primarily as a presidential strategy. Here we look at the presidency reacting to congressional initiative to terminate, in order to bring out the range of presidential roles in curtailment processes, and also because of the relative absence of presidentially initiated terminations under Johnson. In an interview, Presidential Science Adviser Hornig stated he could not recollect a single termination decision of any consequence directly involving Johnson. This may reveal a basic Johnson approach, which was partially to curtail, or to reject, but to avoid the political costs of terminating an ongoing program altogether.

Johnson inherited Mohole. As a science and technology enterprise, Mohole could be traced back to the Eisenhower years. The object of the program was to drill "an unprecedentedly deep hole in the ocean floor for the purpose of studying the composition of the earth's interior."[60] This hole would pierce the earth's crust at the Mohorovicic discontinuity (Moho), the boundary of separation, and reach the mantle beneath. Mohole was the largest project ever undertaken by earth scientists. It took a long time to plan and was taking a longer time to accomplish. It represented a multi-million-dollar effort lasting several years. The goal was pure research; the means, big technology. Mohole entailed huge drilling efforts of a kind never before attempted. The first hole was to be drilled 115 miles northeast of Hawaii's Maui Island through about 14,000 to 17,000 feet of crust in 14,000 feet of water.[61] Mohole was the earth scientists' Apollo; but, instead of NASA to run the project, there was NSF, a basic research agency totally unaccustomed to managing scientific and technological efforts of Mohole's complexity and scale.

As Leland Haworth, director of the National Science Foundation, testified before Congress in 1963, "The Mohole project is a very complicated situation. I have been in some complicated situations in my life, but I have never been in one that approached this for complexity."[62] By the time Johnson came to power, Mohole was in trouble, falling behind schedule, experiencing cost overruns, and embroiled in disputes among scientists, contractors, and government managers. However, it retained strong support in the scientific community and in the key sector of Congress, namely, Albert Thomas of Texas, chairman of the House appropriations subcommittee responsible for NSF's budget. The drilling contractor, Brown and Root, Inc., was Thomas's constituent.

At the level of presidential technoscience, there was ambivalence concerning Mohole. There was at least some talk of terminating the project. In November 1963, at one meeting of concerned individuals, Wiesner, the president's science adviser, was asked whether Mohole would not now be initiated, given what was known about it in relation to other priorities. Wiesner responded, "No." "Then why not abandon the project before incurring further losses?" asked William Carey, a high-ranking BOB official. Wiesner would not fully agree. He went part way, however, in saying that "he would have to raise a flag on Mohole in terms of the best use of NSF funds" if NSF's overall budget ran into serious trouble.[63]

BOB apparently decided not to press the issue. Had it done so in the context of Johnson's search for budgetary cutbacks to keep his $100 billion ceiling intact, there might have been a presidential termination in late 1963. New presidents enjoy a honeymoon period that permits canceling old programs as well as launching new ones. Presidential termination requires that potential victims be brought to a new president's attention. It appears that this was not done in the case of Mohole, although BOB obviously was not oblivious to the possibility.

Thus, whatever its problems, there was no substantial effort to cancel Mohole at the time Johnson took over. Having included it in his first budget, he became identified with its implementation. His new science adviser realized that he, too, would have to deal with this troubled program. On March 10, 1964, Hornig wrote NSF Director Haworth, "So far, I have avoided Mohole, but that can't go on long. I should be most appreciative of a briefing on the Mohole Project."[64] Two months later, he wrote Haworth, "Our office continues to be deeply concerned with problems of Mohole."[65]

Problems notwithstanding, Hornig, like his predecessor, supported Mohole's continuation and worked with BOB in trying to move NSF to deal with the managerial difficulties that were surfacing. By 1965, both he and BOB were feeling better about Mohole. NSF seemed to be learning how to administer this large-scale science and technology program. On September 20, 1965, Hornig told Budget Director Schultze that he would favor Mohole over many other R&D programs in and out of NSF.[66] On October 12, BOB official Hugh Loweth listed for Schultze what NSF had done to strengthen Mohole's management structure:

> At NSF's urging, a new project manager was appointed by Brown and Root, Inc., to replace a man considered weak by the Foundation.
> Steps are being taken by the Foundation with Brown and Root to correct weaknesses in the contractor's staff concerned with electronics and communications.
> Previous weaknesses in Brown and Root systems engineering staff have been corrected.
> NSF has employed a new project manager to work directly with the prime contractor. He is a retired Navy officer with experience in ship construction and an academic background in metallurgy.
> NSF is doubling its [Mohole] staff from 11 to approximately 20. . . .
> The field staff of the Foundation will be given clear responsibility for seeing to it that the prime contractor carries out his responsibility and that the subcontractors perform their roles adequately.
> NSF is buttressing its staff capabilities with consultant advice from other agencies and from private organizations. . . .[67]

Thus, in 1965, the option of cancellation discussed in 1963 and occasionally mentioned in the press was not being considered seriously.[68] The Johnson technoscience presidency was persuaded that

Mohole was becoming a viable program. Then came one of those events that can befall a major program of science and technology, one that so changes its political environment as to alter its course totally. In January 1966, Albert Thomas died. In a brief moment, Mohole's strongest supporter in Congress was succeeded by one of its severest critics, Joseph Evins of Tennessee. While Thomas was in charge of Mohole, Evins could do little against it. Now Evins had the power. His "first major act as chairman was to kill Project Mohole."[69] His subcommittee stated that it had not allowed funds for Project Mohole because it had "progressed slowly with considerable difficulty." It pointed out that, at an estimated cost exceeding $75 million, the project's cost had "greatly exceeded the original estimate and promises to increase still further." It suggested "that the funds of the Foundation can be more advantageously used in other activities, and [thus] no funds are included to continue this project."[70]

Termination was not complete. There was hope through an appeal to the Senate, which had not yet acted on the NSF appropriation. Would the technoscience presidency fight to save Mohole? Who would wage the battle? How much personal energy would Johnson himself give to the contest? The president could be rescuer, or he could be a party to termination through nonaction.

Within the technoscience presidency, there were those who were only lukewarm in their support for the project. There were others who felt that the presidency had to back the project. "You just don't abandon a project of this kind after all the pain and cost," argued William Cannon, a BOB official.[71] Cannon told Schultze that Evins was simply "throwing his weight around in his first term as successor to A. Thomas." He wanted "to twist NSF more in his direction," which was "to spread support to more schools."[72]

A great deal of lobbying ensued on behalf of the stricken program. Many senators were approached, and Johnson assisted in the effort. The fight to avoid termination, led by the technoscience presidency, seemed to be working. The Senate voted to reinstate Mohole. This forced decision making into conference committee, where a number of bargains might be struck that could keep Mohole alive. The president's continued support was critical.

Again, events interceded. Brown and Root's chairman, George Brown, and members of his family contributed a total of $23,000 to the President's Club, a Democratic fund-raising organization. The contribution took place just a few days after Johnson had contacted several legislators in a successful appeal to the Senate to reverse the House action.[73]

Representative Donald Rumsfeld (R, Illinois) made known the

George Brown contribution. Whatever the connection between Johnson's rescuer role and George Brown's $23,000, the appearance was unfortunate, to say the least. It caused considerable embarrassment not only to Johnson but also to those on whom he had prevailed to help save Mohole. Political support diminished. In conference, critics from the House side had the advantage. The Senate joined the House in voting to cancel, and events took their course. In this instance, termination was complete; there was no other drilling project on a scale similar to Mohole, nor was there a political constituency similar to that in the Midwest for 200-BEV demanding another program. The earth scientists and some elements of the techno-science presidency still cared; but there was no way to turn a full termination into a partial termination. You either drill to the mantle, or you do not. In this case, the decision was not to drill. In Apollo, the goal was proclaimed and maintained; in Mohole, it was proclaimed and abandoned.

Conclusion

The curtailment of scientific and technological programs in the era of Lyndon Johnson has been discussed. As the "cut back" literature points out,[74] there are various degrees of curtailment. Some are partial. Minimal curtailment is arrestment, a process of holding a developing program in check until a later, more clear-cut decision can be made. ABM was arrested by Johnson, and further deployment beyond that already accomplished was canceled under Nixon. Reduction involves partial curtailment, often for only one year or so. Programs are cut back, and an agency like NSF cannot provide support as expected; sometimes it even curtails funds for awards already made. Reduction can be temporary or long-term. If the latter, it becomes retrenchment. Large parts of programs do not move forward but are held back, deferred, year after year. Retrenchment entails repeated reductions in a program, to the point where layoffs occur, priority is downgraded, and real capability is lost. NSF survived reduction to bounce back, essentially as it had been before. NASA's retrenchment, begun under Johnson, continued under Nixon until the Space Shuttle gave it a new lease on life. However, when this decision took place, the space program was but a shell of its former self.

Full curtailment was seen in the cases of MURA and Mohole. MURA was a rejected proposal; Mohole was terminated in the implementation stage. In the former instance, the president was the moving force for curtailment; in the latter, it was Congress.

The president can play any of a number of roles in curtailment.

In ABM, he was an arrester; in the NSF case, he was a reducer and a rescuer; in NASA, he was somewhere between a retrencher and a bystander. He made his own cuts and then publicly announced that he would stand by while Congress, led by the House appropriations committee, went still deeper. In MURA, he was the rejecter. In Mohole, he was first the rescuer; then he chose to be a bystander when his rescuing role was linked to the Brown and Root, Inc., political contribution.

Behind presidential decisions and roles in the curtailment process lay the many subpresidential and outside forces. In ABM, the administrator McNamara was the advocate for arrestment and used the scientific estate as his ally; the JCS professionals stood in opposition. In the NSF reduction, the scientists and budgeteers fought for the support of the president. Hornig and the budget director found themselves on opposite sides of this issue, with Hornig pressing for rescue and BOB arguing for cutbacks.

In the retrenchment of NASA, it was administrator Webb who advocated rescue. Again, BOB was in opposition. The president's scientists were not used either to help or to hurt the cause of either party. They were largely bystanders to the contest over post-Apollo. So, too, were the professionals on the National Aeronautics and Space Council. MURA was identified for rejection by the budgeteers in BOB. The science adviser and administrator Seaborg were essentially bystanders while the president made his decisions. The science adviser was made to appear as an advocate of rejection, but this was the president's stratagem, not the reality of the science adviser's position. Finally, in Mohole, there was the unusual situation in which scientists and budgeteers found themselves on the same side of a rescue effort. They had worked so hard earlier to rescue the program from NSF's managerial inadequacies that they obviously had come to see Mohole as their program, too. They got the president on their side briefly, but events they could not control worked against them.

Strategies for (and against) curtailment reflect the political forces surrounding programs. Specific programs, as DeLeon notes, may be easier to diminish or kill than governmental functions, agencies, or policies.[75] But the task is by no means simple, especially where termination is at issue. Sapolsky and I have written elsewhere that "to kill an R&D program, one must weaken the constituency behind it."[76] Decremental budgetary strategies frequently ease the task of terminators by gradually removing elements of the program support system over time. Conversely, rescuers must nurture and attend to those support systems.[77]

Curtailment has a Janus quality. Decisions harmful to one science and technology program may be helpful from another standpoint. For example, arresting ABM was good for arms control, and rejection of MURA paved the way for 200-BEV and its siting in the Midwest. Termination may end one program, but it can make room for the birth of another.[78]

7. Conclusion

This book has used the Johnson administration as a means to probe the presidential management of science and technology policy. This is an important subject. It involves a complex relationship between the federal government and science and technology. Guiding that relationship is the science and technology (technoscience) presidency. The technoscience presidency is a functional cut of the general presidency. A collective entity, it is a management system that includes president and subpresidency. The subpresidency consists primarily of those top officials who help the president, in his chief executive role, to manage science and technology: principals, budgeteers, professionals, administrators, and the vice-president. These actors participate in presidential policy decisions. Like the president, they are influenced by outsiders, such as Congress, bureaucracy, interest groups, and others.

Among those inside and outside the presidency there is a constant jockeying for position and influence. Various participants can seek to influence critical presidential decisions affecting the birth, life, and death of technoscience programs: agenda setting, adoption, implementation, and curtailment. Where program decisions move forward, there must be an advocate or policy entrepreneur, one who builds a favorable coalition of support for a particular decision outcome.

Who is influential as a policy entrepreneur behind the various decisions? How does the answer differ by policy arena—scientific research, technological development, and technological application? This chapter reviews the patterns of cooperation and competition as revealed in the Johnson presidency's management of science and technology and attempts to assess the significance of this experience for the long-term development of presidency/science and technology relations in the United States.

Scientific Research

Earthquake prediction/prevention and oceanography were featured in two cases of agenda setting. The former did not become a presidential agenda item; the latter did. Promoting earthquake prediction/prevention was a faction of the subpresidency's scientific estate. This faction could not win the strong support of the scientific estate, much less other subpresidential actors. The science adviser did not attempt to pursue this as a presidential priority. The triggers were not sufficient in and of themselves to sustain the issue, and there was no well-placed policy entrepreneur to supply the needed push. As a consequence, a possible presidential agenda issue was, in effect, screened out at an early point by the scientific estate's own system of priority setting. Oceanography, on the other hand, did have enough support to be on the agenda, but not enough, initially, to gain presidential priority. With the shift from scientist Hornig to politician Humphrey, oceanography's fortunes rose. Vice-President Humphrey was a strong subpresidential advocate of oceanography and was able to move it forward and upward as a presidential priority.

To change the status of oceanography on the agenda required adoption of a policy that added new machinery specifically on oceanography to the technoscience presidency. This adoption was opposed by the science adviser and budgeteers, but promoted by legislative stalwarts of the field. The latter prevailed, but had to settle for a temporary status for that machinery.

Another adoption involving scientific research was 200-BEV. It took a long time to get this adoption, owing to the great expense of the machine and locational politics. BOB wanted to keep Johnson's options (to say no) open. The core of advocacy within the technoscience presidency included the science adviser and administrator Seaborg, himself a scientist. There was advocacy from outside, in the scientific community, and in the Joint Committee on Atomic Energy.

The science adviser was part of the coalition behind 200-BEV; he was the prime subpresidential advocate behind New Centers of Excellence. The major linkage was between Hornig and the NSF director, by way of the Federal Council for Science and Technology. They got Johnson's attention because the proposed program meshed with his interest in geographical spread and science and education as tools of economic development. To the extent there was any hint of opposition, it came from universities and elite scientists who feared they would lose under the program.

An important case involving implementation of scientific research was that of NIH reorientation. Here the president listened to an outsider and tried to reorient NIH toward more applications in the name of "payoffs" in better health. Opposition from outsider scientists was mirrored inside by opposition from the science adviser, and, more importantly, from the relevant administrator and a more principal aide who dealt with Johnson on health matters. While against the reorientation proposal, the science adviser did not lobby the president directly. Others took the lead in trying to get the policy changed. They succeeded.

MURA, NSF basic research, and Mohole illustrated different aspects of curtailment decisions. In the cases of MURA and Mohole, two big science efforts, the political estate was key. The MURA decision was presidentially derived, with Johnson most important, although the program was identified for rejection by BOB. Johnson was key because the president was subordinating policy for scientific research to policy established for reasons of political symbolism (to hold the budget under $100 billion). On the other hand, Mohole was terminated by a legislative outsider in spite of the president and his aides. The reasons apparently began with a political show of force by the new House appropriations subcommittee chairman responsible for NSF's budget.

As in adoption, in curtailment there was a pulling and hauling within the presidency and between the presidency and Congress. The curtailment of NSF's basic science programs through budgetary cutbacks in the latter years of the Johnson administration was an act by Congress and the budgeteers responding to larger budgetary issues. Both institutions cut back, but the presidency cut less and even tried to restore funds following a particularly severe year. The presidency undoubtedly did so in part because of the protestations of the science adviser. No one else within the presidency was promoting the cause of NSF—or basic science generally—at this time.

In conclusion, it can be said that while there were multiple participants in scientific research policy, some were more influential than others. The scientific estate was a moving force in favor of basic research—for adopting some programs, lessening the impacts of cutbacks on others. Its divisions weakened advocacy of certain initiatives and made it easier for other estates to curtail particular efforts. Its orientation was not applied enough for some outsiders and led them to seek displacement of inside scientists with insiders of another kind in order to affect both the content and process of agenda setting.

However, the basic science orientation did get an audience with the president, and basic science did not fare badly under Johnson.

Over the course of his administration, the president may well have been concerned with his image (as the reversal in stance in the NIH case suggests). Moreover, he shared a faith that science (including basic science) would help solve practical problems. While he may have wanted payoffs sooner than was possible, he did not single out basic research for special negative treatment in harsh budgetary times. Having a science adviser had a measure of importance in this regard. There was an input, at times the "principal" input. Had there not been a science adviser (and had he not played this representational role), a key perspective within the technoscience presidency might well have been missing.

Technological Development

Like policies for scientific research, policies for technological development constitute an arena of cooperation and conflict. From a purely financial standpoint, the nation's stakes are higher. The Johnson technoscience presidency had to contend with a host of large-scale technological programs. The aim of these programs was to produce new capabilities, including such efforts as MOL, the electronic barrier, nuclear desalting, Apollo, SST, ABM, and post-Apollo. Whereas NSF and NIH were key agencies involved in scientific research policy, in technological development, the major funding agencies were DOD, NASA, AEC, DOI, and FAA. Industry was the major performer of technological development, not universities. Many of the decision makers and decision-making processes in technological development were different from those in scientific research.

The policies of the Johnson presidency on technological programs that were discussed were to arbitrate the adoption of MOL; to preemptively adopt and (initially) protectively implement the electronic barrier; to coordinate the implementation of nuclear desalting; to decelerate SST; to maintain Apollo, but retrench where post-Apollo was concerned; and to arrest the deployment of ABM. Who influenced the formation of these policies?

MOL was a technological development that was adopted. The adoption of MOL by the president was a decision in which he arbitrated bureaucratic interests. Johnson was pressed by NASA and the Air Force and their respective allies in the presidency and Congress. The issue was less "whether" than "who." "Who" had to deal with "when." The subpresidency was divided. Johnson had strong views on defense preparedness which were linked to space. These were key to his decision. Thus, he moved to adopt MOL as an Air Force program.

Competition was not an issue in the adoption of the electronic barrier. In that case, there was a proposal from one administrator (McNamara). The president and the Joint Chiefs of Staff went along, and thus a major new development program was launched. In the era of Vietnam buildup and an urgent search for "solutions," achieving adoption in this case was relatively easy, and actually performing the developmental work moved relatively swiftly. While the program was in development, McNamara was able to monitor it closely and protect it from bureaucratic threats. This was not possible later. When the technology moved into the applications arena, the situation was quite different.

Johnson inherited a desalting program from Kennedy and presided over its reconstitution as a nuclear desalting effort. While a number of sources contributed to this decision, there is little question that Johnson himself took a personal interest in this area. Nuclear desalting combined Johnson's interests in water and in nuclear technology. For many reasons, including coordination problems between the Atomic Energy Commission and the Department of Interior, there were gaps between what was policy and what was administrative reality. Given the tensions between AEC and DOI over control, Johnson asked his science adviser to "coordinate." A specific demonstration project was launched and ultimately aborted. This was one of those instances in which the president prematurely made optimistic claims for a new technology. Those involved in the decision to launch the program did not include the operating agency within DOI which had to implement a good part of the desalting aspects of the program. It was not able to fulfill the dreams of Johnson. Nor was it enthusiastic about being "coordinated" by one of his agents. Nuclear technology was ready, but not that for desalting. Getting AEC, through its Oak Ridge National Laboratory, to do more in desalting R&D merely exacerbated the bureaucratic tensions. The science adviser was aware of all the difficulties, including the unwarranted expectations raised by Johnson's rhetoric. There were limits to what the science adviser, as coordinator, could do, however.

The Johnson presidency had pushed forward with nuclear desalting and had attempted to coordinate an interagency program via the science adviser. It decelerated, but also moved forward with SST. Here, also, the decision was to attempt a measure of presidential management when agency-level problems appeared. As a technological development program, SST had been inherited from Kennedy. However, it was still in early implementation when an outside evaluation indicated problems. Johnson received advice from BOB and other subpresidential sources, including his science adviser, and concluded that slowing down might permit time to improve the plane. The decision to decelerate was accompanied by Johnson's creation of an interagency president's advisory committee, known as the McNamara Committee, to manage the program (and FAA) on his behalf.

The scientific estate was linked closely with the McNamara Committee through the science adviser's role in the evaluation of sonic booms. Slowing development and creating an extra layer of administrative apparatus did not help much. The basic problems of SST lay in the technical limits to building a commercially viable supersonic plane. But Johnson had tried. In making decisions on SST, he sought consensus among the various forces in his technoscience presidency. As a presidential principal, Califano played an important role in laying the president's policy options before him. Califano also was used by Johnson as a broker between McNamara and the FAA administrator, Halaby. The budget director was also involved, keeping track not only of SST spending, but also of FAA's straining to escape McNamara Committee control. Johnson himself kept a watchful eye on certain outside forces, especially in Congress. He wanted Congress to be fully checked out before he would issue a major decision that would accelerate SST again, lest he be accused of "denying children milk to build big planes."[1]

In both nuclear desalting and SST, efforts in presidential management had the effect of blurring lines of authority and raising issues of "who is in charge." This was not the case with Apollo. The key participants in decision making on Apollo were Johnson and Webb, the chief executive and the administrator. Webb was the principal aide on Apollo, and Johnson backed him. As president, Johnson was implementing a policy he had helped establish as vice-president. Apollo was viewed as a national goal, one with which he identified completely. He did not pay attention to pleas from within (e.g., BOB) or from outside (e.g., the mayors) to stretch Apollo into the next decade to release funds for other programs in the 1960s.

Other programs included post-Apollo. Here there was less presidential protection and more participation in decision making. The scientific estate was not particularly influential in post-Apollo decisions, although it sought to play a role. Nor were professional aides in the National Aeronautics and Space Council successful in establishing a presence. The primary actors in the post-Apollo policy were president, administrator, budget director, and Congress. Most of the executive branch dialogue took place at the subpresidential level, between the NASA administrator and BOB director. In post-Apollo decision making, Webb did not dominate. When the president acted, he tried to find a middle ground that would keep NASA going, but at a lower budget. However, Congress went for deeper cuts, and the president, concerned about support for a major tax bill, found himself yielding to congressional pressure against post-Apollo at a critical juncture in NASA's history. The president inadvertently tipped the balance from a policy of cutback to one of retrenchment.

Like all presidents, Johnson favored a strong defense capability. He also saw the dangers of nuclear war and the arms race. ABM symbolized this problem. The administrator and the president's scientists were against taking the next step, from development to deployment. They wanted to arrest the technology, to keep it in the R&D phase and not move forward to actual construction of ABM facilities. The military professionals were in favor of deployment. Congress was divided, but Johnson perceived it as leaning toward deployment. The Soviet Union was going ahead. Johnson was concerned that he might be attacked for an ABM gap in the next election campaign. Therefore, in the end, the president decided to opt for a minimal choice that was, in fact, an arrestment strategy. The decision gave the appearance of moving forward while retaining the option of holding back. There would be minimal deployment of a less advanced system (anti-Chinese) while, at the same time, arms control negotiation would continue to be promoted with an aim of holding ABM in check altogether. The principal role of the scientific estate in ABM was to provide legitimacy for some of the arguments that the administrator was using against the system.

It is clear that the scientific estate, while important, was not as significant in technological development as it was in the scientific research arena. There were other actors with claims to expertise, and the political, administrative, and even international aspects of decision making were usually far more salient to the president. Hence, generalist White House aides, budgeteers, and administrators mattered more in subpresidential activities aimed at starting, stopping, or slowing down technological projects. Outsiders, such as Congress and even the independent evaluators of SST, also made a difference.

Johnson himself was a considerable presence. He was not involved on a day-to-day basis, to be sure. But many below him made their choices in accord with what they perceived as his policies. If they tried to evade his policies, they might find a presidential surrogate looking over their shoulders and reminding them of presidential intent (e.g., Halaby in the case of SST). Sometimes, when the agency and the president were closely coupled, a would-be presidential coordinator might find himself bypassed and with diminished power (e.g., Hornig in the case of nuclear desalting). The science adviser, like other policy participants, jockeyed for influence. No one individual or institution always prevailed in the technological development arena, not even the president. There were too many uncertainties. Johnson could not make nuclear desalting or SST viable, nor could he afford both Apollo and post-Apollo. There were limits to presidential power in the arena of technological development. Johnson learned this lesson.

Technological Applications

The third set of policies discussed involves technological applications. The Johnson presidency had its aborts (e.g., the Electric Power Reliability Act). It also had a number of adoptions and implementations. There were three major policy thrusts in this arena: 1. the Great Society; 2. the developing countries; and 3. the Vietnam War.

In the context of the Great Society, the following decision processes were discussed: placing environmental pollution on the Johnson agenda as a priority item; the relatively less successful effort in agenda setting for energy; and the attempt to structure a greater science and technology presence in HUD.

Environmental pollution was the most successful of the Great Society applications programs. There were R&D activities of various kinds concerning environmental pollution when Johnson came to power. Johnson built substantially on these and gave the field a new momentum. While outside advocacy existed, especially in the later 1960s, inside advocacy was more important earlier. Within the presidency, the scientific estate was most instrumental in placing environmental quality on the agenda. Hornig and PSAC allied themselves with Moyers (a principal) and BOB in raising environment as a priority item for Johnson. Johnson tested the winds of public opinion and decided to provide presidential leadership. By the time Nixon became president, he had only to put a capstone on the edifice that the Johnson technoscience presidency had helped to construct.

In contrast to environment stood energy. Energy (or, at least, nonnuclear energy) was a potential applications program that could have been related to the Great Society. It might also have become a scientific research and technological development effort. But it never moved beyond a vague awareness-of-problem stage. Hence, there was no policy adoption, no program of any significance. To the extent there was inside advocacy, it came from the scientific estate. In addition, there was support from Califano and BOB. However, this support was never strong enough to move energy to a priority agenda item (e.g., in the manner of environmental pollution). The constituency outside the presidency was not yet there. The inside advocates saw problems but not a crisis ahead. The president had what he regarded as weightier and more immediate matters with which to deal at the time. Energy surfaced as a possible new presidential initiative, but there was no trigger to catalyze action. The prime policy entrepreneur, the science adviser, was too weak—and more principal aides, such as Califano, too preoccupied—to give the issue the push it required.

In another applications area of the Great Society, housing and urban development, the scientific estate made strenuous attempts to build capacity in the line agency responsible for the mission. The focus of activity for the president's scientists was the effort to include an assistant secretary for science and technology in the HUD management structure. If science and technology had better representation at the highest levels of HUD, it was believed that HUD would be able to develop a substantial program in applying R&D to the problems of cities. Among subpresidential scientists, there was a great desire to make sure that science and technology could be relevant to Johnson social priorities. The problem was seen to be at the HUD level. The HUD administrator, while interested, had other priorities. Many in the staff were resistant to special designation of a science and technology assistant secretary. For a while, OST played a quasi—assistant secretary role itself, reaching into HUD operations, holding meetings, and arranging conferences. While there was some restructuring at a level lower than assistant secretary, the effort to link HUD and technoscience never quite succeeded.

The application of science and technology to the problems of developing countries was another major thrust of the Johnson presidency. As with HUD, however, there was an "institutional problem" in the executive branch, in the view of the president's scientists. That problem was AID. AID would not promote science and technology to the degree the science adviser and his professional associates thought necessary. With the support of the president, the science adviser displaced AID priorities with his own in giving emphasis to technoscience in selected countries. A number of institutional models for building up indigenous science and technology capacity in developing countries were launched. These remained ad hoc, however, given AID's lack of strategy for disseminating these "models" on a widespread basis. Hornig and PSAC decided a separate organization had to be created, but they did not press their view within the technoscience presidency, particularly with Johnson. Hornig bequeathed to his successor the "AID problem." Like HUD,

AID was viewed as a barrier to the innovations the scientific estate wished to see applied.

Finally, there was the application of technology to the Vietnam War. The Johnson presidency did either too much or too little in this respect, depending upon one's view of the war. However, it was a proving ground for new weapons. Among new military technologies used in the war were the electronic barrier, weather modification, and defoliation.

The electronic barrier was closely associated with McNamara in its adoption and initial implementation as a development program. Once it moved to the field, in application to the war, the military professionals took command of the program. It was never completed, as a line; but the electronic and sensing devices were used in combat, in accord with needs of the field commanders.

Weather modification, like the electronic barrier, was adopted in secret by a handful of individuals. Unlike the case of the electronic barrier, the secrecy of its use lasted until after the war. The barrier was initiated by outside scientists who had been gathered at McNamara's behest to find new ways of fighting the war. Weather modification was proposed by scientists inside the Pentagon whose principal allies in selling the program to the president were the Joint Chiefs of Staff. There was no development phase, as was the case with the barrier. It was rapidly put into use, and its application was tightly controlled by military professionals and the scientists working with them.

Defoliation was adopted by Kennedy. Johnson escalated the program. There were numerous protests and petitions from outside scientific critics. These demands for an end to defoliation (as well as other novel military technologies) were brought to Johnson's attention by the key inside scientist, Hornig. The president did not agree with his critics. He wanted his science adviser to put his views across to the opposition, rather than vice versa. Hornig found himself in an increasingly difficult position throughout the war in ways typified by defoliation.

The president wanted science and technology better applied to the war. Many scientific critics were repulsed by the war and argued against lending their talents to an unjust cause. Hornig was in the middle, and his relationship with the president suffered for it. PSAC was hurt even more. As Hornig later wrote, ". . . there is no question that PSAC came to be regarded as not having an identity of interest with the President. And it seems to me that, in many respects, this parting of the ways was related to our own inability to be critics and nevertheless be part of the team at the same time."[2]

Actors

Three arenas of technoscience policy—scientific research, technological development, and technological applications—have been reviewed. Who governed in these arenas? Were any particular policy entrepreneurs more active in one than in another or in certain kinds of decisions than in others?

The President

The president was the prime point of policy decision. He influenced policy, directly and indirectly, in all arenas. He did so in many ways. First, he made critical decisions himself. There are many, many decisions that affect the course of programs. Some are more important than others in that they impact on their birth, major phases of implementation, or curtailment. These critical decisions are ones that Johnson made. Through these critical decisions, he maintained a strong measure of control over the pace and direction of the federal science and technology enterprise. His control was not unlimited, to be sure. He acquiesced, even lost, to Congress on occasion. But as a direct decision maker he was a significant chief executive where technoscience was concerned.

Second, indirectly, he conveyed his attitudes to subpresidential aides. Aides shaped proposals in ways they perceived would be acceptable to Johnson. They also kept certain proposals away from him. This allowed him to retain his later options, including that of saying no.

Third, while an influential chief executive, Johnson exercised that influence in a manner that was ad hoc and reactive. There was no self-conscious plan behind his science and technology policy. To the extent there were consistent themes, these lay in such attitudes as preeminence—Johnson wanted American science and technology to be second to none, especially in space and weapons; geographical spread of scientific resources; and the maximum "payoffs" from R&D investments.

Fourth, however ad hoc and eclectic his science and technology policy, it is a fact that there was a great deal of scientific and technological activity during the Johnson years. He was a tremendously energetic and activistic president, and this activism pervaded all policy sectors. Perhaps this spread science and technology too thinly, as subpresidential scientists felt obliged to make technoscience "relevant" to virtually everything.

Finally, Johnson maintained control over science and technology arenas by not permitting anyone inside or outside the technoscience presidency to gain a privileged position with him in this field. There was no "science czar." If the science adviser did not play this role, neither did anyone else. This absence of a concentrated center of power elevated to Johnson the critical decisions in technoscience. It also made for uncertainty and jockeying below. But this was the Johnson administrative style. It was hyperactive, pushing his aides and the country to achieve more and more, sometimes more than was possible or desirable.

Subpresidency

The subpresidency affected what issues got on the president's agenda, but did not control what was adopted, much less the course of implementation. Because it did not speak with one voice, its leverage on policy was diluted. There was a measure of influence, however, and it could be quite important. The subpresidency included the principals, the professionals (including the scientific estate), the budgeteers, the administrators, and the vice-president. While active in various arenas and decision categories, these actors varied in influence, and alliances and coalitions shifted. Thus, of all the actors, the scientific estate cut the widest swath across all the arenas and decisions. It was a locus of activity in presidential science and technology; it was not necessarily always a locus of power. Its influence was most evident in the relatively narrow field of basic research as it related to academic science, particularly where NSF was involved. In this context, it loomed large in agenda setting, adoption, and implementation. In addition, it played an important role in the defense of basic research in the face of attempted curtailments.

The major challenge to the scientific estate in the arena of research policy came from budgeteers in BOB or from professionals with a more applied orientation. The Marine Council, for example, was created by Congress to replace the scientific estate with a more applied group. Nevertheless, to a considerable extent, the scientific estate did have influence with Johnson in basic research. This was particularly the case when it was sensitive to his political needs, as it was in the New Centers of Excellence program. In this instance, at least, Hornig was a presidential principal as well as a White House professional. Basic research was an arena in which the scientific estate was accorded a legitimate place. When it came to other arenas, it had to establish its credentials.

There was plenty of competition for the scientific estate from other professionals in non–basic science matters. The Marine Council staff, led by the vice-president, captured oceanographic policy from the science adviser and his retinue. The military specialists believed they knew more about technological applications to Vietnam; and, if they needed scientific advice, they had their own experts. Deference might be paid to the scientific estate by military professionals on certain new technologies still in development; but the closer to application those technologies came, the more confidence military professionals had in decision making. The Joint Chiefs readily challenged the dominant scientific view about the readiness of ABM for deployment. Who knew more about when a technology was ready than the users? For them, the technology was ready enough.

Most of the White House aides who were principals were generalists whose portfolios cut across several policy sectors. Moyers was one of these. He helped blend advice from the scientific estate with that from others into options that reflected the personal goals of the president. In the forging of an environmental policy, for example, the scientific estate placed environmental pollution on the agenda, but Moyers helped to adapt it so that the president would see a positive legislative outcome. Hornig, as a White House aide, was a principal in appearance, but rarely in substance. When he raised the problem of energy, he had to seek Califano's help to get Johnson's attention. Cater was not as much a principal as Califano, but he was closer to Johnson than Hornig when it came to health science matters. When Johnson damaged his image in seeking to reorient NIH basic research, Cater worked with Gardner in successfully inducing the president to reverse himself. The science adviser had only indirect influence, through others, in this decision. Like others who were relatively close to Johnson, Cater approached the issues from the perspective of the president's personal interests. Professionals could also consider the politics as well as the substance of policy, but presumably did not do so as much as did the principals. The president expected a principal, such as Califano, to help him consider options. In doing so, Califano, unlike the professionals, explicitly discussed the president's political stakes.

The administrators, such as Seaborg of AEC, Webb of NASA, Udall of DOI, McNamara of Defense, Haworth of NSF, Halaby of FAA, and others varied in their roles vis-à-vis presidential decision making. Their influence, in some cases, was quite deep. Thus, when Johnson thought of space, he thought about Webb. When he thought about atomic energy, the referent was Seaborg. While deep, the influence of such administrators was typically narrow. With the exception of McNamara, whose portfolio extended beyond DOD to SST and some other matters, these administrators had influence only within the realm of their agency's activities. Sometimes (e.g., Halaby at FAA) even this was limited. To the extent that the president was not interested in a particular agency or its activities, the administrator did not participate directly in presidential decision making. Thus, Haworth was seldom in Johnson's subpresidency.

McNamara had the broadest scope within the subpresidency. Webb, Udall, Seaborg, and Halaby fell between McNamara and Haworth. Managers of agencies, they were also on call as advisers to the president. More than other estates in the subpresidency, they were seen as advocates—most were. To some extent—perhaps because of the special advocacy role of the Joint Chiefs—McNamara was perceived as an exception. He frequently came across as a restraint on his agency's weapons proposals. Other administrators greatly promoted the interests of space, atomic energy, SST, or desalting, depending upon their organizational identification.

Johnson no doubt expected this. He assumed that administrators would advocate the interests of their agencies. At times, it mattered little, when the interests of the president and administrator were identical, as in the case of Apollo. Johnson also expected administrators to recognize that there might be occasions when what was good for the agency was not necessarily good for the president. In the case of post-Apollo, the president and Webb split; and, while Webb was loyal to Johnson, their relationship was inevitably affected. Johnson found it necessary and useful to let the budget director get between Webb and himself on post-Apollo.

Similarly, Johnson used McNamara as a buffer between himself and Halaby of FAA. Buffers are frequently necessary when presidents are making unpopular decisions that affect agency heads. This is because, while they are presidential appointees, administrators lead agencies with strong linkages to Congress and other important interests in society. Sometimes a president wants to be directly and visibly linked with decision making (e.g., maintaining Apollo); at other times he wishes to keep one step removed (e.g., decelerating SST) or wishes to cast blame on someone else (e.g., Wiesner in the case of MURA accelerator rejection).

No buffers served Johnson better than the budgeteers. Like the science adviser, the budget director cut across all policy arenas: scientific research, technological development, and technological applications. On matters relating to money, his influence was usually greater than that of the science adviser. BOB's influence impinged upon programs at all stages, particularly in the beginning when "new starts" were reviewed. It also affected programs especially at their end, and often was most responsible for their termination. The budget director was the most significant force in the subpresidency in matters relating to financial curtailment. Most presidential participants under Johnson were geared to expansion of programs. Certainly, this was typically true of the scientific estate (for basic research) and most administrators (for whatever their agency did). BOB began with skepticism, a "show-me" attitude. The budgetary process is deliberately adversarial. Issues that cannot be worked out between the budget director and the administrator are elevated to the president for resolution. When the president starts with a decision to cut back in general, BOB can be formidable indeed. Aware that, once begun, programs can prove hard to contain or terminate, BOB seeks to limit presidential commitments, endorsements, and "blessings" of reports issued by other estates, including the scientific. It wants to hold options open for the president, particularly the option to say no. Thus, the budget director's power is enhanced as well as his opportunity to be a presidential principal.

Finally, there is the vice-president, whose role is perhaps unique. It is as much or as little as the president wishes it to be. For Humphrey, the technoscience role was limited to a few areas. In one, oceanography, he was a presidential principal and helped raise the priority of the field on the president's agenda. In another, space, he was not as important to Johnson as the administrator or budget director.

Each of these subpresidential groups has a perspective or expertise that provides a measure of influence with the president under various conditions: the scientific estate in certain choices affecting basic research; the budgeteers in cutback management; the JCS in weapons matters, particularly at the applications stage; the administrators in all arenas, but mainly in questions relating specifically to their agency; and the vice-president as one who can see the electoral stakes of technoscience decisions. Some estates also have constituencies other than the president, and this provides an extra measure of influence beyond mere expertise: administrators with their lines to Congress and interest groups can fall into this category. The science adviser also has a constituency, but not necessarily a particularly influential one. Other units have constituencies—as the Marine Council did in Congress. While having an outside constituency can help an aide, it can just as easily hurt. When push came to shove, Johnson expected his aides to be loyal to the president, not to some outside interest. If he surmised that this was not the case, he would banish the individual or group to the outer circle of the presidency, as Hornig suggests was the fate of PSAC in the latter Johnson Vietnam years.

The Political Setting

Neither president nor subpresidency operates in a vacuum. They seek to influence forces in their environment, and these, in turn, seek to influence them. Congress, bureaucracy, interest groups, foreign nations, and others, formally outside the presidency, attempted to influence Johnson's decision making in science and technology. There were two routes—the direct one to Johnson himself, and the indirect one via the subpresidency.

The direct route was preferred, but less attainable. Those outside the presidential institution most likely to gain direct access were those most like the president—members of the political estate. As Price notes, an estate constitutes an association of organizations and individuals who are distinguished not by formal public office, or by economic or class interest, but by differences in training and skills.[3]

Institutions of government can be organizationally separate. Similarly, the public and private sectors are set apart from one another. But there are forces that work to ease conversation across institutional boundaries, and among these are the shared attitudes and experiences based on common training and skills. They helped in gaining special access to the president, access not accorded to those of other outside estates. Members of Congress were also colleagues of the president in the sense of belonging to the political estate. But access is not necessarily influence, and Johnson did not forget that they had interests different from his own. The midwestern senators pushing the MURA accelerator could gain a hearing for their cause, but they did not get the decision they sought.

For others seeking to assert their claims, direct approaches to Johnson were possible, but usually more difficult. It took relationships of the kind Mary Lasker had with the Johnson family to obtain meaningful direct access. In that instance, access did mean influence, as Johnson sought to reorient NIH's research policies in accord with Lasker's request.

By far the dominant mode of seeking presidential favor was indirect, through the subpresidency as intermediary. Here, again, it helped if the estate inside the presidency had ties with one outside. The hope of outsiders was to make the insider a channel to the president.

For senior bureaucrats, including military officers, this channel was useful. The Joint Chiefs were part of the subpresidency where the war was concerned, and those favoring the application of novel technologies to that effort could get to the president through this intermediary. Most bureaucrats did desire similar channels. They used their agency administrators, seeking to turn the president's appointees into advocates on their behalf.

For the scientific estate, there was easy access to the subpresidency. The science adviser listened to claims ranging from more money for NSF to petitions to end Vietnam defoliation. The channel was there; it provided the possibility of influence.

In the absence of subpresidential channels, outside interests sought to create them. That was the rationale behind restructuring the subpresidency to separate oceanography from other science advice. It was a matter not of administration, but of politics—the politics of access.

This discussion points up the twofold role of the subpresidency. Viewed from the oval office, it is a vehicle for achieving the president's will in policy management. Viewed from outside, it is, at minimum, a route to the president; at best, it is influence itself.

Central Issues

What implications does presidential management of science and technology under Johnson hold for presidential management in general? Four central issues of presidential management that are particularly highlighted by the science and technology area were raised at the outset of this study. They are 1. dispersion of the function; 2. the sequential nature of decision making; 3. the need for integration of knowledge; and 4. the desirability of a strategic approach to policy. The cases and discussions in the various chapters illuminated these issues in different ways.

Dispersion

First, there is the problem of dispersion. Science and technology policy is dispersed owing in part to its having dimensions of research, development, and applications. These aspects may flow together intellectually, but they do not necessarily do so organizationally. Certainly, they do not do so in this country. Different federal organizations are specialized around each of these components. Within each component, one agency focuses on, for example, developing this technology, while a second agency deals with another technology, and so on. Even where the technology may seem similar, as with atomic energy, it may be applied differently (e.g., to military or civilian needs). The further along the continuum from scientific research to technological applications, the more dispersed becomes the domain of science and technology to be managed. At a certain point, that domain ceases to be one of science and technology and dissolves into the operations of an applications area.

Yet that continuum can be seen as a whole, an enterprise in itself, that can be managed. It is a "front end" to many other operational policies, creating options and problems that are new to the operating organizations. Science and technology can be stimulated or retarded, directed one way or another. If the presidency does not provide policy management, some other entity will. Science and technology may be dispersed as a governmental enterprise, but it is not out of control. The question lies in whose control it is.

The science and technology enterprise that Johnson inherited was indeed a dispersed activity, as compared with other governmental policy spheres. Under Johnson, this enterprise was managed toward an even greater fragmentation. In part, this was a consequence of the ebbing of the momentum of Sputnik and the Apollo decision. The post-Sputnik emphases on science and technology as a goal unto itself, stimulated further by the drive for "preeminence" in science and technology symbolized by Apollo, had created a special surge that elevated technoscience as a national and presidential priority. This surge, with its massive and accelerated outlays of research and development monies, could not be maintained indefinitely and came to an end under Johnson.

Science and technology became another priority rather than a particular priority. As such, its emphasis derived more from its associations with other missions of government. It became, in effect, a less central priority; it also became more dispersed.

Johnson continued to fund basic research through NSF and NIH. He supported technological development (as well as mission-oriented basic and applied research) through DOD, NASA, and AEC. However, he was interested more in domestic social reform, until he became embroiled in a war in Southeast Asia and, eventually, economic problems. He was not confronted with a need to make immense science and technology decisions, on the order of Apollo. But he did make many important decisions, and sought initiatives, while carrying out several science and technology programs inherited from Kennedy.

Thus, there had been talk, and some action, under Kennedy, to relate science and technology more to social goals. But there had been little time for follow-through. With Johnson, and the Great Society, a variety of efforts were launched to broaden the base of science and technology support—for purposes of application. This was seen in situations involving the new domestic agencies established by Johnson, such as HUD.

It was during the Johnson years that the question was raised most forcefully: "If we can go to the moon, why can't we . . ." It was an appropriate question, and one whose spirit would be conveyed repeatedly in a variety of ways to a range of visitors to the oval office. This gave a strong applications orientation to Johnson's technoscience policies, and a heightened dispersion to them. Science and technology was seen as useful for all missions of government. For example, it could be related as a new tool for an old problem with which Johnson was quite familiar, water, via nuclear desalting. If we can go to the moon, we can make the deserts bloom!

Where government went, so also went this tool, this "technological fix." Johnson wanted it deployed not only in the cities, but also abroad, and accordingly sent Hornig on missions to one developing country after another. If science and technology could help the United States to modernize, it could help Korea, India, South America, and every developing nation.

And, of course, there was Vietnam. What could be used to build could also be used to destroy, in order to rebuild later. Electronic gadgetry, weather modification, and supertoxic chemical defoliants could all be, and were, applied to the war effort. They worked and they did not work, much as the efforts to apply science and technology to problems of domestic society sometimes were effective and sometimes were not. Questions of match and appropriateness for the setting at hand were not asked much in the 1960s. There was a technological hubris in this era. It was not always appreciated that, in many ways, it was easier to go to the moon than to deal with problems on earth. There were no people, or institutions, or determined adversaries to get in the way.

So Johnson contributed to the dispersion of the science and technology enterprise. As science and technology was applied beyond its traditional areas, it became more and more an object of criticism. The urban interests questioned its relevance. Critics of the war indicted science and technology as part of the problem, rather than a solution. There was a great deal of antitechnology writing in the 1960s, much of it claiming technology was out of control.[4] In part, this was a consequence of the extreme dispersion and multiplicity of decision centers influencing technoscience at the time. The Johnson management style contributed to this kaleidoscopic sense. In a number of cases, the programs that were launched and implemented did move beyond the control of the president in whose name they were undertaken.

Sequence

All government programs involve a sequence, in the sense of a beginning, middle, and (possible) end. But science and technology efforts, especially large-scale technological development projects, seem to bring out relevant policy management issues with particular clarity. This is because the programs involve tangible hardware creations (a new missile, or spaceship, or nuclear reactor). A product is being planned, designed, built, and ultimately deployed.

The research/development/applications continuum was noted above. This cycle has a time dimension. Small decisions made at the outset of a program can have immense consequences (intended and unintended) later on. Programs launched under one president may have to be implemented or curtailed by another. A given president may adopt a program, and then become its implementer. He may find himself changing and reorienting that which he helped to conceive. In adopting late in his administration, he provides a program (and possible problems) for a successor. He himself must deal with the problems caused by a previous president's decision, problems visible only once the program is well into implementation. The sequential nature of science and technology complicates presidential decisions.

Johnson was embroiled (willingly or inadvertently) in the continuum of technological change over and over again. The decision to augment spending in nuclear desalting was essentially a decision to move a slow-paced DOI research effort into a development program geared to AEC nuclear reactors. The decision on ABM was whether a massive development program should shift into an even larger operational effort—that is, whether ABM should be deployed.

The Apollo program was in the development stage. From a policy management standpoint, this meant implementation. However, late in development, when testing was under way, the Apollo fire disaster occurred, and three astronauts died. Johnson could have used the fire as an occasion to slow down the program, saving money at a time when he desperately needed to do that, and to extricate himself from a presidential commitment he had inherited. He chose, instead, to hold to the course, and treat the fire as an aberration, rather than a problem requiring substantial program reorientation.

In contrast, Johnson inherited, as implementer, another project being developed: SST. This time he made decisions that decelerated the program and reoriented it to more design than hardware construction. He came back to decide again, later, whether the program was ready to move into the actual stage of building a prototype plane. He decided affirmatively. But knowledge born of hindsight says that even the later decision was premature.

It is easiest for a president to end a program at the outset, when a technology is young—indeed, not yet developed. Even here, as with the MURA nuclear accelerator, a technology intended for basic research, the controversy attending death-at-birth can be considerable. And when termination takes place in connection with a program in implementation, the decision may well have even more presidential costs. Perhaps that is why Johnson, like most presidents, preferred to cut back ongoing efforts, but not cancel them outright. This was good from the standpoint of holding to long-term commitments over the stages of innovation. It was bad from the standpoint of perpetuating programs which were not evolving in the manner expected at their start. Congress, not the president, ended Mohole in the development/implementation stage.

Thus, science and technology has a life cycle that can be embodied in governmental programs. The president makes decisions that affect the birth, life, and death of a program. These decisions occur in stages, and the earlier in the technoscience life cycle such a decision takes place, the easier it is to cancel a program. In later stages, it is easier to maintain, reorient, or curtail than to terminate altogether. It is hardest of all for a president to telescope stages into an early decision, so that he will anticipate problems in advance and take the necessary precautions. President Johnson, like others, dealt with decisions as they came up to him, whether they were generated by the pressures of technology or those of politics.

Integration

The third issue is the integration of knowledge necessary for decision. Integration points up the role of the subpresidency. The subpresidency must help the president to integrate scientific, administrative, budgetary, political, and other knowledge. If it does not do this, who does? Perhaps the most significant issue is: who leads the subpresidency in its integrating responsibility? Specifically, is the science adviser a "principal" in this regard? Should he (or she) be? There are two aspects of this issue: 1. integration through science adviser/president direct relationships; and 2. integration through relationships at the subpresidential level, an indirect means.

First, the question of direct advice. Before Sputnik, there was little conscious attention to the integration of scientific knowledge with other ingredients of policy advice. With the rise of science and technology as a function of government, and consequent elevation of scientists within the presidency, it was natural in the late 1950s and early 1960s to see the science adviser as a principal on the White House staff, with an overarching role in rendering science advice to the president. The decentralized model of advice—in which the president receives inputs from multiple sources—was to some extent replaced by a more centralized approach in which this one source played a special role. While in no sense having a monopoly on access, the science adviser as principal was placed in a position of being the prime integrator of scientific advice, and of having at least the opportunity to synthesize scientific and nonscientific information required for technoscience decisions. Kennedy, like Eisenhower, used this centralized model. The informal (not the formal) status and power of the science adviser was the key factor.

Johnson shifted to a different approach. Hornig was seldom treated as a presidential principal, although he formally retained senior White House status. To some extent this was because of factors already noted, such as the increasing dispersion of the function within the executive branch. Any science adviser would have been spread quite thinly. The very desire to adapt to the president moved Hornig into areas new to him, already occupied by other potential advisers. This was especially true of the large-scale technological programs. Moreover, Johnson and his science adviser had problems relating to one another. As Hornig noted, "He listens to me very seriously; he's responded on what I thought were major issues . . . but there has never been any easiness about it."[5]

While "human chemistry" may have had something to do with the difficulties in the Johnson-Hornig relationship, there was also an organizational element involved. As director of OST, Hornig had an institutional role to perform. This role was new, having come into being only in 1962, under Kennedy. Since Kennedy was relatively close to his science adviser, this institutional role did not get in the way of the advisory relationship. But it may have done so in the case of Hornig.

Hornig was not only a personal adviser to the president; he was also a leader of an agency within the institutional presidency. As such, he was expected to testify before Congress on behalf of OST, negotiate with BOB, deal with other executive professionals, and work with (and against) the agencies. OST began with twelve professionals in 1962. By the end of 1968, the number had doubled. Hornig's institutional role was a centrifugal force on the president/science adviser nexus. Hornig noted as much: "The biggest problem—the central issue—is to define the right boundary line between a small, nimble top group which is very responsive to the president, and a more formalized structure which can in fact do something in greater depth to study the complete range of things from time to time he gets into."[6]

Other aides might have similar problems of balancing personal and institutional roles. The national security adviser has this dilemma, for example. But whereas, under Johnson, Rostow saw the president day to day and retained his personal status as a presidential principal, Hornig saw Johnson less and less as time passed and found his institutional role a detriment to membership in the president's inner circle of advisers.

Another problem Hornig had—and any science adviser has—is the balance between "neutral" advice and advocacy of the interests of the scientific community. Is the adviser the advocate of science to the president, or the president's advocate to the scientific community? The issue came up on the occasion of budget cutbacks in basic research—one key issue where the interests of science and the president diverged in the Johnson years. In that instance, Hornig chose to defend science against the budgeteers, thereby creating friction with BOB. He sought to persuade the president that his interests in curtailing government spending were not well served by cutting basic research, particularly in NSF.

The science adviser's problems as an adviser and "representative" within the subpresidency of a constituency are also illustrated in the matter of Vietnam defoliation. There the science adviser attempted to be a neutral broker, transmitting Johnson's view of the war to his scientific critics and carrying the critics' position back to Johnson. Vietnam turned out to be a no-win situation for the science adviser. The critics wanted him to help them with Johnson, and Johnson expected the adviser to "deliver" his constituency on the issue that counted most.

Hence, under Johnson, the direct science adviser/president relation gave way to an indirect approach. The end was the same—integrating scientific and technological knowledge into broader sets of considerations necessary to presidential decision making. But the means inevitably became more complex, because more parties were involved.

With Johnson, the indirect means became dominant. The science adviser began working with various aides. He had to determine which were principals, on which issues. Alliances were struck among science adviser, budget bureau chief, and other senior White House aides as necessary. These horizontal relationships were key to vertical influence with the president. A factor that weakened the science adviser's direct relationship—namely, his role as an "institutional man," heading OST—helped him with other subpresidential officials. OST staff interacted with staff from BOB; one member of the OST staff wore an additional hat as a member of the NSC staff; Hornig and other executive office officials worked with agency administrators in coordinating, monitoring, and evaluating bureaucratic performance from a presidential standpoint. In various ways, networks of human relationships served as an informal means for transfer of various kinds of knowledge. The science adviser lost much of his visibility as a personal and principal adviser to the president. He melded into the organizational processes of subpresidential decision making. A measure of integrated knowledge at that level blended into further integration at the presidential level. A new model for integration of scientific with nonscientific advice was thus developed in the Johnson years.

Succeeding presidents have used various versions of these direct and indirect approaches in their science and technology decisions. Nixon, who concentrated so much power in so few aides, at the start of his first term adopted the indirect approach inherited from Johnson. The science adviser had to reach the president through the generalists who served as principals. When these individuals ceased to listen, however, or received information they did not wish to hear, the science adviser was unofficially dropped as an aide to the president. At the beginning of Nixon's second term, the science advisory apparatus was abandoned more officially. Technically, the NSF director was to serve as science adviser, but the reality was abandonment of the concept—a subpresidency in which science and technology was so peripheral as to be essentially without access.

This model lasted only a brief time. Ford, Carter, and Reagan decided they needed more central sources of advice and institutional assistance in managing science and technology. The science adviser, and his staff, now called the Office of Science and Technology Policy (OSTP), reappeared. Other parts of the apparatus, such as a presidential science advisory committee, also came back, but in a less formal and less elevated way.

Carter, with his strong technical background, had a close working relationship with his science adviser, Frank Press. Even so, this individual was more often than not part of a diffuse organizational process that provided integration indirectly rather than a direct and sole adviser/integrator. Horizontal rather than vertical relationships were dominant, and these were apparently effective with Carter. Reagan also used a science adviser, George Keyworth, who succeeded in adapting to the president's style. He was a principal on some issues, but just another subpresidential professional on most. His capacity to work with and through aides who were closer to the president, even on matters of science and technology, determined his effectiveness. Moreover, the Reagan adviser, more than others, served as an advocate to outside interests, particularly Congress and the scientific community, on behalf of certain of the president's more controversial programs, such as the MX missile and "star wars" space defense system.

Thus, it would appear that the model of science adviser/president relations that evolved in the era of Lyndon Johnson was a precedent. At the time, Hornig received criticism for having let the status of the position he inherited slip. In reality, what was under way had less to do with personalities and more with the routinization of a governmental innovation. What had been new to the president and presidency, namely, science advice as a distinct input to decision making, became more a part of the White House scene.

As the president and others in the presidency became more accustomed to dealing with science and technology issues, they gained confidence. The science adviser seemed less "special," certainly less awe-inspiring. Science and technology and the need to integrate science advice with other forms of knowledge remained. Hence, the symbol of this need continued. But the capacity of the science adviser to lead in the integrating effort depended less on his special knowledge than on his ability to relate, day to day, to his peers in the subpresidency, and to serve the needs of the president as that individual saw them.

Strategy

The fourth issue of presidential management is strategic decision making. Science and technology is a force to be developed and applied in the nation's interest. Formulating a coherent national strategy for science and technology entails long-range decision making, a concept of goals, and willingness to keep an eye on the larger issues that ought to concern presidents. A strategy provides a set of criteria in weighing which programs to initiate and implement, and how fast. It is also a means to decide which to curtail or terminate. It is a guide and discipline to decision making and resource allocation. Was Johnson's science and technology policy strategic? Was there, in short, a policy to be managed?

The nature of the policy (or policies) to be managed constitutes the fourth issue. In many ways, it embraces the others. For a strategic policy would be comprehensive and long-range. It would deal with the matter of dispersion. It would link the sequential decisions, particularly in terms of anticipating decisions to be made, rather than simply responding to events, ad hoc. It would integrate scientific, political, and other considerations in presidential decision making. Without such a linkage, a strategic policy addressing science and technology in terms of national needs is not feasible.

Defined thus, there was no strategic science and technology policy in the era of Lyndon Johnson. There were policies that dealt with particular programs and agencies, but none that drew them together in any systematic framework.

To a large extent, this reflected the reactive style of Johnson policy making in general. There was no strategic national policy to which a science and technology component might have been related. PSAC had the capability to think long-range and to anticipate the new science and technology—intensive problems on the horizon. OST, in combination with BOB, could provide some of the necessary follow-up in implementation. The science adviser, however, was not, in any consistent sense, a principal in the Johnson White House.

Hence, what was missing was not so much knowledge as power. Without that, little was possible in the way of a comprehensive approach. The science adviser, rather than thinking strategically, necessarily looked for opportunities among the many science and technology issues that came his way. Policies sometimes resulted, and these could be worthwhile. However, they were not linked to an overall strategy. This reality, however, was a function of the way the Johnson presidency worked in general. That, in turn, reflected Johnson's interests and style.

Science and technology policy prior to Johnson was somewhat more strategic, in part because U.S. goals involving science and technology were more limited and clear-cut—primarily, preeminence in the Cold War. Also, science and technology was viewed as matching that goal quite well. As national goals became more diffuse, and as science and technology's negative impacts became more salient, the need for a strategic policy grew. This was especially the case as money became tighter, and it was more essential to choose.

No president since Johnson has produced a strategic science and technology policy. Nixon made sure he would not do so by disassembling the subpresidential machinery of science and technology. Ford resurrected and Carter retained the machinery. Both made statements and some attempts at strategy, but these remained more rhetorical than real. Reagan's science and technology policy was narrower. In a sense, it could be said to have been more strategic. It definitely reflected the philosophy of the president: to achieve preeminence in defense, support "excellence" in selected areas of basic research, and encourage, in sharply limited ways, the private sector to develop technologies for economic recovery. Critics would argue that ideology is not necessarily strategy; and a policy that excludes too much is no more strategic than one that is overly inclusive. Certainly, the Reagan and Johnson approaches provide polar extremes in science and technology policy.

What is needed is an approach that reflects both discipline and breadth. To have such a strategy requires a president who is oriented to the future. That is, it requires one who consciously seeks to shape the future and sees science and technology as a means for doing so. Such a president would place the issues of dispersion, sequence, and integration in a context of long-term planning, inheriting past programs and developing a strategy amidst the politics of the present. But if his eye was toward the future, he would have science and technology at the forefront of his thinking. This is because trends in technoscience are one of the most tangible indicators available of future options—good and bad—for society. Science and technology is not the only indicator, and its uses must be considered along with others. What is possible is not always desirable.

But science and technology is certainly a critical—maybe the critical—factor in the society of today and tomorrow. Hopefully, such a president would develop a coherent strategy to bring about the more positive future that is possible. He (or she) would have to mold the necessary subpresidential infrastructure to help create programs from possibilities. Such a president would begin, however, with a vision of what could be.

The foresight and skills of the president remain the key to any presidency. This is as true for science and technology as for other policy areas. It was the case in Lyndon Johnson's day. It is the case today; and it will be the situation beyond the year 2000—or as long as the president is the focal point of American democracy.

Notes

1. Introduction

1. Hugh Heclo, *Studying the Presidency: A Report to the Ford Foundation* (New York: Ford Foundation, 1977), p. 30.

2. James David Barber, *The Presidential Character*, 2d ed. (Englewood Cliffs, N.J.: Prentice-Hall, 1977).

3. Hugh Heclo, "Introduction: The Presidential Illusion," in Hugh Heclo and Lester M. Salamon, eds., *The Illusion of Presidential Government* (Boulder, Colo.: Westview, 1982), p. 14.

4. Thomas E. Cronin, *The State of the Presidency*, 2d ed. (Boston, Mass.: Little, Brown and Company, 1980), p. 145.

5. Hugh Heclo and Lester M. Salamon, eds., *The Illusion of Presidential Government*. This section includes the following chapters: Lester M. Salamon, "The Presidency and Domestic Policy Formulation"; Roger B. Porter, "The President and Economic Policy: Problems, Patterns, and Alternatives"; Anna Kasten Nelson, "National Security I: Inventing a Process (1945–1960)"; and I. M. Destler, "National Security II: The Rise of the Assistant (1961–1981)."

6. The literature on science and technology policy, discussed here to some extent, is large. Much of it is concerned with specific fields, such as nuclear energy, space, and, recently, genetic engineering. For nonspecialists in this policy area, who are primarily interested in presidential and governmental matters, the bibliography in James Everett Katz, *Presidential Politics and Science Policy* (New York: Praeger, 1978), would be useful.

7. C. P. Snow, *Science and Government* (Cambridge, Mass.: Harvard University Press, 1960).

8. Robert Gilpin, *American Scientists and Nuclear Weapons Policy* (Princeton, N.J.: Princeton University Press, 1962).

9. Don K. Price, *The Scientific Estate* (Cambridge, Mass.: Harvard University Press, 1965), p. 122.

10. George B. Kistiakowsky, *A Scientist in the White House* (Cambridge, Mass.: Harvard University Press, 1976).

11. James R. Killian, Jr., *Sputnik, Scientists, and Eisenhower* (Cambridge, Mass.: MIT Press, 1977).

12. Edward J. Burger, Jr., *Science at the White House: A Political Liability* (Baltimore: Johns Hopkins University Press, 1980).

13. *Technology in Society* 2, nos. 1 and 2 (1980): 47.

14. W. Henry Lambright, *Governing Science and Technology* (New York: Oxford University Press, 1976).

15. Katz, *Presidential Politics and Science Policy.*

16. Graham T. Allison, *Essence of Decision: Explaining the Cuban Missile Crisis* (Boston: Little, Brown and Company, 1971).

17. Harold Lasswell, *A Pre-View of the Policy Sciences* (New York: Elsevier, 1971), especially chapter 2.

18. Gary Brewer, "The Policy Sciences Emerge: To Nurture and Structure a Discipline," *Policy Sciences* 5 (September 1974): 239–244.

19. Charles O. Jones, *An Introduction to the Study of Public Policy,* 2d ed. (North Scituate, Mass.: Duxbury Press, 1977).

20. Ernest S. Griffith, *The Impasse of Democracy* (New York: Harrison-Hilton Books, Inc., 1939), p. 182.

21. Douglass Cater, *Power in Washington* (New York: Random House, 1964).

22. J. Leiper Freeman, *The Political Process: Executive Bureau–Legislative Committee Relations* (New York: Random House, 1965).

23. For a good discussion of this and related issues, see Harold Seidman, *Politics, Position, and Power: The Dynamics of Federal Organization,* 2d ed. (New York: Oxford University Press, 1975).

24. Hugh Heclo, *A Government of Strangers: Executive Politics in Washington* (Washington, D.C.: Brookings, 1977).

25. See David Easton, *A Framework for Political Analysis* (Englewood Cliffs, N.J.: Prentice-Hall, 1965) for an elaboration upon the concept of "system" as applied to political science.

26. Destler, "National Security II: The Rise of the Assistant (1961–1981)."

27. Cronin, *The State of the Presidency,* p. 145.

28. Cronin uses the term "subpresidency" to refer to the functional presidency or policy sphere. I use it in the same way as Emmette S. Redford and Marlan Blissett, *Organizing the Executive Branch: The Johnson Presidency* (Chicago: University of Chicago Press, 1981), to refer to a set of actors in the executive presidency "under" the president.

29. Price, *The Scientific Estate,* p. 122.

30. Donald F. Hornig, "The President's Need for Science Advice: Past and Future," *Technology in Society* 2, nos. 1 and 2 (1980): 47.

31. Ibid.

32. Emmette S. Redford, *Democracy in the Administrative State* (New York: Oxford University Press, 1969), p. 69.

33. Lambright, *Governing Science and Technology.*

34. Because some cases involve two different stages of the development of certain programs, there are twenty-four cases drawn from twenty-two programs.

2. Agenda Setting

1. Press release, White House, 2 May 1964, cited in *The Office of Science and Technology during the Administration of President Lyndon B. Johnson, November 1963–January 1969*, II, J2, p. 1, LBJ Library; hereafter cited as *OST Administrative History*.

2. "Earthquake Prediction—A Proposal for a Ten Year Program of Research," presented to PSAC on 8 June 1965 by an Ad Hoc Panel on Earthquake Prediction, cited in *OST Administrative History*, II, J2, p. 2, LBJ Library.

3. Memo, Donald F. Hornig to the president, 16 September 1965, cited in *OST Administrative History*, II, J2, p. 3, LBJ Library.

4. *OST Administrative History*, II, J2, p. 3, LBJ Library.

5. Ibid., p. 5.

6. Earthquake prevention, like earthquake prediction, remained a potential scientific research program. The president's attention was not strongly sought, in part because there was never a cohesive constituency for earthquake prediction or prevention within the subpresidency's scientific estate.

7. *OST Administrative History*, II, J2, p. 1, LBJ Library.

8. David Z. Robinson, "Politics in the Science Advisory Process," *Technology in Society* 2, nos. 1 and 2 (1980): 160.

9. "LBJ and Hornig: Close Ties Exist as Science Adviser Starts Third Year," *Science* 151 (28 January 1966): 431.

10. Memo, Hornig to president, 11 November 1965, Papers of Donald F. Hornig, LBJ Library; hereafter cited as Hornig Papers.

11. "Northeast Power Failure November 9–10, 1965—A Report to the President by the FPC," 6 December 1965, cited in *OST Administrative History*, II, J2, p. 2, LBJ Library.

12. Memo, Joseph A. Califano, Jr., to president, 6 January 1966, Ex UT2, WHCF, LBJ Library.

13. Memo, Califano to Hornig, 14 October 1966, cited in *OST Administrative History*, II, J2, p. 3, LBJ Library.

14. Letter, Hornig to Califano, 23 November 1966, Hornig Papers, LBJ Library.

15. Memo, Hornig to Califano, 2 December 1966, "Electric Power" folder, Files of Joseph A. Califano, Jr., LBJ Library; hereafter cited as Califano Files.

16. Memo, Hornig to Joseph Califano, 3 December 1966, "Electric Power" folder, Califano Files, LBJ Library.

17. *OST Administrative History*, II, J2, p. 7, LBJ Library.

18. Memo, Hornig to James F. C. Hyde, Jr., 1 May 1967, Hornig Papers, LBJ Library.

19. Memo, Califano to president, 7 June 1967, Ex LE/UT2, WHCF, LBJ Library.

20. *OST Administrative History*, II, J2, p. 7, LBJ Library.

21. Ibid.

22. Letter from Donald F. Hornig to Honorable Lucien Nedai, 19 May 1964, Hornig Papers, LBJ Library.

23. The events concerning to ICO/OST/FCST are related in an unpublished study entitled "Planning and Coordinating Oceanographic Programs," LBJ Library.

24. Memo, Philip S. Hughes to Bill D. Moyers, 18 December 1964, Files of the Director of the Bureau of the Budget, National Archives; hereafter cited as BOB Files.

25. Memo, Moyers to Kermit Gordon, 22 December 1964, Ex SC6, WHCF, LBJ Library.

26. *OST Administrative History*, II, F, p. 5, LBJ Library.

27. Edward Wenk, Jr., *The Politics of the Ocean* (Seattle: University of Washington Press, 1972), pp. 90–91.

28. Ibid., p. 91.

29. Letter, Hornig to Representative Herbert C. Bonner, 6 May 1965, Hornig Papers, LBJ Library.

30. U.S. Congress, House, Committee on Merchant Marine and Fisheries, *Hearings before a Subcommittee on Oceanography*, 81st Cong., 1st sess., 10 August 1965.

31. Memo, Hornig to president, 19 August 1965, Hornig Papers, LBJ Library.

32. Memo, Hornig to president, 1 April 1966, Hornig Papers, LBJ Library.

33. Address by Hornig before the Banquet Session of the Marine Technology Society, Second Annual Conference on "Exploiting the Ocean," 28 June 1966, Hornig Papers, LBJ Library.

34. Memo, president to vice-president, 16 July 1966, Ex FG 11-7, WHCF, LBJ Library.

35. Wenk, *The Politics of the Ocean*, p. 102.

36. Memo, vice-president to president, 14 October 1966, Ex FG 11-7, WHCF, LBJ Library.

37. Memo, vice-president to president, 19 November 1966 (11:30 A.M.), Ex FG 11-7, WHCF, LBJ Library. Also, a second memo, vice-president to president, 19 November 1966 (1:30 P.M.), Ex FG 11-7, WHCF, LBJ Library.

38. Wenk, *The Politics of the Ocean*, p. 150.

39. Ibid., p. 153.

40. Memo, vice-president to president, 19 November 1966, Ex FG 11-7, WHCF, LBJ Library.

41. Wenk, *The Politics of the Ocean*, p. 150.

42. Bryce Nelson, "Hubert Humphrey's Scientific Role: From Ocean Depths to Outer Space," *Science* 155 (24 February 1967): 981–983.

43. Ibid.

44. Wenk, *The Politics of the Ocean*, p. 152.

45. Memo, vice-president to president, 12 December 1967, Ex FG 11-7, WHCF, LBJ Library.

46. Wenk, *The Politics of the Ocean*, p. 153.

47. Memo, Hornig to Califano, 4 March 1967, Hornig Papers, LBJ Library.

48. Wenk, *The Politics of the Ocean*, p. 117.

49. Memo, Wenk to Califano, 8 January 1969, Ex FG 11-7, WHCF, LBJ Library.

50. A. B. Cambel et al., *Energy R&D and National Progress: Findings and Conclusions*, cited in Barry M. Casper, "The Experts' Silent Trumpet," *Bulletin of the Atomic Scientists* 32, no. 7 (September 1976): 24–25.

51. Memo, James T. Bonner to Walter W. Heller, 8 October 1963, records from the Council of Economic Advisers, Roll G, LBJ Library, as cited in James L. Cochrane, "Energy Policy in the Johnson Administration: Logical Order versus Economic Pluralism," in *Energy Policy in Perspective: Today's Problems, Yesterday's Solutions*, ed. Craufurd D. Goodwin (Washington, D.C.: Brookings, 1981), p. 344.

52. Cochrane, "Energy Policy in the Johnson Administration," p. 345.

53. Memo, Charles J. Zwick to Hornig, 21 January 1966, BOB Files, National Archives.

54. Cambel et al., *Energy R&D*, cited in Casper, "The Experts' Silent Trumpet," pp. 24–25.

55. Ibid.

56. Ibid.

57. Ibid.

58. Memo, Hornig to president, 7 October 1966, Hornig Papers, LBJ Library.

59. *OST Administrative History*, II, J, p. 6, LBJ Library.

60. Ibid.

61. Robert Stobaugh and Daniel Yergin, eds., *Energy Future* (New York: Random House, 1979), p. 3.

62. Ibid.

63. Memo, Hornig to Califano, 20 December 1966, Chron. File, Box 4, Hornig Papers, LBJ Library.

64. Ibid.

65. "Special Message to the Congress: Protecting Our Natural Heritage" (30 January 1967), in *Public Papers of the Presidents of the United States: Lyndon B. Johnson, 1967* (Washington, D.C.: Government Printing Office, 1968), p. 100; hereafter cited as *Public Papers*.

66. Memo, Califano to Zwick, 16 December 1968, BOB Files, National Archives.

67. Memo, Zwick to Califano, 21 December 1968, BOB Files, National Archives.

68. Memo, Hornig to president, 3 January 1969, Hornig Papers, LBJ Library.

69. Donald Hornig, participant Session II, "National Dimensions," the Second Franklin Conference: Science Policies for the Decade Ahead (Philadelphia, Pa.: Franklin Institute, October 1975), p. 60, as cited in William G. Wells, Jr., *Science Advice and the Presidency, 1933–1976* (Ann Arbor, Mich.: University Microfilms, 1978), p. 600.

70. Particularly, Senator Edmund S. Muskie (D, Maine) was an early leader on behalf of environmental issues.

71. President's Science Advisory Committee, *Use of Pesticides* (Washington, D.C.: Government Printing Office, 1963).

72. Letter, Hornig to Moyers, 29 May 1964, Hornig Papers, LBJ Library.

73. Memo, Califano to president, 18 February 1966, Ex FG 165-6-1/A, WHCF, LBJ Library.

74. "Special Message to the Congress on Conservation and Restoration of Natural Beauty" (8 February 1965), *Public Papers,* 1965, I: 162.

75. *OST Administrative History,* II, D, p. 7, LBJ Library.

76. Ibid.

77. Ibid.

78. "Special Message to the Congress on Conservation and Restoration of Natural Beauty," p. 164.

79. President's Science Advisory Committee, *Restoring the Quality of Our Environment* (Washington, D.C.: Government Printing Office, 1965).

80. Cited in letter, Elmer Staats to Orville Freeman, 8 December 1965, BOB Files, National Archives.

81. Ibid.

82. The chairman of CEA, Gardner Ackley, headed a Committee of Economic Incentives for Pollution Abatement. This committee, which had a number of task forces, also developed a legislative program in the area of air and water pollution, which dealt with organizational, standard setting, and enforcement problems, as well as economic incentives. Memo, Joseph Califano to Gardner Ackley, 31 July 1965, Legislative Background, Water Pollution, Box 1, LBJ Library.

83. Memo, Hornig to Califano, 15 December 1967, "Agricultural Pollution" folder, Files of James A. Gaither, LBJ Library.

84. Memo, Hornig to John Macy, 8 March 1969, Hornig Papers, LBJ Library.

85. Roger W. Cobb and Charles D. Elder, *Participation in Amerian Politics: The Dynamics of Agenda-Building* (Boston: Allyn and Bacon, 1972), pp. 85–86.

86. Charles O. Jones, *An Introduction to the Study of Public Policy,* 2d ed. (North Scituate, Mass.: Duxbury Press, 1977), pp. 37–39.

87. Paul C. Light, *The President's Agenda* (Baltimore, Md.: Johns Hopkins University Press, 1982), p. 220.

88. Memo, Califano to president, 18 February 1966, Ex FG 165-6-1/A, WHCF, LBJ Library.

3. Adoption

1. As it happened, delays in starting and pleas for additional time meant that, once in being, the apparatus was extended through successive amendments that permitted the Marine Council and Advisory Commission to continue, at least for a while, into the Nixon administration.

2. Edward Wenk, Jr., *The Politics of the Ocean* (Seattle: University of Washington Press, 1972), p. 98.

3. *The Office of Science and Technology during the Administration of President Lyndon B. Johnson, November 1963–January 1969,* II, H3, p. 4, LBJ Library; hereafter cited as *OST Administrative History.*

4. Cited in memo, F. C. Schuldt to the director of the Bureau of the Budget, 22 January 1965, Files of the Director of the Bureau of the Budget, National Archives; hereafter cited as BOB Files.

5. Memo, Donald F. Hornig to president, 27 March 1964, Papers of Donald Hornig, LBJ Library; hereafter cited as Hornig Papers.

6. *OST Administrative History*, II, H3, pp. 5–6, LBJ Library.

7. Memo, Schuldt to the director of the Bureau of the Budget, 22 January 1965, BOB Files, National Archives; emphasis in original.

8. Ibid.

9. Ibid.

10. Memo, Hornig to president, 25 January 1965, Hornig Papers, LBJ Library.

11. U.S. Congress, Joint Committee on Atomic Energy, *High Energy Physics Research, Development, and Radiation*, 89th Cong., 1st sess., 2–5 March 1965.

12. David Z. Robinson, "Politics in the Science Advising Process," *Technology and Society* 2, nos. 1 and 2 (1980): 158.

13. *OST Administrative History*, II, H3, p. 8, LBJ Library.

14. Memo, Schuldt to the director of the Bureau of the Budget, 11 April 1966, BOB Files, National Archives.

15. Memo, Charles L. Schultze to president, 31 August 1965, Ex FG 202, WHCF, LBJ Library.

16. Memo, Califano to president, 14 March 1966, filed with a memo, Schultze to president, 31 August 1965, Ex FG 202, WHCF, LBJ Library.

17. Ibid.

18. Anton G. Jachim, *Science Policy Making in the United States and the Batavia Accelerator* (Carbondale: Southern Illinois University Press, 1971), pp. 121–122.

19. Memo, Schuldt to the director of the Bureau of the Budget, 5 April 1966, BOB Files, National Archives.

20. Robinson, "Politics in the Science Advising Process," p. 158; emphasis in original.

21. Bryce Nelson, "200 BEV: Close Senate Vote Defeats Effort to Delay Weston Project," and "Scientific Luxury," *Science* 157 (21 July 1967): 295.

22. *OST Administrative History*, II, H3, p. 9, LBJ Library.

23. Memo, Hornig to Schultze, 8 December 1967, Hornig Papers, LBJ Library.

24. Ibid.

25. Thomas P. Murphy, *Science, Geopolitics, and Federal Spending* (Toronto, Canada: D.C. Heath, Lexington Books, 1971), p. 475. Chapter 15 contains a good discussion of MOL.

26. Ibid.

27. Memo, Military Division of the Bureau of the Budget to the director, 27 November 1964, BOB Files, National Archives.

28. Murphy, *Science, Geopolitics, and Federal Spending*, p. 475.

29. U.S. Congress, House, Committee on Government Operations, *Government Operations in Space*, 89th Cong., 1st sess., 1965, p. 1011.

30. U.S. President, "The President's News Conference of 25 August 1965," in *Public Papers of the Presidents: Lyndon B. Johnson* (Washington, D.C.: Government Printing Office, 1966), pp. 917–918; hereafter cited as *Public Papers*. When the Manned Orbital Laboratory (MOL) was terminated

by President Nixon on 10 June 1969, approximately $1.5 billion had been spent on the project, and MOL still needed much more developmental work.

31. Memo, General Thomas White to president, 30 August 1965, filed with memo, president to General White, 3 September 1965, Ex OS, WHCF, LBJ Library.

32. *The Pentagon Papers*, Gravel ed. (Boston: Beacon Press, 1971), pp. 420–424. Details of the seeding program and decision-making process can be found in formerly secret testimony made public in the U.S. Congress, Senate, Committee on Foreign Relations, Subcommittee on Oceans and International Environment, *Hearings: Weather Modification*, 93rd Cong., 2d sess. (Washington, D.C.: Government Printing Office, 1974), pp. 87–123.

33. Memo, Schultze to Califano, 17 February 1966, Ex LE/SC 2–3, WHCF, LBJ Library. See also memo, Schultze to Califano, 10 February 1966, filed with Schultze memo to Califano, 17 February 1966. There was a specific request from Senator Clinton Anderson to the president that he let Congress debate the weather modification issue and not push an approach favored by the Department of Commerce and the committees of Congress that related to the department. See letter, Senator Anderson to the president, 14 March 1966, filed with memo, Mike N. Manatos to Anderson, 16 March 1966, Ex LE/SC 2–3, WHCF, LBJ Library.

34. Briefing on "Popeye," 31 March 1967, Appointments Book, filed with Hornig Papers, LBJ Library.

35. W. Henry Lambright, *Governing Science and Technology* (New York: Oxford University Press, 1976), pp. 63–64.

36. A thorough account of the electronic barrier is found in Paul Dickson, *The Electronic Battlefield* (Bloomington and London: Indiana University Press, 1976).

37. Memo, Robert McNamara to president, 14 October 1966, cited in Neil Sheehan et al., *The Pentagon Papers* (New York: Bantam, 1971), p. 544.

38. Memo, General Earl G. Wheeler to Robert McNamara, 14 October 1966, in Sheehan et al., *The Pentagon Papers*, pp. 552–553.

39. Interview, Walt Rostow, 16 June 1981, LBJ School of Public Affairs.

40. Dickson, *The Electronic Battlefield*, pp. 49–50.

41. The barrier was never completed. One reason is that electronic equipment was successfully diverted for use in higher-priority areas where the fighting was most intense. Another was that the operating personnel in the military (the users) did not find a linear technological concept particularly relevant to a war that they were fighting on a 360-degree battlefield.

42. U.S. Congress, Committee on Armed Services, Subcommittee on Preparedness, *Hearings: Investigation into the Electronic Battlefield Program* (Washington, D.C.: Government Printing Office, 1970).

43. Charles O. Jones, *An Introduction to the Study of Public Policy*, 2d ed. (North Scituate, Mass.: Duxbury Press, 1977), p. 80, points out that policy formulators attempt to link a conception of what a policy problem is with the "hard political realities" of getting it legitimated.

4. Implementing the New

1. This section is based to a large extent on the account in Paul Dickson, *The Electronic Battlefield* (Bloomington: Indiana University Press, 1976).

2. Ibid., p. 35.

3. Ibid.

4. Ibid., pp. 35–36.

5. Ibid., pp. 32–33.

6. Ibid., p. 54.

7. Donald F. Hornig, address at Temple University Convocation, "Scientific Progress and Democratic Choice," 21 March 1964, Papers of Donald Hornig, LBJ Library; hereafter cited as Hornig Papers.

8. Memo, Hornig to Bill D. Moyers, 8 August 1964, filed with memo, Hornig to president, 28 August 1964, Ex FG 726, WHCF, LBJ Library.

9. Memo, Hornig to president, 28 August 1964, Hornig Papers, LBJ Library.

10. Letter, Haworth to Donald F. Hornig, 19 May 1965, cited in *The Office of Science and Technology during the Administration of President Lyndon B. Johnson, November 1963–January 1969*, II, H1a, p. 1, LBJ Library; hereafter cited as *OST Administrative History*.

11. Memo, Donald F. Hornig to president, 27 August 1965, cited in *OST Administrative History*, II, H1a, p. 1, LBJ Library.

12. Ibid.

13. Ibid.

14. Memo, Horace Busby, Jr., to Hornig, 14 September 1965, Hornig Papers, LBJ Library.

15. Memo, Hornig to president, 29 September 1965, Hornig Papers, LBJ Library.

16. Donald F. Hornig, "Universities and Federal Science Policies," *Science* 142 (12 November 1963): 849.

17. William G. Wells, Jr., *Science Advice and the Presidency, 1933–1976* (Ann Arbor, Mich.: University Microfilms, 1978), pp. 566–567.

18. Memo, Hornig to president, 15 March 1966, Hornig Papers, LBJ Library.

19. Memo, president to Hornig, 15 March 1966, cited in *OST Administrative History*, II, H1a, p. 5, LBJ Library.

20. Ibid.

21. Daniel Greenberg, "Share the Wealth: LBJ Directive Beginning to Show Some Effects," *Science* 154 (30 December 1966): 1628–1629.

22. "An Assessment of Large-Scale Nuclear Powered Seawater Distillation Plants," cited in *OST Administrative History*, II, E2, p. 2, LBJ Library.

23. *OST Administrative History*, II, E2, p. 3, LBJ Library.

24. Memo, Hornig to president, 9 July 1964, Hornig Papers, LBJ Library.

25. Memo, Hornig for the record, "Conversation with the President," 9 July 1964, Hornig Papers, LBJ Library.

26. The Oak Ridge National Laboratory had technical skills relevant to water desalting, in general, not just nuclear applications. It was, in Hornig's view, fully capable of displacing OSW from a technical standpoint (interview, Donald F. Hornig, 9 December 1981, Harvard School of Public Health).

27. Memo, Resources and Civil Works Division/Military Division to Kermit Gordon, 31 July 1964, Files of the Director of the Bureau of the Budget, National Archives; hereafter cited as BOB Files.

28. Memo, Hornig to Gordon, 7 September 1964, BOB Files, National Archives.

29. Memo, Donald F. Hornig and Kermit Gordon to president, 19 October 1964, *OST Administrative History*, II, E2, p. 8, LBJ Library.

30. James T. Ramey et al., "Nuclear Energy—Potential for Desalting," paper presented at First International Symposium on Water Desalination, Washington, D.C., 3–9 October 1965, p. 4. ("Desalination" was used interchangeably with "desalting" in references at the time.)

31. *OST Administrative History*, II, E2, p. 10, LBJ Library.

32. "Remarks at the Signing of the Saline Water Conversion Act" (11 August 1965), in *Public Papers of the Presidents of the United States: Lyndon B. Johnson, 1965* (Washington, D.C.: Government Printing Office, 1966), p. 865; hereafter cited as *Public Papers*.

33. *Administrative History of the Atomic Energy Commission*, 1:viii, LBJ Library.

34. Memo, Hornig to Jack J. Valenti, 14 September 1965, Hornig Papers, LBJ Library.

35. Memo, S. Douglass Cater to president, 30 September 1965, Files of S. Douglass Cater, LBJ Library.

36. Lyndon B. Johnson, "First International Symposium on Desalination," 7 October 1965, *Weekly Compilation of Presidential Documents* 1, no. 1 (Washington, D.C.: Government Printing Office, 1965), p. 381.

37. Memo, Lee White to president, 20 January 1966, Ex AT2, WHCF, LBJ Library.

38. Memo, Lee White to president, 12 August 1965, Ex AT2, WHCF, LBJ Library.

39. Memo, Lee White to president, 20 January 1966, Ex AT2, WHCF, LBJ Library.

40. Memo, W. Marvin Watson to president, 1 September 1966, LBJ Library.

41. *OST Administrative History*, II, E2, p. 17, LBJ Library.

42. Letter, President Dwight D. Eisenhower to president, 28 July 1967, LBJ Library.

43. Letter, president to President Eisenhower, 31 July 1967, Ex UT4, WHCF, LBJ Library.

44. Memo, Secretary Udall to president, 24 August 1967, Ex UT4, WHCF, LBJ Library.

45. Memo, Hornig to Califano, 22 December 1967, Hornig Papers, LBJ Library.

46. Letter, Hornig to Glenn Seaborg, 25 August 1967, Hornig Papers, LBJ Library.

47. *OST Administrative History*, II, E2, p.18, LBJ Library.

48. Memo, Hornig to president, 4 November 1965, Hornig Papers, LBJ Library.

49. Letter, Hornig to Robert C. Weaver, 6 February 1966, Hornig Papers, LBJ Library.

50. Memo, Hornig to president, 12 August 1966, Hornig Papers, LBJ Library.

51. *OST Administrative History*, II, K1, p. 5, LBJ Library.

52. Letter, Hornig to Weaver, 17 September 1968, Hornig Papers, LBJ Library.

53. Letter, Hornig to Lee DuBridge, 24 December 1968, Hornig Papers, LBJ Library.

54. *OST Administrative History*, II, N1, p. 13, LBJ Library.

55. Memo, Hornig to president, 18 May 1965, Hornig Papers, LBJ Library.

56. Memo, Busby to Hornig, 20 May 1965, Hornig Papers, LBJ Library.

57. Letter, president to Hornig, 19 May 1965, Hornig Papers, LBJ Library. Hornig recollects an earlier occasion on which Johnson turned to him for ideas in the foreign policy realm. On 12 January 1965, the president phoned Hornig at home to complain about the preparations for the visit the next morning by the prime minister of Japan. He wanted a good idea to present. After all-night telephone discussions around the country, Hornig presented Johnson with a proposal the next morning while they waited for the prime minister to arrive for the meeting at the White House. Hornig suggested that the United States and Japan mount a coordinated effort to deal with the diseases that ravage Asia and the Pacific area. Politically designed to improve the relations of both Japan and the United States with the countries of Asia, the program was enthusiastically welcomed by Prime Minister Sato. One hour later, the U.S.-Japan Medical Program was born. It was announced in a joint communiqué issued the same day (13 January 1965). It is a program still very much alive today (Hornig, personal communication, 7 February 1984).

58. Memo, Busby to Hornig, 7 July 1965, Hornig Papers, LBJ Library.

59. Memo, Hornig to president, 4 August 1965, Hornig Papers, LBJ Library.

60. Press release, White House, 5 August 1965, cited in *OST Administrative History*, II, N1, p. 16, LBJ Library.

61. Memo, Hornig to president, 4 August 1965, Hornig Papers, LBJ Library.

62. Letter, Hornig to Winthrop Brown, 10 August 1965, Hornig Papers, LBJ Library.

63. Memo, Hornig to president, 13 December 1965, Ex CA (11/22/63), WHCF, LBJ Library.

64. Letter, Hornig to William Gaud, 27 February 1967, Hornig Papers, LBJ Library.

65. Memo, Hornig to president, 3 April 1967, Hornig Papers, LBJ Library.

66. Letter, Hornig to Sol Linowitz, 29 March 1967, Hornig Papers, LBJ Library.

67. Memo, Hornig to president, 16 November 1967, Hornig Papers, LBJ Library.

68. Memo, Hornig to Charles L. Schultze, 29 November 1967, Hornig Papers, LBJ Library.

69. Letter, Hornig to Gaud, 5 December 1967, Hornig Papers, LBJ Library.

70. Letter, Hornig to David Bell, 23 January 1968, Hornig Papers, LBJ Library.

71. *OST Administrative History*, II, N1, LBJ Library.

72. Ibid.

73. Letter, Hornig to DuBridge, 30 December 1968, Hornig Papers, LBJ Library.

74. Ibid.

75. Ibid.

76. See Jeffrey L. Pressman and Aaron B. Wildavsky, *Implementation* (Berkeley: University of California Press, 1973); Frances E. Rourke, *Bureaucracy, Politics, and Public Policy* (Boston: Little, Brown, 1969); Eugene Bardach, *The Implementation Game* (Cambridge: MIT Press, 1977); and Robert T. Nakamura and Frank Smallwood, *Politics of Policy Implementation* (New York: St. Martin's Press, 1981).

77. See Pressman and Wildavsky, *Implementation*, pp. 133ff., for a good discussion of coordination and its problems.

5. Carrying Out the Old

1. Lyndon B. Johnson, *The Vantage Point* (New York: Popular Library, Inc., 1971), p. 279.

2. "Annual Message to the Congress on the State of the Union" (8 January 1964), in *Public Papers of the Presidents of the United States: Lyndon B. Johnson, 1964* (Washington, D.C.: Government Printing Office, 1965), p. 117; hereafter cited as *Public Papers*. Also, "Annual Budget Message to the Congress, Fiscal Year 1965" (21 January 1964), *Public Papers, 1964*, p. 186.

3. Letter, James E. Webb to president, 30 November 1964, Files of the Director of the Bureau of the Budget, National Archives; hereafter cited as BOB Files.

4. Daniel Greenberg, "Space: A White House Endorsement and a NASA View of the Attitudes of Scientists toward the Program," *Science* 147 (12 March 1965): 1369–1370.

5. Ibid.

6. Arthur Levine, *Future of the U.S. Space Program* (New York: Praeger Publishers, 1975), pp. 94–95.

7. Johnson, *The Vantage Point*, p. 283.

8. Memo, Charles L. Schultze to president, 11 August 1967, BOB Files, National Archives.

9. Interview transcript, James E. Webb Oral History, 29 April 1969, pp. 31–32, LBJ Library.

10. The principal investigations of the Apollo fire by Congress were carried out by the relatively friendly House and Senate Space committees.

11. Johnson, *The Vantage Point*, p. 283.

12. Stephen P. Strickland, *Politics, Science, and Dread Disease* (Cambridge, Mass.: Harvard University Press, 1972), pp. 184–185.

13. Elinor Langer, "Presidential Medicine: Johnson Panel, Law and Medical, to Study Heart Disease, Cancer, and Strokes," *Science* 143 (20 March 1964): 1398–1409.

14. Strickland, *Politics,* p. 207.

15. Letter, Mary Lasker to president, 14 June 1966, National Institutes of Health File, Ex FG 165–6, WHCF, LBJ Library.

16. U.S. President, "Remarks at a Meeting with Medical and Hospital Leaders to Prepare for the Launching of Medicare (15 June 1966)," in *Public Papers, 1966* (Washington, D.C.: Government Printing Office, 1967), p. 610.

17. Ibid.

18. Elinor Langer, "NIH: Demand Increases for Applications of Research," *Science* 153 (8 July 1966): 149.

19. *New York Times,* 28 June 1966, p. 35. See also James E. Katz, *Presidential Politics and Science Policy* (New York: Praeger Publishers, 1978), p. 162; Strickland, *Politics,* pp. 207–209.

20. Strickland, *Politics,* pp. 207–208.

21. Memo, Irving Lewis to Douglass Cater, 18 August 1965, LBJ Library.

22. *New York Times,* 2 October 1966, p. 84; Strickland, *Politics,* p. 208.

23. Memo, Donald Hornig to Douglass Cater, 6 June 1967, Papers of Donald F. Hornig, LBJ Library; hereafter cited as Hornig Papers.

24. Elinor Langer, "LBJ at NIH: President Offers Kind Words for Basic Research," *Science* 157 (28 July 1967): 403–405.

25. Memo, Douglass Cater to president, 19 July 1967, Cater Aide File, LBJ Library.

26. Memo, Philip Lee to Cater, 10 May 1967, LBJ Library.

27. Elizabeth Drew, "The Health Syndicate," *Atlantic Monthly* (December 1967): 78.

28. Seymour M. Hersh, *Chemical and Biological Warfare* (Indianapolis: Bobbs-Merrill, 1968), p. 149.

29. Roger Hilsman, *To Move a Nation* (Garden City, N.J.: Doubleday, 1967), pp. 442–443.

30. U.S. Congress, House, Committee on Science and Astronautics, Subcommittee on Science, Research, and Development, *Report: A Technology Assessment of the Vietnam Defoliant Matter: A Case History,* 91st Cong., 1st sess., p. 1.

31. Ibid., p. 16.

32. Ibid., pp. 41–47.

33. Letter, Hornig to the Federation of American Scientists, 1 July 1964, Hornig Papers, LBJ Library.

34. "Scientists Protest Viet Crop Destruction," *Science* 141 (21 January 1966): 309.

35. Hersh, *Warfare,* pp. 166–167.

36. Ibid.

37. Letter, Hornig to Matthew Meselson, 13 March 1967, Hornig Papers, LBJ Library.

38. Stockholm International Peace Research Institute, *The Problem of Chemical and Biological Warfare, The Rise of CB Weapons* (New York: Humanities Press, Inc., 1971), I: 164.

39. U.S. Congress, House, Committee on Science and Astronautics, *Report: A Technology Assessment,* p. 34.

40. Ibid.

41. "Remarks at Colorado Springs to the Graduating Class of the U.S. Air Force Academy (5 June 1963)," in *Public Papers of the Presidents of the United States: John F. Kennedy, 1963* (Washington, D.C.: Government Printing Office, 1964), pp. 440–441.

42. Don Dwiggins, *The SST: Here It Comes, Ready or Not* (New York: Doubleday, 1968), p. 139.

43. Ibid., p. 142.

44. Ibid., p. 138.

45. Letter, Gordon Bain to president, 28 February 1964, BOB Files, National Archives.

46. Letter, Najeeb Halaby to president, 4 March 1964, BOB Files, National Archives.

47. Ibid.

48. Memo, president to Halaby, 23 April 1964, WHCF, LBJ Library.

49. Press release, White House, 20 May 1964, BOB Files, National Archives.

50. Memos, Bill D. Moyers to president, 14 May and 15 May 1964, C.F. CA, WHCF, LBJ Library.

51. Memo draft, R. G. Prestemon to Kermit Gordon, 17 June 1964, BOB Files, National Archives.

52. Memo, Gordon conversation with Halaby, 19 June 1964, BOB Files, National Archives.

53. Letter, Gordon to Halaby, 30 October 1964, BOB Files, National Archives.

54. Memo, Gordon conversation with Halaby, 28 November 1964, BOB Files, National Archives.

55. Memo, president to Halaby, 2 December 1964, C.F. FG 718, WHCF, LBJ Library.

56. Ibid.

57. Memo, Halaby to president, 23 December 1964, LBJ Library.

58. *Case Study: Managing the U.S. Supersonic Transport Program* (Cambridge, Mass.: Harvard Business School, 1977), p. 6. See also Mel Horwitch, *Clipped Wings* (Cambridge, Mass.: MIT Press, 1982).

59. Dwiggins, *SST*, p. 160.

60. Memo, Joseph A. Califano, Jr., to president, 3 August 1965, LBJ Library.

61. Letter, Hornig to Robert S. McNamara, 11 September 1965, *The Office of Science and Technology during the Administration of President Lyndon B. Johnson, November 1963–January 1969*, II, C2, pp. 26–30.

62. *Case Study: Managing the U.S. Supersonic Transport Program*, p. 9.

63. There had been some supersonic flights over cities before (e.g., Oklahoma City), but Hornig regarded these as inconclusive from the standpoint of scientific evaluation (letter, Hornig to McNamara, 30 December 1965, Hornig Papers, LBJ Library).

64. Memo, Hornig to president, 23 April 1966, Hornig Papers, LBJ Library.

65. Memo, Schultze to president, 23 April 1966, LBJ Library; emphasis in original.

66. Memo, General W. F. McKee to W. Marvin Watson, 21 April 1966, LBJ Library.

67. Memo, Califano to president, 27 April 1966, Ex CA, WHCF, LBJ Library.

68. *Case Study: Managing the U.S. Supersonic Transport Program*, p. 9.

69. Memo, Hornig to president, 8 September 1966, Hornig Papers, LBJ Library.

70. Letter, Hornig to McNamara, 1 November 1966, with the "Report of the OST Coordinating Committee on Sonic Boom Studies, November 1, 1966," cited in *OST Administrative History*, II, C2, p. 29.

71. Memo, president to Schultze, 24 March 1967, BOB Files, National Archives.

72. Press release, White House, 29 April 1967, BOB Files, National Archives.

73. Memo, Everett Hutchinson to president, 14 February 1968, BOB Files, National Archives.

74. Graham T. Allison and Morton H. Halperin, "Bureaucratic Politics: A Paradigm and Some Policy Implications," in Raymond Tanter and Richard H. Ullman, eds., *Theory and Policy in International Relations* (Princeton: Princeton University Press, 1972), p. 54; and Graham T. Allison, *Essence of Decision: Explaining the Cuban Missile Crisis* (Boston: Little, Brown and Company, 1971).

75. Eugene Bardach, *The Implementation Game: What Happens after a Bill Becomes a Law* (Cambridge, Mass.: MIT Press, 1977), pp. 42–43.

76. Ibid., pp. 57–58.

77. Ibid.

6. Curtailing Science and Technology

1. Robert S. McNamara, *The Essence of Security* (New York: Harper and Row, 1968), p. 196.

2. William G. Wells, Jr., *Science Advice in the Presidency, 1933–1976* (Ann Arbor, Mich.: University Microfilms, 1978), p. 586.

3. W. W. Rostow, *The Diffusion of Power* (New York: Macmillan, 1972), pp. 386–387.

4. The meeting was engineered by McNamara, who went to great lengths to make sure all the scientists could be there. He had a plane sent to the Caribbean to pick up Hornig, where he was vacationing with his family (interview, Donald F. Hornig, 9 December 1981, Harvard School of Public Health).

5. Herbert F. York, *Race to Oblivion* (New York: Simon and Schuster, 1970), pp. 194–195.

6. Morton H. Halperin, *National Security Policy Making* (Lexington, Mass.: Lexington Books, 1975), p. 129.

7. Ibid., p. 131.

8. Hornig suggests that PSAC, which had noted this option in a report

(nonpublic), may have been the source of this idea (interview, Donald F. Hornig, 9 December 1981, Harvard School of Public Health).

9. Halperin, *National Security Policy Making*, p. 135.

10. *The Office of Science and Technology during the Administration of President Lyndon B. Johnson, November 1963–January 1969*, II, H1.6, p. 4, LBJ Library; hereafter cited as *OST Administrative History*.

11. Memo, Donald F. Hornig to Charles L. Schultze, 22 November 1967, Papers of Donald Hornig, LBJ Library; hereafter cited as Hornig Papers.

12. Memo, Schultze to Hornig, 4 December 1967, Files of the Director of the Bureau of the Budget, National Archives; hereafter cited as BOB Files.

13. Memo, Hornig to president, 22 December 1967, Hornig Papers, LBJ Library.

14. Ibid.

15. Doris Kearns, *Lyndon Johnson and the American Dream* (New York: Signet, 1976), p. 315.

16. Memo, Hornig to president, 11 May 1968, Ex FG 265, WHCF, LBJ Library.

17. Memo, Joseph A. Califano, Jr., to president, 21 May 1968, LBJ Library.

18. Memo, Califano to president, 12 August 1968, Ex FG 265, WHCF, LBJ Library.

19. Memo, Hornig to Charles J. Zwick, 26 September 1968, Hornig Papers, LBJ Library.

20. Memo, Hornig to president, 3 October 1968, Hornig Papers, LBJ Library.

21. Letter, David Henry to president, 25 October 1968, LBJ Library.

22. Memo, Hornig to James A. Gaither, 8 November 1968, Hornig Papers, LBJ Library.

23. Memo, Gaither to Califano, 29 November 1968, LBJ Library.

24. Memo, Hugh Loweth to Zwick, 13 November 1968, BOB Files, National Archives.

25. Handwritten note at bottom of memo, Loweth to Zwick, 2 December 1968, BOB Files, National Archives.

26. Memo, Hornig to president, 2 December 1968, Hornig Papers, LBJ Library.

27. James E. Webb, John Diebold Lecture on Technological Change and Management, Harvard University Graduate School of Business Administration, "NASA as an Adaptive Organization," 30 September 1968, Boston Massachusetts, cited in *Preliminary History of NASA, 1963–1969* (Washington, D.C.: National Aeronautics and Space Administration, 15 January 1969), p. II-53.

28. Cited in Emmette S. Redford and Orion F. White, *What Manned Space Program after Reaching the Moon? Government Attempts to Decide: 1962–1968* (Syracuse: N.Y.: Interuniversity Case Program, 1971), p. 152; memo, Hornig to president, 29 January 1964; letter, president to James E. Webb, 30 January 1964, cited in *OST Administrative History*, II, C1, pp. 3–4.

29. Cited in Arthur Levine, *Future of the U.S. Space Program* (New York: Praeger, 1975), p. 119.

30. Ibid.

31. Note by president written at bottom of memo, Jack J. Valenti to president, 30 March 1965, LBJ Library.

32. *Preliminary History of NASA*, p. II-16.

33. Memo, Webb to president, 16 May 1966, C.F. FG, WHCF, LBJ Library.

34. Letter, Webb to president, 26 August 1966, Ex OS, WHCF, LBJ Library.

35. Memo, Schultze to president, 1 September 1966, LBJ Library.

36. Ibid.

37. Memo, Schultze to president, 16 December 1966.

38. Ibid.

39. Memo, Webb to president, 14 December 1966, BOB Files, National Archives.

40. Memo, Hornig to president, 22 December 1966, Hornig Papers, LBJ Library.

41. *Preliminary History of NASA*, p. II-17.

42. U.S. Congress, Senate, *NASA Appropriations Hearings on H.R. 12474*, 90th Cong., 1st sess., 1967.

43. U.S. Congress, House, Committee on Appropriations, Subcommittee on Independent Offices, *Hearings: NASA Appropriations for 1968*, 90th Cong., 1st sess., 1967.

44. Redford and White, *What Manned Space Program?*, p. 207.

45. Memo, president to Webb, 29 September 1967, C.F. FG, WHCF, LBJ Library.

46. Memo, Webb to Califano, 1 December 1967, LBJ Library.

47. Memo, Hornig to president, 26 September 1968, Ex OS, WHCF, LBJ Library.

48. Memo, president to Hornig, 26 September 1968, Ex OS, WHCF, LBJ Library.

49. Memo, John F. Kennedy to Kermit Gordon, 6 August 1963, BOB Files, National Archives.

50. Memo, William Connel to Walter W. Jenkins, 3 December 1963, BOB Files, National Archives.

51. Memo, Gordon to Jenkins, 7 December 1963, BOB Files, National Archives.

52. Daniel Greenberg, *The Politics of Pure Science*, Plume ed. (New York: New American Library, 1967), pp. 260–261.

53. Memo, Jerome B. Wiesner to president, 19 December 1963, Ex AT2, WHCF, LBJ Library.

54. Greenberg, *Politics*, p. 261.

55. Letter, Elvis Stahr to Senator Hubert H. Humphrey, 21 December 1963, LBJ Library.

56. Letter, Birch Bayh to president, 24 December 1963, LBJ Library.

57. Letter, president to Humphrey, 16 January 1964, LBJ Library.

58. Memo, Elmer Staats to president, 18 January 1964, LBJ Library.

59. Greenberg, *Politics*, p. 264.

60. Ibid., p. 171.

61. *Comptroller General, Report to Congress, Administration of Proj-*

ect Mohole by the National Science Foundation (Washington, D.C.: General Accounting Office, 1968), p. 4.

62. Greenberg, *Politics*, p. 170.

63. Note, William Carey to Gordon, 4 November 1963, BOB Files, National Archives.

64. Letter, Hornig to Leland Haworth, 10 March 1964, Hornig Papers, LBJ Library.

65. Letter, Hornig to Haworth, 7 May 1964, Hornig Papers, LBJ Library.

66. Memo, Hornig to Schultze, 20 September 1965, BOB Files, National Archives.

67. Memo, Loweth to Schultze, 12 October 1965, BOB Files, National Archives.

68. Memo, president to Hornig, 12 August 1965, Hornig Papers, LBJ Library.

69. Greenberg, *Politics*, p. 189.

70. Report No. 1477, Independent Offices Appropriations Bill, 1967, U.S. House, 89th Cong., 2d sess., p. 14. In U.S. House of Representatives, *Reports on Public Bills, House Reports 1413–1547, with Exceptions*, 89th Cong., 2d sess. (Washington, D.C.: Government Printing Office, 1966).

71. Route slip memo, William Cannon, 11 May 1966, BOB Files, National Archives.

72. Memo, Cannon to Schultze, 17 May 1966, BOB Files, National Archives.

73. Greenberg, *Politics*, p. 206.

74. See Charles Levine, ed., "A Symposium: Organizational Decline and Cutback Management," *Public Administration Review* 38 (July/August 1978); and Robert D. Behn, ed., "A Symposium: Leadership in an Era of Retrenchment," *Public Administration Review* 40 (November/December 1980).

75. Peter DeLeon, "Public Policy Termination: An End and a Beginning," *Policy Analysis* (Summer 1978): 369–392.

76. W. Henry Lambright and Harvey M. Sapolsky, "Terminating Federal Research and Development Programs," *Policy Sciences* 7 (June 1976): 199–213; see also Eugene Bardach, "Policy Termination as a Political Process," *Policy Sciences* 7 (June 1976): 123–131.

77. Ibid.; see also Robert D. Behn, "How to Terminate a Public Policy: A Dozen Hints for the Would-Be Terminator," *Policy Analysis* (Summer 1978): 393–413.

78. DeLeon, "Public Policy Termination," pp. 369–392.

7. Conclusion

1. Memo, president to Charles Schultze, 24 March 1967, Files of the Director of the Bureau of the Budget, National Archives.

2. Donald F. Hornig, "The President's Need for Science Advice: Past and Future," *Technology in Society* 2, nos. 1 and 2 (1980): 47.

3. Don K. Price, *The Scientific Estate* (Cambridge, Mass.: Harvard University Press, 1965), p. 135.

4. See, for example, the section of readings, entitled "Technology and Philosophy," in Albert H. Teich, ed., *Technology and Man's Future*, 2d ed. (New York: St. Martin's, 1977).

5. Hornig Oral History Interview, Tape 1, LBJ Library, p. 19.

6. Ibid., p. 33.

Index

Bureau of the Budget (BOB), 13; and aid to developing countries, 98; and Apollo, 105; and atomic energy, 40, 41; and basic research, 136–137, 139–141; and energy, 29, 30, 38, 43, 171; Health and Welfare Division, 110; Hornig and, 185, 186; and HUD, 92; Johnson and, 14; and Mohole, 158–160; and MOL, 66; and MURA, 152–153, 157, 166; and NASA, 162, 169, 177; and New Centers of Excellence program, 81; and NSF, 162; and nuclear desalting, 86, 87, 91; and oceanography, 31–32, 55–56; and pollution, 45, 46, 171; role of, 177–178, 189; and scientific estate, 175; and space, 142–144; and SST, 118–119, 121–122, 124–125, 168, 169; and 200-BEV, 59–61, 63, 74, 165

Burger, Edward J., Jr.: *Science at the White House*, 3

Busby, Horace, 82; and aid to Korea, 95

Califano, Joseph: and basic research, 138–140; and domestic affairs, 36; and energy, 29–30, 42–43, 171, 172, 176; and HUD, 92; and nuclear desalting, 90; and pollution, 45, 47, 48; as principal, 13, 176; and space, 148; and SST, 123, 124, 169; and 200-BEV, 62, 64, 74

California Institute of Technology, 94

Cambel, Prof. Ali Bulant, 38

Cambel report, 38–41, 43, 50

Cannon, William: and Mohole, 160

Carey, William: and Mohole, 158

Carson, Rachel: *Silent Spring*, 44

Carter, Jimmy: and science adviser, 9, 187; and technoscience policy, 3, 189

Cater, Douglass: and health, 110–112, 176; and nuclear desalting, 88; *Power in Washington*, 10; as

principal, 176; on subgovernments, 10

Cavanaugh, James, 106

Central Intelligence Agency (CIA): and SST, 119; and weather modification, 69

CERN (Switzerland), 63

Chicago, University of, 156

China, 134, 135, 170

Cities. *See* Urban problems

Cloud-seeding. *See* Weather modification

Cobb, Roger W.: *Participation in American Politics*, 48

Cohen, Wilbur: and basic research, 139

Cold War, 67, 189

Commerce, Department of: and NOAA, 37; and SST, 119–123

Committee on Academic Science, 82

Committee on Aeronautical and Space Sciences: Anderson as chair of, 17

Committee on Government Operations (House): Subcommittee on Military Operations, 67

Concorde, 116–118, 120, 127

Congress: and ABM, 133, 135, 136, 170; and adoption, 19, 54, 174; and aid to developing countries, 98; and Apollo, 104, 107, 170; appropriations committees of, 17, 67, 69, 147, 150, 152; and basic research, 136–138, 140–141; and curtailment, 131; and energy, 29–30, 42–43, 51; and health research, 108, 110; and HUD, 93, 94, 101; and implementation, 76, 77, 79; Johnson and, 12, 72–73; and Marine Council, 175; and modes of adoption, 72–74; and Mohole, 157, 158, 160–161, 184; and MOL, 65–67, 167; and MURA, 151, 152, 154, 156, 166; and New Centers of Excellence program, 82, 83–84; and NSF, 166; and nuclear desalting, 87,

103–104, 130; and NIH, 165–166; and nuclear desalting, 87, 168; of SST, 117, 119, 120, 126, 127, 129, 168; strategies reviewed, 99
India, 97, 182
Industry: and aid to developing countries, 97; and HUD, 92; and oceanography, 31, 55; and SST, 117, 118, 120, 121, 123, 125; and technological decisions, 21, 167
Initiating agenda. *See* Agendas, initiating
Institute of Industrial Technology and Applied Science, 95, 96
Institutional presidency: subpresidency and, 12, 13
Integration: of knowledge, 5, 180, 184–188, 190
Interagency Committee on Oceanography (ICO), 31–32
Inter-American Foundation for Science and Technology, 97
Interdepartmental Energy Steering Committee, 38
Interior, Department of, 35; and energy, 38, 50; and nuclear desalting, 85–87, 89, 100, 168, 183; and pollution, 46, 47; and technological development, 167, 176
International Decade of Ocean Exploration (IDOE), 36
International Desalination Conference, 88
Intervention: and implementation, 80, 99, 102, 111, 112
Israel, 86

Jackson, Sen. Henry "Scoop": and MURA, 154–155
Japan, 95, 201n
Jenkins, Walter: and MURA, 152–153
Johnson, Lyndon B.: activism of, 7, 174; and administrators, 15; and Apollo, 5, 104–108, 117; and Congress, 11, 45, 55; and energy, 51; and environment, 51; and

growth of R&D, 8; and health research, 108–112; life of, 11; and NASA, 104–108; and nuclear desalting, 85; and oceanography, 55–56; "Protecting Our National Heritage," 42; and science adviser, 14, 185–189; and space, 65, 67; Special Message on Natural Beauty, 45, 46; *The Vantage Point*, 105; "Water for Peace," 88, 100
Joint Chiefs of Staff: and ABM, 133–136, 162, 176; and defoliation, 113, 115, 129; and electronic barrier, 78, 168; and weather modification, 69–70, 73, 173
Joint Committee on Atomic Energy (JCAE), 17; and nuclear desalting, 86; and 200-BEV, 57, 59–62, 64, 165
Joint Task 728, 77
Jones, Charles O.: *An Introduction to the Study of Public Policy*, 10, 48–49, 51

Katz, James Everett: *Presidential Politics and Science Policy*, 3
Kennedy, John F.: and Apollo, 5, 7, 65, 104–107, 127; and atomic energy, 58; and defense, 133, 135; and energy, 38; and health research, 108, 127, 128; and MURA, 151–153; and NSF, 136; and nuclear desalting, 168; and oceanography, 55, 56; and organization of science and technology, 8, 181; and PSAC, 85; and science adviser, 14, 185; and space, 60, 150; and SST, 116–118, 120, 125, 127, 168; and Vietnam, 112, 113, 127–129, 173
Keyworth, George: as science adviser, 187–188
Killian, James R., Jr.: and ABM, 134; *Sputniks, Scientists, and Eisenhower*, 3
Kistiakowsky, George B.: and ABM,